Religion and]
in the Marvel
Cinematic Universe

Religion and Myth in the Marvel Cinematic Universe

MICHAEL D. NICHOLS

McFarland & Company, Inc., Publishers
Jefferson, North Carolina

This book has undergone peer review.

ISBN (print) 978-1-4766-8159-7
ISBN (ebook) 978-1-4766-4208-6

Library of Congress and British Library
cataloguing data are available

Library of Congress Control Number 2021001816

Front cover image © 2021 Shutterstock

Printed in the United States of America

*McFarland & Company, Inc., Publishers
Box 611, Jefferson, North Carolina 28640
www.mcfarlandpub.com*

For Jeanette, Xander, and Luka,
and for my mother and father

Table of Contents

Preface and Acknowledgments

In the summer of 2012, as I was drafting my first book (an adaption of my doctoral dissertation on the evolving forms of the figure of Māra throughout Buddhist mythic discourses), I found the time to take in a viewing of *Marvel's The Avengers* during its theatrical release. Because I had been a fan of Marvel superheroes and comics since boyhood, the film was naturally of interest, but multiple aspects of the experience registered with me on a professional level, as well. First, my work on the transformations of Māra in Buddhist narratives had taken me into manifestations of the figure in television and film, which led into the scholarship on religion in popular culture. As a result, one could say I was primed to detect potential symbolism and philosophical valences in the film.

Second, during the course of the film and then subsequent home viewings of the preceding entries in what has become known as "Phase One" of the Marvel Cinematic Universe, the interconnected nature of the storylines and the true extent of the unifying, overarching narrative became evident. This extensive and intentional interconnection closely mimicked the dialogue between the narratives of Indian religions that had formed the basis of my graduate studies, thus further piquing my interest.

Finally, though it is purely anecdotal, and hence by definition unscientific, I was struck by the strength of the audience reaction during the showing of *Marvel's The Avengers*. On two occasions (when Captain America and Iron Man first appeared on screen together, and also when the Hulk battered the film's villain, Loki) the audience erupted into cheers and applause, a rare phenomenon in my previous movie-going experiences. Altogether, it seemed that something truly unique was occurring in this film franchise, something that might have ancient corollaries, powerfully deep roots, and potential significance for my field of Religious Studies.

This book is the result of my investigations into those connections and resonances. During the course of my research, which covers the first three so-called "Phases" of the Marvel Cinematic Universe (at times referred to collectively as the "Infinity Saga" due to their concern with mythic objects which the films call "Infinity Stones"), those comparisons and resemblances gradually expanded to include myths and religious traditions from every corner of the globe. Showing the extent of these comparisons is critical for understanding the extensive depth of connections between the Marvel films and other world traditions. Since my own expertise and linguistic knowledge is focused on certain European and Indic languages (such as German, Sanskrit, and Pāli), I have relied on dependable translations and other sources for works outside of those areas. Beyond the necessity of using such a wide variety of sources, it is also my hope that employing good translations will increase accessibility for a popular audience potentially interested in this topic. The correspondence between prominent themes in the film series and classic theoretical works in the Religious Studies field similarly grew. The pairs of quotations at the beginning of most chapters are intended to show those parallels.

Overall, the contribution of this study is to show how the Marvel Cinematic Universe both rests in a long lineage of worldwide mythic and religious narratives and also serves as a new iteration of commentary on ancient human concerns. Though many scholars have rightfully pointed out the blind spots and shortcomings of his works, Joseph Campbell is still the source of valuable insights into the perennial appeal of mythic narratives and the cultural tendency to re-envision and redeploy ancient narratives. In his most famous work, *The Hero with a Thousand Faces*, he summarizes that trend in his characteristically rhapsodizing way: "The latest incarnation of Oedipus, the continued romance of Beauty and the Beast, stand this afternoon at the corner of Forty-Second Street and Fifth Avenue, waiting for the traffic light to change."[1] While all myths and all cultural experiences are clearly not the same, some aspects of human experience are nevertheless universal: we are all born, we all have parents and families, and we all die. Within the unquestionable diversity of global traditions, common threads reacting to these shared issues are detectable across world myths and religious traditions that also, as this book will demonstrate, surface in the Marvel film series.

Even while I finished my first book, I began compiling notes for this project and as I did so, I shared elements of it in courses I was teaching, particularly the courses "Symbols of Evil in World Religions" and "Religion and Popular Culture." The immediate enthusiasm of my students was yet another indication of the relevance and merit I saw in the book. I am grateful for their comments and for ongoing conversations with three former students in particular: Jose Arteaga, Kyle Hodge, and Shannon Kiley.

There are many other people and influences I need to thank for helping to make this book possible. Looking deeper into the past, this book has grown out from two intellectual taproots that I must acknowledge. The first is the graduate training in Religious Studies and Comparative Religion that planted the seeds for my love of the field. Preeminent on this score was the Master's training I received at Miami University of Ohio, where I underwent a "boot camp" in the theory and method of the study of religion with Julie Gifford and learned firsthand how to carry out careful, sensitive comparative work in seminars led by James Hanges and Peter Williams. Most of all, Liz Wilson, my adviser at Miami University, was a sagacious overseer of my work and has been a steadfast supporter (and friend) ever since. During my doctoral studies at Northwestern University, Sarah McFarland Taylor further refined my training in theory and method (and shared my budding interests in popular culture connections), Stuart Sarbacker acted as an eager mentor on the broad interrelations of Indian religions (as well as the vagaries of graduate school life), and George Bond served as a gracious and patient mentor for my specialization in Buddhist Studies. Though I have thanked all these individuals elsewhere, I do not believe I can ever do so enough, or adequately.

The second intellectual root for this book project comes from a special kind of academic curriculum that I had the honor and pleasure to participate in both as a student and a faculty member while at Saint Joseph's College in Rensselaer, Indiana. Called the "Core Curriculum," this program was a sequence of ten interconnected courses taken by all students at the College throughout their entire undergraduate study, from first year to graduation. Eminently interdisciplinary, these ten seminars served as the student's general education training, but in a holistic manner, combining philosophy, literature, science, economics, history, and many other ways of knowing and viewing the world, all into a sequence of classes calibrated to help students develop keen critical thinking and moral reasoning skills. As an undergraduate, the Core Curriculum stimulated my love of interconnected fields of knowledge, of looking through as many lenses as possible on a given issue, which in turn led me to Religious Studies, one of the most interdisciplinary fields in the Academy. Later, after earning my doctorate, I had the great fortune to return to Saint Joseph's College as a professor of Religion and Philosophy, allowing me to teach in the Core Curriculum. There I was immersed alongside colleagues from multiple fields, benefiting from their knowledge of history, classics, psychology, and other disciplines, all of which have helped to inform this book and my approach to its topic.

Tragically, in May 2017, Saint Joseph's College was forced to close due to financial distress. Along with this closure, the Core Curriculum, the College's distinguishing academic program for nearly fifty years, sadly came to an end. However, I would like to think that in its own humble way, through its interdisciplinary focus, broad cross-cultural comparison, and concern for things essentially human and humane, this book carries on aspects of the Core Curriculum's intellectual tradition. Without a doubt the Core Curriculum formed who I am intellectually and, consequently, this book would not have existed without it.

Additionally, two professorial colleagues, Mike Malone and Maia Hawthorne, deserve special recognition for providing constructive and supportive comments on the work as well. A portion of Chapter Four, in an earlier and differently-conceived version, was previously published as an article in the journal *Cosmos and Logos*. I am grateful to the editors of that journal for permission to reprint those ideas. The staff of the Mother Theresa Hackelmeier Memorial Library at Marian University in Indianapolis have also been incredibly helpful in interlibrary loaning and otherwise getting hold of materials that I needed for the research going into this book. I also owe great thanks to Layla Milholen, my editor at McFarland, for her enthusiasm and dedication to this project. It has been a pleasure working with you, Layla. Closer to home, my father and mother, John and Connie Nichols, have been an unflagging source of support and love. My sons, Xander and Luka, and my wife, Jeanette, went on this journey with me, watching and re-watching all the Marvel films while discussing theories and ideas, making the process of writing the book a pure joy. Words cannot express how much I love all three of you.

In the spirit of transparency, I come to this subject as both an academic and a fan, a scholar and an enthusiast. It is my hope that both elements come through in this work and that both audiences appreciate the analysis and discussion that follows.

Introduction

A Myth in the Making
and Making the Case for a Myth

You think you're the only superhero in the world?
Mr. Stark, you've become part of a bigger universe.
You just don't know it yet.
    —Nick Fury, played by Samuel L. Jackson,
            Iron Man (2008)

The world becomes apprehensible as world, as cosmos, in the
measure in which it reveals itself as a sacred world.
   —Mircea Eliade, *The Sacred and the Profane*, p. 64

With the words given in the first quotation above, Marvel Studios inaugurated the most successful shared cinematic universe, not to mention movie franchise, in film history. As Tony Stark's "Iron Man" became part of the larger universe that Nick Fury promised—pulling in famous characters such as "Captain America," "Thor," the "Incredible Hulk," and others—audiences around the world did as well, experiencing a series of films with unparalleled interconnection, continuity, and overlap. Indeed, rather than compose a chain of sequels and primarily independent films, Marvel Studios essentially created an imagined world of interacting superheroes, layered with decades of backstory and past history in which each entry contributed to an overarching narrative as episodes in a larger story.

Eleven years and twenty-two films later, the Marvel Cinematic Universe (hereafter abbreviated as "MCU") has concluded this first storyline—termed the "Infinity Saga"—with *Avengers: Endgame* (2019), capitalizing on that first post-credits scene's promise of a "bigger universe." In terms of audience response and box office yields, the results have been nothing less than record-breaking. As of the time of this writing, the entire MCU has grossed over twenty billion dollars, with more than one billion of that total coming in receipts from the opening weekend of *Avengers: Endgame* alone.[1] Beyond dollar signs, the MCU has permeated popular culture, generating spin-offs in other media (including television, digital shorts, and video games), dominating news headlines with each release, and creating an enormous fan base which, if social media videos are to be believed, broke into near hysterics during pivotal moments of *Avengers: Endgame*.[2]

Given the MCU's immense popularity and its emerging status as a defining popular culture phenomenon, it is only right that it has become the subject of academic attention. To this point, the growing body of scholarship on the MCU, as well as on superheroes in general, has tended to focus on the ideological and geopolitical contexts of the films. In this light, Terence McSweeney, for example, argues,

> The films of the MCU emerge as embodiments of national fantasies and consolidate a range of decidedly American views on the world to the extent that a more comprehensive literalization of American exceptionalism would be hard to find.[3]

Rather than ascribe the motivation simply to nationalism, McSweeney argues specifically for the terrorist attacks of 9/11 and the subsequent, so-called "War on Terror" as inciting events for the MCU's assertion of American exceptionalism through the narrative of the superhero. He is not alone, as critics and scholars have been quick to interpret the events and symbolism of the MCU films, as well as all recent superhero movies, as stemming from the cultural trauma of 9/11 and its ensuing conflicts. Jeffrey Brown, for instance, argues that "in response to the cultural anxieties and fears of a weakened America caused by 9/11, superhero films have presented new, hyper-masculine, white male bodies capable of protecting the nation."[4] Other examples of this scholarship abound and, from this vantage, the MCU franchise has achieved its success by expressing the wishes of its audience for a triumphant, super-powered America, while at the same time smoothing out and mending past wounds and conflicting emotions regarding 9/11 and its successive wars.

The presence and influence of these political themes in the MCU is beyond contest. To give a few prominent examples from the films, all three of the *Iron Man* films deal in some way with terrorism or national security, the primary villain of *Guardians of the Galaxy* is a fundamentalist who seeks to exterminate another culture he deems impure, and the final battle of *Marvel's The Avengers* features an attack on New York City, depicted with scrambling civilians, first responders, and crumbling skyscrapers. Beyond the geopolitics of 9/11, commenters have delved into other socio-political angles of the MCU. This has particularly been the case with interpretations of later films, such as *Captain Marvel* and *Black Panther*, on issues of gender and race.[5]

This book does not argue that these interpretations of the MCU from a political angle are inaccurate. On the contrary, they reveal important aspects of the film's cultural context. However, while these prevailing political arguments and interpretations are persuasive and fascinating, they do not exhaust the potential meanings of the MCU, nor perhaps even adequately speak to its widespread popularity. Indeed, these films have been enjoyed by not only an American audience but by fans around the world, many of whom are too young to remember 9/11 or were not yet even born at the time of those attacks. Solely approaching the MCU from the perspective of 9/11, the War on Terror, or simply politics in general, while leading to perceptive insights, also tends to reduce the franchise's appeal to contemporary or recent politics, leaving out other potential levels of significance. In this book, I argue that there are also deeper, more timeless themes and symbols at work in the MCU which tap into fundamental questions about what it means to be human. The MCU, therefore, in addition to any political commentary it may be making or informed by, also falls (as the second quotation at the beginning of this introduction suggests) under the umbrella of mythology. In his groundbreaking essay on the epic Anglo-Saxon work *Beowulf*, J.R.R. Tolkien argued that while criticism and analysis of that poem from the perspectives of history, politics, and other fields had been ample, there had been very little by the way of studying "the poem as a poem."[6] In the following chapters, I intend to investigate the mythology of the MCU as a mythology using the tools of Religious Studies, a field especially well-equipped to delve into the symbolic layers of such stories.

Importantly, Religious Studies (a field sometimes also referred to as "History of Religions" and/or "Comparative Religion") is distinct from Theology. While Theology in general tends to interpret subjects from the point of view of a particular tradition, often Christianity, Religious Studies draws on academic tools and perspectives from a wide variety of disciplines (such as anthropology, sociology, philosophy, psychology, and comparative literature and mythology) to examine religious phenomena from a more cross-cultural standpoint. By employing this mode of interpretation to the MCU, the deeper and more mythic valences of the films emerge to resonate with religious narratives from around the world, helping perhaps to explain the popularity of the franchise not only in the United States, but around the globe. My goal, then, simply put, is to use broad cross-cultural comparison to illuminate the ways in which the MCU delves into timeless themes, symbols, and issues akin to more ancient religious and mythic narratives, like the *Epic of Gilgamesh*, the *Iliad*, or the *Mahābhārata*, and thus expresses something profound about the human condition.

Before proceeding further, a book that proposes comparing myths and religions across many cultures should pay due attention to the nature and definition of "myth," its place within Religious Studies and religious traditions, and the very viability of the enterprise of cross-cultural comparison. Primarily this is due to schools of thought within Religious Studies (and allied disciplines) that call all of these factors into question in the wake of postmodern movements that have assailed the very possibility of cross-cultural categories like "myth." Ivan Strenski, for example, has argued that due to the variety of narratives to which the term has been applied, effectively, "[T]here is no such 'thing' as myth."[7] Amid this multiplicity, still others have seen ulterior motives, such as Bruce Lincoln and Russell McCutcheon, who have written extensively about the political and power dynamics they perceive at work behind every scholarly attempt to work in the realm of myth or even to define it.[8]

These useful correctives aside, there are no shortage of definitions of "myth," although in common parlance and everyday language, the notions of myth as a falsehood, an untruth, or widely held misunderstanding (i.e., "it's just a myth that everyone needs to drink eight glasses of water a day") have stubbornly persisted.[9] Still, within Religious Studies and other fields, particularly Anthropology, understandings of the meaning of "myth" tend to share a common core and do, in fact, apply to a wide variety of traditions and narratives from around the world. For instance, Alan Dundes has provided a classic characterization: "a myth is a sacred narrative exploring how the world and [humanity] came to be in their present form."[10] For his part, anthropologist Bronislaw Malinowski accepts this foundation, but adds that myths further distinguish themselves from other narratives by their connection to rituals, social structures, and moral codes.[11] Further building on these ideas, Robert Ellwood adds that while myths are often about "gods, heroes, or other exceptional beings" and are set in "primordial times," they also simply "tend to be the kind of stories that deal with basic themes of life in such a dramatic way that one can read or listen to them over and over."[12] Elsewhere, Ellwood goes even further, arguing, "Myth, like all great literature, can become universal, transcending particular cultural settings to provide general models of the human predicament."[13] So, to summarize these overlapping definitions, myths can be understood as narratives cultures or traditions consider sacred, dealing often with the origins of rituals, social structures, moral codes, and other timeless concerns of the human condition.

This definition of myth allows us to understand its connection to the wider phenomenon of religion. As eminent scholar of religion and myth Wendy Doniger puts it, myth is the communication of religious questions in narrative form. "Certain questions," she writes, "recur in myths which I would call religious questions: Why are we here? What happens when we die? Is there a God? How did men come to be different from women?

Questions such as these, which are the driving force behind myths, have no empirical answers."[14] Myth is thus the human religious impulse, our drive to wrestle with timeless and overwhelming questions, put into narrative form. As I will show, the MCU asks and deals with many of these enduring questions, corresponding in a multitude of ways with mythic traditions from around the world.

On that note, the project of cross-cultural comparison has also been assailed by post-modern critics who contend that any attempt to compare religions or myths from across the world is inherently problematic. Russell McCutcheon, for instance, critiques any category used for comparison (such as "myth," "sacred," or "ritual") as a means for scholars to reproduce hierarchies of control and power.[15] In similarly pointed fashion, Jonathan Z. Smith targets the methodological mechanics of comparison as the tendency to elide differences between cultures for the sake of making patterns that may exist only in the eye of the beholder.[16]

Other scholars, though, have leapt to the defense of comparison, noting its necessity, first of all from a purely cognitive standpoint: the human brain cannot function without categories and to put information and data into categories requires comparison.[17] More specific to Religious Studies, William Paden contends that the discipline as a whole would collapse without the comparative method:

> There *is* no study of religion without cross-cultural categories, analysis, and perspective. Knowledge in any field advances by finding connections between the specific and the generic, and one cannot even carry out ethnographic or historical work without utilizing transcontextual concepts. Like it or not, we attend to the world not in terms of objects, but in terms of categories. Whenever there is a theory, wherever there is a concept, there is a comparative program.[18]

Moreover, if comparison is unavoidable and also inescapably fundamental to Religious Studies, we cannot shy away from embracing the commonalities and similarities we encounter, for to do so would mean only noting distinctions and differences, rendering each culture, narrative, or religion irreducibly alien to one another, sequestered, as Kimberley Patton puts it, "in its own little box."[19] Rather, while still being attentive to distinctions and diversity, why not affirm the correspondences and resonances we find for what they reveal about each tradition in question, as well as our common humanity? Reflecting on the metaphor of the "implied spider," which forms the title of one of her many books on the study of myth, Doniger suggests that if one sees webs of connections and common threads between the myths, religions, and cultures of the world, we can intuit that it is "the shared humanity, the shared life experience that supplies the web-building material of narrative to countless human webmakers who gather up the strands that the spider emits."[20]

This book proceeds from these positive premises on myth and the comparative enterprise, arguing that the MCU is a new—perhaps the newest?—example of one of these mythic threads, of a response to the varied conundrums of human existence. By putting the MCU into comparison with traditions from across the world, this book shows how these films about superheroes delve into truly timeless issues and elements properly deemed religious and mythic.

To be sure, past works have noted the link between superheroes and myth. Marco Arnaudo, for example, writes, "From the very beginning, the superhero comic has maintained a strong relationship with myth and religion."[21] Similarly, Peter Coogan has argued that "superheroes are the closest thing our modern culture has to myths," while Chris Knowles focuses on parallels and potential connections between comic book figures and the epic heroes of ancient civilizations like Sumer, Egypt, and Greece.[22] Others have seen ancient figures such as Hercules and Samson as the forerunners of certain superhero characters, suggesting an almost genetic narrative link.[23] The most sustained effort along these comparative lines, however, has most likely been carried out by Don Lo Cicero who, in *Superheroes and Gods: A Comparative Study from Babylonia to Batman*, surveyed a host of comic book characters for their similarities to past figures in world (primarily western) mythology.[24]

While taking a cue from these past studies, this book pursues a different tack from previous works. For one, my emphasis is narrower in that my concern is entirely focused on the MCU as a self-contained mythic text. Though I will draw at times from comic source materials (such as Jim Starlin's *The Infinity Gauntlet*) when they have direct bearing or influence on the MCU, my primary interest throughout will be the first twenty-two films of this cinematic universe. This standard applies as well to the various loosely-affiliated television series such as *Jessica Jones*, *Daredevil*, and *Agents of SHIELD*, which are largely extraneous to the central narrative of the MCU.

The MCU's unparalleled level of interconnection and intentional cinematic world-building, which, in the words of one cultural critic "no other movie studio has ever really attempted before," warrants such focused scholarly attention for the unique artifact it has produced.[25] Indeed, whereas other attempts at cinematic universes (such as Universal's "Dark Universe," the "Pacific Rim" franchise, the DC Expanded Universe, and "Ghostbusters") have largely foundered, the MCU has experienced only wild success, leading some to speculate that the degree of intentional interconnectivity and long-range narrative planning is the secret behind its popularity and resulting financial achievement.[26]

As perhaps an unintended consequence, the MCU's narrative focus and interconnection actually greatly facilitates scholarly study. When studying superheroes in general, even when focusing on a single figure, the context is often sprawling, involving decades of material, legions of authors, and multiple variants and forms. As a deliberately self-contained narrative with a limited number of identifiable creators (primarily figures such as Marvel Studio's head Kevin Feige and writer/directors Joe and Anthony Russo), as well as a clear beginning, middle, and end, these distinct boundaries facilitate scholarly analysis and simplify the process of comparison with other mythologies. To a degree, Richard Reynolds appears to have anticipated this parallel, arguing that one of the few aspects separating superhero narratives from these earlier, ancient mythologies was the kind of interconnectivity the MCU has achieved.[27]

Without a doubt, the pantheons of the mythic traditions of ancient Greece, Egypt, Japan, and India, as well as the mythic stories regarding figures such as Gilgamesh, Odysseus, the Buddha, and Rāma are themselves not always cleanly demarcated and definitely not without their variants. Yet, it is also true that over time the myths of these figure have gone through a process of "settling" in which, despite numerous strands of narrative, definable plotlines and events have emerged.[28] The very compactness of the MCU narrative thus allows for us to put it in fruitful comparison with other well-defined world religious traditions and narratives.

While my focus is narrower than past studies by concentrating solely on the narrative world of the MCU, my argument is also broader than past approaches in that, as mentioned above, the theoretical toolbox I employ through Religious Studies includes classic works from anthropology, sociology, psychology, philosophy, and comparative mythology. From that vantage, I will be putting the MCU in conversation with other mythic texts from around the world (including Greek, African, Hindu, Buddhist, Medieval European, and other traditions), but also the wide-ranging theoretical perspectives of scholars and thinkers such as Victor Turner, René Girard, Mary Douglas, Friedrich Nietzsche, and Carl Jung, among others. Importantly, though I will interpret the MCU as a mythology, it is outside the purview of this work to determine whether the MCU, or superheroes in general, are a new religion in and of themselves. Rather, my investigation looks into the MCU as a new vehicle in a new media for very old mythic questions, themes, and ideas going back to the dawn of humanity. As Danny Fingeroth has written, comic and superhero figures "play out our own problems and challenges in bigger than life, operatic terms," putting into relief issues and dilemmas with which cultures and peoples throughout time and geography have struggled.[29] By placing the MCU, the scholarship of Religious Studies, and these older mythologies in dialogue, we

The Avengers assemble for the first time in *Marvel's The Avengers* (2012). The crossover of characters from multiple individual films inaugurated the MCU's trademark—and unprecedented—level of narrative interconnection. From left to right: Chris Hemsworth as Thor, Scarlett Johansson as Natasha Romanoff/Black Widow, Jeremy Renner as Clint Barton/Hawkeye, Mark Ruffalo as Bruce Banner/Hulk, Chris Evans as Steve Rogers/Captain America, and Robert Downey, Jr., as Tony Stark/Iron Man.

experience a kind of alchemy of ideas along the lines of what Kimberley Patton and Benjamin Ray have described:

> In the act of comparison, the two original components juxtaposed in scholarly discourse have the potential to produce a third thing, a magical thing, that is different from its parents. Not only is it "different," but it can illuminate truths about both of them in ways that would have been impossible through the exclusive contemplation of either of them alone.[30]

In the following chapters, what this comparison of the MCU to world religions and mythologies reveals is that, although I will often compare the MCU superheroes to gods, god-like figures, and epic heroes, the superheroes of the MCU are more like religious virtuosos, specialists of the sacred, people touched by divine powers who now mediate with the divine. Rather than wholly human or wholly god-like, the superheroes in the MCU are portrayed as beings existing in (or thrust into) marginal, in-between categories and positions. By playing this role within the narrative, to a degree, the MCU's superheroes mirror the role Ben Saunders argues that they hold outside their various narratives as cultural figures: "Superheroes do not render sacred concepts in secular terms for a skeptical audience ... they deconstruct the opposition between sacred and secular, religion and science, god and man, the infinite and the finite by means of an impossible synthesis."[31]

At times within the MCU itself, characters attempt to resolve this "impossible synthesis" by ascribing divine status to the superheroes. When warning Steve Rogers ("Captain America") not to intervene during an altercation involving Iron Man, Thor, and Thor's brother Loki, Natasha Romanoff affirms, "These guys come from legend. They're basically gods."[32] Similarly, when the Avengers are temporarily residing in their safe-house home, Laura Barton (wife of Clint Barton, "Hawkeye") remarks, in response to her husband's need to stay on the team, "They're gods and they need someone to keep them down to earth."[33] While these comments appear to locate the superheroes in the godly realm, they also suggest a more problematic arrangement. Being "basically" a god, for instance, is not the same as being a god. Far more indicative of the role the superheroes play in the MCU, and the mythical template which they tend to copy, is the position alluded to in a speech SHIELD director Nick Fury delivers to the assembled heroes: "There was an idea ... called the 'Avengers Initiative.' The idea was to bring together a group of remarkable people, see if they could become something more. See if they could work together when we needed them to, to fight the battles we never could."[34] In this way, the Avengers (and by extension, the entirety of superheroes in the MCU) act as intermediaries between humanity and forces and powers entirely beyond their comprehension. In the language of world religions and mythology, they would thus be considered "religious virtuosos," or those individuals considered particularly gifted with abilities to specialize in handling the sacred and dangerous powers which populate the universe.

Attendant to the presence of religious specialists though, and owed to their intermediary status of occupying both the human world and the world of the divine, are certain problems and dangers. Internally, the religious virtuoso can be either symbolically or literally divided into "light/dark" and "good/evil" halves. Externally, while his or her expertise can be called on to solve supernatural problems, the invocation of those powers can also create and foster instability. The inherent ambiguity of straddling the line between the supernatural and the human (or the superhuman and the human, in the case of the MCU figures) can create a situation where, as Jeffrey Kripal has expressed with his usual flair for wordplay, the "sacred" hits instead in the register of the "scared."[35] For the superheroes of the MCU mythos, even as they protect humanity from intergalactic attacks and supernatural threats, their activities and even their very existence create additional challenges and calamities. Joe Russo, one of the key filmmakers behind the MCU, in an interview with the *New York Times* expressed awareness of this pressure and duality regarding the series' superheroes: "Ultimately, what you'll see by the end of the movies is, what does it cost to be a hero in a world where there are no easy answers? I think that's the world we live in."[36]

The lack of easy answers extends not just to the role the superheroes play in society, but also in their attempts, like the religious specialists they parallel in world mythologies, to wrestle with questions, dilemmas, and issues that have perennially plagued humanity. In the course of the MCU, along with fending off alien invasions and terrorist organizations, the superheroes also mediate perpetual cultural issues such as justice, identity, and good versus evil. Paramount among the timeless themes that the MCU superheroes confront, however, is the problem of death. Arising early in the MCU and returning to unmistakable prominence at its conclusion, is a concern with human mortality, found in the dramatic struggle with the very fact of death, personified by the figure of the villain Thanos, whose very name literally means "death." In his landmark work, *Magic, Science, and Religion*, Bronislaw Malinowski wrote, "Of all the sources of religion, the supreme and final crisis of life—death—is of the greatest importance."[37] Similarly, in the introduction to their work on views of death across world religions, Frank Reynolds and Earle Waugh position religion as the universal "language" humans use to talk about death.[38] Death quite literally stalks the MCU and the entire narrative is structured as a myth detailing how a group of religious virtuosos struggle against all odds to stave off humanity's oldest, most implacable and invincible enemy. In this way, I will argue that, in both the roles ascribed for the superheroes and the timeless issues they confront, we can see the MCU as part of a species-long, mythic conversation about the factors impinging on the human condition, putting it in the same family as the *Epic of Gilgamesh*, the *Iliad,* the *Mahābhārata* and other classic religious narratives.

To carry out this study, the book is broken into the following chapters to deal more or less chronologically with the tripartite, three "Phase" structure of the MCU. This means that while I follow the development of the MCU as much as possible from its inception to the conclusion of its storylines, some themes appear recurrently and will entail comparing, for instance, films in Phase One with films from Phase Three, or films across all three Phases. In Chapter One, I concentrate primarily on "Phase One" of the MCU, covering films running from *Iron Man* (2008) to *The Avengers* (2012). Using the anthropological theories of Arnold van Gennep, Victor Turner, and others, Chapter One applies the scheme of rites of passage to the origin narratives of the MCU heroes, showing that, just as liminality and death symbolism signify these traditional rituals, the characters of the MCU are similarly marked, injecting an element of instability, not to mention inherent mortality, into the narrative from its inception. Additionally, in that chapter we will see that the origin stories of the superheroes closely resemble the initiatory experiences described of shamans, the intermediary and ambiguous religious figure of many traditional societies. Chapter Two looks at the villains with whom the heroes contend during the Phase One (and later) films, drawing on Jung's concept of the "Shadow-self" and the Religious Studies subfield of "Monster Theory" to show that these enemies are represented as mirror-like inversions of their heroic counterparts. This parallels closely with the mythic journeys of figures like the Buddha, Beowulf, and Jesus, who each had to contend with monsters or demons who represented the darker portions of their nature.

With Chapters Three and Four, the book more substantially considers "Phase Two" and "Phase Three" of the MCU, which run from *Iron Man 3* (2013) to *Ant-Man* (2015), and *Captain America: Civil War* (2016) to *Avengers: Endgame* (2019), respectively. The narrative and the universe it describes has become increasingly more complicated and, therefore, more unstable by this point. Chapter Three details this instability by applying the work of Mary Douglas on purity and pollution to the prominent theme of infection, contamination, and corruption that defines the Phase Two movies. For instance, during the course of the Phase Two films, Iron Man must deal with the "Extremis" Virus, Captain America learns that Hydra has infiltrated SHIELD, and Thor learns the supernatural "Aether" has infected Jane Foster. While Phase One illustrated the heroes' creation and ascendancy, the pervasiveness of the theme of pollution throughout Phase Two signals the beginning of their decline. Chapter Four follows this thread to discuss how, in the Phase Three films *Captain America: Civil War, Spider-Man: Homecoming, Guardians of the Galaxy: Vol. 2, Thor: Ragnarok, Black Panther,* and *Captain Marvel,* the heroes have begun fighting amongst themselves or with their elders. This parallels the stories of the Hindu *Mahābhārata,* Greek *Iliad* and *Theogony,* among other myths, which, particularly through René Girard's work, can be seen as deploying the horrors of internecine and intergenerational warfare as allegories for societies coming apart at the seams, a process which the heroic fraternities of the MCU are suffering at this point in the larger narrative. Throughout this chapter, we see the continuing issue of confused and disrupted identity as the superheroes face difficulties not only in determining their true antagonists, but also their true selves. This aligns with the larger trajectory in the MCU, for at this point in its narrative, the superheroes struggle against primarily internal rather than external enemies.

In the final chapters of the book, I focus entirely on the two films *Avengers: Infinity War* and *Avengers: Endgame,* respectively. Chapter Five looks at the former, primarily analyzing the figure of Thanos, whose reappearance in the MCU signals the return of death, which has been the latent threat to the heroes since their origin stories in Phase One. As a conquering titan who utterly defeats the heroes arrayed against him, Thanos resembles such monstrous figures as the Hindu demons Rāvaṇa and Tāraka, the Greek monster Typhon, and the Egyptian chaos-dragon Apophis, but also personifications of death around the world, including Hades and Māra. These comparisons bring out both the mythic similarities, but also the universal anxiety undergirding all these figures: irresistible chaos and the fear of life's instability and eventual end. Chapter Six examines the events of *Avengers: Endgame*, in which the heroes, refusing to accept the reality of death, go on a time-bending adventure in the hopes of undoing Thanos' victory. This journey is quite similar in both motivation and content to the quests undertaken by Gilgamesh, Odysseus, Orpheus, and others to their culture's version of the Underworld, either to undo death or seek its counsel. In the final battle that this quest precipitates with Thanos, we can see the end (and the moral) to which the entire MCU mythic narrative has aimed since its first film: death haunts us all as a fact of the human condition, but by opposing it and defining oneself against it, a kind of peace and transcendence is possible. The concluding chapter, in addition to summarizing the main ideas of the book, also takes a look at the twenty-third MCU movie, *Spider-Man: Far from Home*, and other proposed MCU projects, for hints of how the series' mythology may progress after the end of its first saga, as well as discuss once again how this project contributes to the wider field of Religious Studies.

Through these discussions, this book reveals the deeper mythic themes and symbols of the MCU. As author Grant Morrison has written,

> We live in the stories we tell ourselves. In a secular, scientific, rational culture lacking in any convincing spiritual leadership, superhero stories speak loudly and boldly to our greatest fears, our deepest longings, and highest aspirations.[39]

In the following chapters, I show how the MCU taps into precisely those same deep wells of wonder (and terror) regarding the human experience.

ONE

The Ritual Birth—and Death—of a Superhero

Rites of Passage and Initiation in the MCU Origin Stories

There was an idea ... called "the Avengers Initiative." The idea was to bring together a group of remarkable people, see if they could become something more. See if they could work together when we needed them to, to fight the battles we never could.
—Nick Fury, played by Samuel L. Jackson,
Marvel's The Avengers (2012)

After initiation, the shaman demonstrates various powers in public rites for the benefit of the community ... the shaman is also a mediator between the supranormal and normal worlds and so restores a proper balance.
—Margaret Stutley, *Shamanism: An Introduction,* p. 7

Whether through miracles, divine parentage, virgin births, or other means, myths around the world often herald the origin of a hero through spectacular fashion. In this way, the Buddha, Lao Tzu, Arjuna, Hercules, Jesus, Sundiata, Sweet Medicine, Huitzilopochtli, and countless others come into the world immediately marked as extraordinary individuals, separate and somehow different from the rest of their communities. To introduce and similarly delineate its superheroes, the MCU draws on the structure and symbolism of the mythical-ritual complex known as the "rite of passage." As anthropologists have long observed, rites of passage—rituals signifying a person's movement from one state of life to another—are ubiquitous in cultures around the world. Catherine Bell, in her detailed discussions of ritual types and processes, describes the significance of such ceremonies in this way:

Sometimes called "life-crisis" or "life cycle rites," [rites of passage] culturally mark a person's transition from one stage of social life to another. While these rites may be loosely linked to biological changes like parturition and puberty, they frequently depict a sociocultural order that overlays the natural biological order without being identical to it.[1]

Though articulated differently depending on the culture, formal recognition of the importance of life's transitions—from youth to adulthood, single to married, living to dead, and so on—helps the individual and the society at large acknowledge changing roles, relationships, and responsibilities. Near the turn of the twentieth century, pioneering researcher Arnold van Gennep argued that, around the globe, rites of passage tend to follow a common pattern of separation, transition, and reincorporation: the person(s) going through the ritual are marked as separate, put through the rites of the ceremony, and then integrated back into the larger community.[2] This framework can be found in birth customs, baptisms, weddings, graduation celebrations, military training, funerals, and a host of other societal activities.[3]

In another landmark work, *The Hero with a Thousand Faces*, Joseph Campbell borrowed heavily from van Gennep's three-part conceptualization of rites of passage to argue that a similar pattern (which he deemed the "monomyth") recurs in stories of the "hero's journey" across cultures.[4] Within the superhero genre, the personal journey and transformation that van Gennep and Campbell would recognize as the rite of passage or monomyth, respectively, often most explicitly occurs in the very first episode of the superhero's career: his or her origin story. Usually forming a critical part of his or her identity, the origin story frequently establishes the values, struggles, and character arc that the superhero will experience.[5] This structure applies equally well to the characters of the MCU, who, as they are first introduced throughout the film series, are shown undergoing journeys and transformations that establish the fundamental aspects of their personalities. These origin stories in the MCU bear all the hallmarks of the rite of passage ritual, with its attendant religious and mythic symbolism. What is more, the depictions found in the MCU bear an additional resemblance to the general outline of the rite of passage initiation for the religious specialist known in many cultures as the "shaman." As individuals put through trials not necessarily of their own choosing, whose resulting special powers and position often put them on the margins of their community, the shaman serves as a particularly interesting parallel to the unstable situations often held by the superheroes of the MCU.

First, before launching into that specific comparison, it is useful to apply the general outline of the rite of passage to examples from the MCU, starting with the first film in the franchise, *Iron Man*. As the movie begins, billionaire Tony Stark is portrayed as an egotistical, philandering, technological genius who makes his living by inventing and selling weapons through the corporation his father founded. In a typically cynical, jingoistic moment, during a weapons demonstration in Afghanistan he makes the following declaration to a group of United States army officials:

> They say that the best weapon is the one that you never have to fire. I respectfully disagree. I prefer the weapon you only have to fire once. That's how Dad did it, that's how America does it....[6]

Following the demonstration, his military convoy is ambushed and he is taken prisoner by an insurgent group deep in a series of caves. Shrapnel from the attack on the convoy having pierced his heart, Stark is kept alive only by the operation performed by fellow prisoner Yinsen, who has placed a small generator in his chest. The insurgents insist Stark build weapons for them to aid in the takeover of their country. Planning several steps ahead of his captors, Stark works with Yinsen to instead build a powerful suit of armor. Immune to bullets and with enhanced strength, he uses the armor to escape. Once back in the United States, Stark finds the experience has changed him and he risks his life to turn his company around and keep others from abusing the technology he has created.[7]

From this summary, the structure of the rite of passage is obvious. Separated from society, Stark undergoes an ordeal that forces him to transform, and, upon his return to his community, he achieves a new status: superhero. Importantly, the transformation is composed of two parts. One is a physical aspect, in that Stark is now marked by his chest injury and the need to wear a portable mini-reactor to keep his heart beating. The other is in the mental and moral dimensions, for as a result of his experience, he has fundamentally altered the way he views the world. In a dual sense, Tony Stark has gained a new heart.

Looking more closely, other common features of the rite of passage also stand out from the film. One is the conspicuous role of an elder or teacher. In *Iron Man*, Tony Stark owes his life to Yinsen in many ways: for originally stabilizing his condition with the operation, for buying him time to power up the suit when the insurgents begin to suspect a plot, and, perhaps most of all, for planting the seeds of his incipient moral center. Commenting on Stark's current lifestyle, Yinsen chides, "So you are a man who has everything ... and nothing." Not willing to leave the situation quite so philosophical, he further, and even more bluntly, laments what Stark has done with his life: "Those are your weapons ... in the hands of those murderers! Is this what you want? Is this what you wish the legacy of the great Tony Stark to be?" When Yinsen is mortally wounded in the escape, Stark acknowledges the debt he owes to him and the role Yinsen has played in turning his life around:

> TONY STARK: Thank you for saving me.
> YINSEN: Don't waste it ... don't waste your life, Stark.[8]

Yinsen's response further motivates Stark to remake his life, to eventually take on the superhero mantle, and thus underscores the role that this teacher figure has played in this rite of passage.

A second conspicuous element of Stark's rite of passage is symbolism very strongly suggestive of what anthropologist Victor Turner called "liminality," or the "in-between." Fleshing out and expanding van Gennep's categories, particularly the intermediary "transition" period, Turner argued that across cultures the initiation stage is marked by practices and symbols of inversion and ambiguity. Turner explains that this is due to the fact that "liminal entities are neither here nor there; they are betwixt and between positions assigned and arranged by law, custom, convention, and ceremony."[9] During the rite of passage, at the intermediary transition or initiation stage, the initiate belongs officially to neither the before nor the after of the social realm they are traversing, thus meaning he or she is also ambiguously in-between or outside the social rules and mores of both of those realms. In his fieldwork with the Ndembu of Zambia, Turner noted that this liminal period was consequently marked by the suspension of usual regulations: those of high status were abused by the low, the rich dressed like the poor, the living pretended to be dead, and so on.[10]

Even more frequently, as the initiate was (at least metaphorically) dying to one role and being reborn in another, the liminal period was characterized by language and symbols evoking death. Mircea Eliade made the same observation, noting that "often rituals illuminate the symbolism of initiatory death. Among some peoples candidates are buried or laid in newly dug graves, or they are covered with branches and lie motionless like the dead."[11] Across world religions, other symbolisms of death during rites of passage abound. In Southeast Asian Theravāda Buddhism, the induction to monastic life involves shaving the head and dressing in robes that either replicate or are explicitly gathered from cemetery grounds.[12] In Islam, during the Hajj (the ritual pilgrimage to Mecca), participants exchange their regular clothes for plain white robes, cut their nails and hair, and go without shoes—all traditional ways of preparing a dead body in the Middle East.[13] Myriad other examples could be cited, however, the main point is that, following Turner and Eliade, ritual traditions around the world invoke death symbolism to show how the initiate is dying to an old life and being born anew.

As we might expect from the prevalence of this imagery, *Iron Man*

Taking on the new form of Iron Man, Tony Stark (Robert Downey, Jr.) emerges from the cave where he has been held captive, symbolizing his figurative death and rebirth. From *Iron Man* (2008).

participates in the same symbolism of liminality and death. After the attack on the convoy, Stark is reduced from a tailored, expensive suit to wearing dusty, torn rags. Though an exceedingly wealthy, elitist member of global society, he is abused and treated with scorn by his captors. Most tellingly, though, his place of confinement is a cavern tunneled deep into the earth, resembling nothing so much as a grave. For all intents and purposes, Stark has been buried or, rather, his old egotistical self has been broken down and buried. Through the ordeal and his bonding with Yinsen, the cavern grave becomes also a womb in which he transforms into a new person.[14] When Stark reemerges, it is as an entirely different being who, rather than wearing a suit from Armani, wears a suit of armor and goes by a new name (though he has yet to pronounce it): Iron Man. In this way, his old self has died, giving birth to a new identity.

Once recognized, the pattern of the rite of passage and the symbolism of liminality and death are widespread in the MCU origin stories. The resonance is particularly strong in *Thor* (2011). While Thor is, of course, a pre-existing figure from Norse traditions, the comic history of the character draws on but also deviates significantly from the mythic source material, marking a path of distinct representation that the MCU follows as well. For example, besides introducing new characters and personalities, the comics, particularly in the early years, provided Thor with a human secret identity, Dr. Donald Blake. While the MCU does not inject this facet of the comics into its films (other than with an aside, where Blake is referenced as Jane's ex-boyfriend and his identity employed briefly as a cover for Thor) it still suggests that the Asgardians are more otherworldly, powerful beings rather than the gods of Norse legend. Partly this is communicated by the recurrent theme, brought up both by Jane Foster and later by Thor himself, that magic is merely science that has not yet been understood.

Like Tony Stark, at the beginning of the film, Thor is portrayed as morally-deficient: he is brash, conceited, and quick to anger. During an early scene when his father, Odin, is preparing to name him king-in-waiting of Asgard, Thor is shown marching through the crowd, indecorously soaking up the applause, and performing tricks with his hammer. When the ceremony is interrupted by an incursion of Frost Giants, the traditional enemies of the Asgardians, Thor argues vehemently for a punitive strike into their home realm of Jotunheim. In response to Odin's refusal, Thor petulantly throws over a table, then leads his own private raid, putting the tenuous peace with Jotunheim at risk. The attack goes badly and Odin must intervene to save Thor and his companions.

As if this were not bad enough, throughout the confrontation with the Frost Giants and after, Thor finds himself referred to not as an adult, but as a child. Laufey, king of Jotunheim, mocks Thor prior to the battle, saying, "You're nothing but a boy, trying to prove himself a man," and then, to Odin, "Your boy sought this out." Tellingly, Odin does not disagree: "These are the actions of a boy, treat them as such." Back in Asgard, in response to Thor's continuing protests, Odin offers one further chastisement along these lines: "You are a vain, greedy, cruel boy!"[15] Seeing that his son is too immature for his station and responsibilities, Odin strips him of his powers and exiles him to Earth, sending the hammer as well, albeit conditioned with the enchantment that only one truly worthy can wield it.

On Earth, Thor endures a series of reversals emphasizing the liminal, topsy-turvy space he has entered. Once a prince upon whom others doted, he is tasered, sedated, and restrained by various authorities, to which he can only offer the now impotent protest that the "mighty Thor" should not be treated in this way. Most humiliating and heartbreaking, though, is the realization that even after he has finally located his hammer on Earth, he cannot lift it. Slowly and painfully, he learns humility and the extent of his ignorance. When his adopted brother Loki (who has been scheming to take the throne) sends the fearsome Destroyer to Earth, Thor is a changed person. Rather than let the Destroyer maraud among innocent bystanders, he offers himself as a sacrifice, telling Loki:

> Brother, whatever I have done to wrong you, whatever I have done to lead you to do this, I am truly sorry. But these people are innocent. Taking their lives will gain you nothing. So take mine and end this.[16]

With that, the Destroyer strikes and kills Thor, but his selfless act has made him worthy of the hammer and its power returns him to life. Having discovered a moral center, Thor returns to Asgard and, where once he sought to punish the Frost Giants, he recoils in horror from Loki's plan to annihilate them. Defeating Loki and reconciling with his father, Thor demonstrates that he has undergone a fundamental change.

Using the film's own language, through the trials and ordeals he endured, Thor has transitioned from a boy to an adult. As with Stark, an elder was key to this transformation, in this case Odin, whose decision to exile his son, in retrospect, was less a punishment than the instigation of a rite of passage. Finally, accentuating the extent of the change Thor undergoes, the borderline between the old personality and his new perspective is death: the new Thor only emerges after he has been struck dead by the Destroyer.

While the entirety of *Thor* can be seen as detailing the character's rite of passage, the imagery is just as powerful in two other MCU films, though neither devotes quite as much space to its development. In *Captain America: the First Avenger* (2011) and *Black Panther* (2018), from Phase One and Phase Three respectively, we find obvious liminal imagery, though the characters' developmental trajectories are also quite different from both Thor and Stark. For the first third of *Captain America*, Steve Rogers lives life as a physically frail man unable to act on his desire to fight alongside his friends in the Second World War. When an experimental "super-soldier" procedure becomes available, the scientist Abraham Erskine, who invented the serum, learns of Rogers and tests his motivation by asking if he wants to fight so that he can "kill some Nazis." Rogers responds, "I don't want to kill anyone. I just don't like bullies. I don't care where they're from."[17] Satisfied with this response and confident that Rogers is a "good man," Erskine puts him forward for the procedure, which involves painful injections and bombardment by mysterious energies, all while lying restrained and prone in an enclosed capsule that resembles a coffin. When he emerges, Rogers is several inches taller, many pounds heavier in muscle, and possesses greatly enhanced reflexes and strength. For the rest of its run-time, the film takes several opportunities to underscore that, despite the physical transformation brought on by this near-death experience/experiment, Rogers' conscience and motivation remain the same, though his assertiveness has obviously increased. When battling the Red Skull, he remarks, "I can do this all day," which was his rejoinder to a more mundane bully earlier in the film, underscoring both the ways he has remained the same, but also the distance he has come. Additionally, when his file is closed after going missing in action, the picture kept in the folder is not of the more recent super-powered physique, but an enlistment photo showing the smaller, frailer Steve Rogers.[18] Though this suggests a kind of continuity, it also emphasizes the fact that the man he was is also gone.

In this sense, Rogers' rite of passage is the inverse of Thor's: while

Within the enclosed pod, Steve Rogers is bombarded with mysterious rays and absorbs the "super-soldier" serum that will turn him into Captain America. Note how the pod closely resembles a coffin, suggesting that Steve Rogers must encounter death in order to attain his new persona. From *Captain America: The First Avenger* (2011).

the former possesses brawn, but not heart, Rogers is all heart, but no brawn. When both symbolically die as part of their respective rituals, these deficits are balanced out by what is gained through the ordeal. Rogers' journey is like Stark's and Thor's, however, in the role played by an elder: besides enabling the procedure, Erskine encourages Rogers to, no matter what else happens, make sure that he remains a good person.

In *Black Panther* (2018), the rite of passage is innately tied to the role of the elders and ancestors, though it portrays the evolution of that relationship differently from the other films we have analyzed. At the start, T'Challa has inherited the throne of the African nation of Wakanda upon the death of his father, T'Chaka. After prevailing in a ceremonial challenge, T'Challa is laid in a pit of red dirt with his arms crossed. Zuri, the royal priest, administers the magical heart-shaped herb that will make him the "Black Panther" while onlookers bury him in the sandy red soil. T'Challa finds himself in the midst of a vision, arising out of the ground in a white robe, evoking what we observed earlier about the use of such clothing in Islamic, Buddhist, and other traditions to treat the deceased, the pilgrim, or the initiated. T'Challa then encounters the spirit of his father who expresses pride in having prepared his son to be king. "Have I ever failed you?" the father asks, and T'Challa replies, "Never."[19]

This turns out not to be the case, though, when N'Jadaka, a long-lost cousin of T'Challa's who was kept secret by T'Chaka, appears and badly beats him in another ceremonial challenge. Cut, stabbed, and comatose from a long fall, T'Challa lies in a coma when his family finds him. Administering the herb again, they once more bury T'Challa and he lapses into a second vision with his father. Again clothed in a white robe, the son this time reproaches his father for omitting the truth of this cousin and, along with his ancestors, for turning away from helping the rest of the world.

T'Challa revives, his experience in the liminal realm between life and death giving him renewed strength to defeat N'Jadaka. Though we will discuss the complicated family dynamics of *Black Panther* in much more detail in Chapters Two and Four, for now, it is interesting to note, in the current context of rites of passage, that T'Challa's seeming first initiation is perhaps better seen as the start of an ongoing ritual. Somewhat like Thor, from that moment on, all of T'Challa's choices seem to go awry: he is unable to capture a wanted criminal, he loses the trust of friends, and he is beaten in the first fight with N'Jadaka. Following these ordeals and having gained more knowledge, T'Challa admonishes his father in the second vision, establishing himself as his own person with his own ethical standards. This moral transformation signals the end of the rite of passage and, rather than the resumption of his reign, more accurately depicts its true beginning.

On that point, one further element appears in all of these MCU origin stories. As Eliade notes, at the end of the ritual, "candidates are given new names, which will be their new names henceforth."[20] After taking back the mantle, T'Challa is the "Black Panther." Similarly, Steve Rogers becomes "Captain America" and, during the final scene of his film, Tony Stark declares, "I am Iron Man." In other cases, characters are more reluctant to lay claim to their new identities. Scott Lang, for instance, when asked to become the "Ant-Man" first says, "Can we do something about the name?" and, when introducing himself by that moniker, adds, "It wasn't my idea."[21] Bruce Banner, given his violent tendencies as "the Hulk," is even more reticent to use the name, referring instead to "the other guy" throughout *Marvel's The Avengers.*[22]

One of the most complicated instances of ritual naming involves Captain Marvel. Originally born as "Carol Danvers," she is badly injured in a military plane crash and taken by an alien race called the "Kree" to be exploited for her powers. Able only to read the last few letters of her dog tag, the Kree refer to her as "Vers," which she accepts until their duplicity and manipulation is revealed. Then, she reclaims her own name and, it is implied, also the name of her mentor: "Mar-vell."[23]

Altogether, the prevalence of the tripartite ritual structure (separation, transition, and reincorporation), the treatment of liminality, and the obvious death symbolism in these MCU movies shows that the religious pattern of the rite of passage informs these superhero origin stories. Given the ubiquity of such rituals, the use of this template at once imbues the story of each character with a universal mythic quality and also guarantees the relatability of these figures: though one may lack the technical skill of Iron Man, the indefatigable spirit of Captain America, or the strength of Thor, their struggles and ordeals to become better in the face of challenges can be reminiscent of our own trials.

Beyond rites of passage in general, as mentioned at the beginning of this chapter, the particular ritual figure which the MCU figures resemble more than any other in their origin stories is the so-called "shaman." First, it is worthwhile to touch on the long and fraught history of the study of shamanism in Religious Studies. Used at one time to refer to traditions from areas as disparate as Native America, Australia, South America, Africa, and Northern and Central Asia, shamanism as a term has described those religious specialists who are "able to travel to the other worlds to communicate with the gods and spirits ... and mediate between the various worlds."[24] The linguistic origin of the word "shaman" is hotly disputed, with various hypotheses placing it as Chinese, Turkic-Mongolian, Siberian, or Indic in derivation.[25] In light of this linguistic uncertainty and diffuse geographic background, some have wondered about the usefulness of the term and whether it serves merely as a catch-all phrase for a variety of traditions and practices. Peter Knecht, for instance, writes:

> It could well be that the academic terms "shaman" or "shamanism" impose on the elements they are meant to identify a meaning that does not correspond to the meaning of the local terms, even if, in the eye of the outside observer, these elements appear similar to those in other areas.[26]

In other words, "shamanism" as a cross-cultural category may be too amorphous to do anything other than conflate unrelated phenomena and elide crucial practical and theoretical differences.

At the same time, there is little doubt that even if practices across these geographical regions are not identical, substantive and fascinating commonalities do appear to exist.[27] For a long period of time, Mircea Eliade's *Shamanism: Archaic Techniques of Ecstasy* was the seminal work in the field, though his wide-ranging phenomenological style has been the subject of multiple criticisms along the lines Knecht offers above. However, despite this appraisal, as Witzel points out, while Eliade's descriptions and categories have been found wanting when applied to Australian and African practices, his work on other parts of the world has been confirmed by later ethnographers.[28] As a broad and loose category, then, employed carefully and for comparative purposes in conversation with more contemporary ethnographic evidence, the concept of the "shaman" still remains relatively tenable.

The common elements in the experience that compose that concept, as reported not only by Eliade but others, begin with a moment of crisis. The incipient shaman is caught up either by a disturbing dream, a prolonged and debilitating illness, or an injury, and is subsequently pulled into a vision in which he or she sees spirits, demons, and/or ancestors. These beings pull him or her into a range of dimensions, including the sky, the underworld, or other supernatural realms apart from regular human experience. During this time, the initiate will also experience "dismemberment of the body, followed by renewal of the internal organs," all as part of the trial and spiritual education by these beings and ancestors.[29] At times, the prospective shaman is even taken apart down to the skeleton before being reconstructed.[30] Heyne reports the following from his study of the Evenki in Siberia:

> The soul of the candidate traveled into the other world. There it was killed and cut into pieces by the spirits. In the process the young shaman experienced his being made into a skeleton. The spirits consumed his flesh and afterwards reassembled his bones. He was revived and fully returned with the capacity to act as a fully established shaman for the benefit of his community. Now he was in a position to leave this world, if need be, and converse with beings in the otherworld.[31]

We find similar language in *The Tibetan Book of the Dead*, the origination and symbolism of which Geoffrey Samuel locates among the shamanism of the ancient Indo-Tibetan and Nepalese region.[32] Used traditionally in a set of rituals for the deceased while he or she is in the liminal state of the *Bardo* (the dimension between death and rebirth), *The Tibetan Book of the Dead*'s prayers and incantations are meant to initiate and guide the individual into higher consciousness and rebirth while in that condition. During this initiation, the text cautions, imposing and frightful beings will materialize and "cut off your head, tear out your heart, pull out your entrails, drink your blood, eat your flesh and gnaw your bones; but you cannot die, so even though your body is cut into pieces, you will recover."[33] If the initiate can maintain equanimity during this and other experiences in the liminal *Bardo*, he or she will achieve manifold spiritual insights, transitioning to a higher plane of existence.

After the spirits have cut up, then refashioned and reassembled the shaman initiate's body anew, ceremonially killing and then resurrecting him or her, the individual is returned to the human world and, in the words of Margaret Stutley, he or she:

Demonstrates various powers in public rites for the benefit of the community. He or she is now a psychotherapeutic healer, having undergone both mental and physical suffering and long training that enables him or her to train others. The shaman is now a mediator between the supranormal and normal worlds.[34]

In this capacity, the shaman is frequently called upon for assistance in times of illness for others, to facilitate the smooth transition of souls to the afterlife, or to rescue souls prematurely taken to the other worlds.[35]

Despite the service the shaman thus delivers to his or her community, they are also, as reported by ethnographers, often viewed ambivalently: the forces they control and interact with are ambiguous at best, while the fact of their in-between status is sometimes thought to be the source of some of the very problems they are called upon to solve, namely sickness and death.[36] The shaman's role is thus defined in many ways by death: his or her near-death experience at the beginning of the shamanic career, then a lifelong mediation between the worlds of life and death thereafter.

Shamanic initiations thus contain all the elements of the broader rite of passage, such as the tripartite separation/transition/reincorporation structure and symbolic death/resurrection. On the latter, in his ethnographic studies of the Evenki, Heyne found that shamans were considered to have been born twice, once from a mother and again from spirits, to the extent that they were not the same people they were before: they had died and come to life again with new powers.[37] Simultaneously, these rituals also stand apart as entrances to a closed society. Though some rites of passage are more or less universal for any individual in a given group (for instance, birth or puberty rites), a shamanic initiation is set aside only for a chosen few, and often those who have not necessarily chosen the role but been selected for it due to the vision or crisis they have experienced. This establishes the shaman as both the religious virtuoso of the community and also as someone set very much distinct and apart from other members of that same society.

On that basis, we can see an immediate similarity to the function and character of the superhero, which is founded on the fundamental difference between those individuals and the rest of humanity, who by definition do not possess the same supernatural abilities. Like the shaman, it is the superhero's responsibility (again invoking Nick Fury's words from earlier in the chapter) to "fight the battles we never could" and on behalf of his or her community, assume the burden of interacting with the otherworldly. In the world of ritual initiations, the superhero is a restrictive, selective group not unlike a secret society, open only to the chosen few.

Again like the shaman, when it comes to superheroes, the chosen, however, do not always choose themselves. The superhero is just as often drawn into his or her role by powers, forces, or circumstances outside their control. Though some shamans are part of hereditary traditions or sought out their powers intentionally via a vision quest, as we saw above, most come to the position as the result of an unexpected crisis that heralds the intervention of the spirits or ancestors. In the MCU, for every Steve Rogers who pursues extraordinary abilities, there is a Tony Stark, Bruce Banner, or Carol Danvers who has power thrust upon them unexpectedly, pulling them into a world which they did not intend to join.

Indeed, just as a sudden crisis and a painful refashioning of the body usually marks the beginning of the shaman's career, we find the same with the MCU superheroes. In Tony Stark's case, after the unforeseen ambush, he is subjected to an excruciating operation where his heart is augmented by metal, wires, and a battery. Though the Hulk's origin is shown only briefly in the opening credits of *The Incredible Hulk*, we learn that due to Bruce Banner's laboratory accident, he is exposed to an amount of gamma radiation that permanently alters his body, so much so that when angered his body entirely transforms into a massive, green behemoth.[38] As Stark tells Banner later, "that much gamma exposure should have killed you," but instead, it leaves Banner with an ongoing bodily state where, under certain conditions, his body seemingly rips open, manifesting his latent rage and fury, leaving him exposed, he says, "like a nerve."[39]

The women of the MCU likewise undergo torturous, shaman-like physical ordeals as part of their initiation into the status of superhero. In *Avengers: Age of Ultron*, we learn that Natasha Romanoff (also known as "Black Widow") as part of her training as an assassin in Russia, was treated brutally, including being forcibly sterilized.[40] Carol Danvers similarly endures invasive treatment at the hands of the Kree who, in addition to physical training, transfuse Kree blood into her body and install a chip in her neck meant to shut down her incipient powers. In some ways, Danvers' experience is stereotypically shaman-like, as she is literally carried off into the sky realm to gain tutelage in space from otherworldly entities. Though the Kree have their own interests in mind rather than those of Earth or Danvers, this is not inconsistent with the shaman's experience: at times, the beings who come to claim and or instruct the initiate can be terrifying or even malign.[41] Finally, when Danvers confronts what the Kree call their "Supreme Intelligence," she is hurled through a wall that turns liquid, and spirals into an explosion of colors and streams of her own memories. This phantasmagoria of light and sound, out of which Danvers forcefully asserts her own personality, strikes a chord similar to that described in stories of shamanic otherworldly journeys. These ecstatic visions of the heavenly, astral, trans-dimensional, or underworlds are often accompanied by jarring auditory experiences, varieties of luminous figures or shapes, random animal, insect, or human forms juxtaposed, or other amalgamations of lightning and fire.[42]

Two other heroes introduced later in the MCU also have nearly text-book shamanic experiences, even with corollaries to the hallucinogenic visions explained above. After Scott Lang steals Hank Pym's "Ant-Man" suit, he tries it on out of curiosity, stepping into his apartment's bathtub for privacy. When he experiments with a button on one of the gloves, he suddenly finds himself reduced to minuscule size. To add to the mystery of the situation, seemingly out of nowhere a voice (that of Hank Pym's) begins to talk to him. "The world sure seems different from down here, doesn't it, Scott?" Pym says, causing Lang great consternation, akin to the disembodied voices at times reported by shamans during their initiations, and also later throughout their lives.[43] "It's a trial by fire, Scott, or in this case, water," Pym continues, as one of the roommates enters, turning on the bathtub's faucet, sending Lang hurtling to the floor and into a crack in the tile to the floor below. He lands in a dance club, spinning on a turnta-ble before falling further down through a vent to be sucked up by a vacuum cleaner and chased by a rat, which, from the perspective of his diminished size, seems to be of monstrous proportions. At the end of the experience, when Pym tells him he has done well and can keep the suit, Lang responds, "No, no, no! I don't want to!"[44] From the utter disorientation to the myste-rious observer/teacher, not to mention his initial reluctance to assume the role, Lang's experience neatly parallels shamanic vision accounts. While he has not received a new body following a dismemberment, he has received a new body in the form of the size-changing suit taken (and then gifted) from Hank Pym. Lang's reluctance to accept the initiatory invitation corre-sponds to the reaction observed by certain ethnographers, who have seen prospective shamans sicken, then deteriorate in health as they resist the supposed call of the spirits, only improving (as does Lang's mentality, and life in general) when they fully embrace their new role in life.[45]

Disorienting as it was, this foray into the miniature world is only the beginning of Lang's shamanic adventure. Later in the film, in order to defeat a villain with a similar suit, Lang shrinks far past levels considered by Pym to be safe, entering the Quantum Realm. As molecules and atomic struc-tures form kaleidoscopic shapes and colors all around, Lang struggles to maintain his grip on reality, barely finding the presence of mind to reverse the process and return to the regular-sized world. Like Danvers' experi-ence with the Kree, this trip through what the MCU terms the "Quantum Realm" mimics the "otherworldly journeys" described by shamans in their trances or initiation stories.

Stephen Strange's story in *Doctor Strange* (2016) equally parallels the shaman's initiation, though his ultimate reaction is somewhat different and his training rather more extensive. A bit like Tony Stark, Strange begins the film as an arrogant, self-absorbed person, working as a neurosurgeon primarily for the fame that he may gain through pioneering new techniques and treatments. Following a car crash, his hands are mangled and the prospects that he will ever operate again are slim. With the failure of conventional and experimental treatments, Strange travels to Nepal where he meets with the "Ancient One," who previously healed a paralyzed man. Rather than cutting edge cellular biology, the Ancient One instead speaks of "reorienting the spirit to heal the body," causing Strange to scoff in sarcastic skepticism. She reacts by separating Strange's astral form from his body, sending it hurtling up past the Earth's atmosphere and through tunnels of psychedelic colors where he grows millions of tiny hands all over his body and has visions of throbbing, glowing balls of color and energy not unlike Lang's visions in the Quantum Realm. In addition to realms of light, the Ancient One also shows Strange, in words that almost deliberately invoke the otherworldly spirits against which shamans must defend their peoples, "dark places where powers older than time live ravenous and waiting." During the experience, Mordo, one of the Ancient One's apprentices, remarks that Strange's heart rate has gotten dangerously high, showing the strain put on him by this trip through the untapped realms of the universe. At the end, however, rather than recoil, as Lang does originally, Strange instead begs the Ancient One to teach him.[46]

Once he begins this training, Strange's period of ordeals has only just begun. To help him overcome difficulties in casting his first spells, the Ancient One decides to motivate Strange by stranding him near the peak of Mt. Everest, where he will freeze to death or suffocate if he does not produce an escape portal. Even after learning spells at a rate that astounds his teachers and fellow students, Strange must still defeat the evil sorcerer Kaecilius, who has allied himself with Dormammu, ruler of the Dark Dimension. Strange can only do so by transporting himself to the Dark Dimension and trapping Dormammu in a time loop where the dark being eviscerates, disembowels, and otherwise kills him over and over again. This mimics the aspect of the initiation in which the prospective shaman is ritually tortured, though with a twist: despite the agony he endures, Strange exerts control over the situation by trapping Dormammu in the time spell. In order to be released from this loop, Dormammu betrays Kaecilius and his followers.[47] In addition to this repeated death and resurrection, once Strange has mastered the mystic arts, he effectively replaces his once crippled hands with ones powered instead by magical energy.

In this way, the shamanic template of crisis, bodily torture, and training is repeated throughout the MCU. The origin stories of the films, which consist of individuals becoming superheroes, is neatly modeled on the pattern of humans becoming religious virtuosos. Beyond the beginning stage of achieving their respective statuses, we ought to remember the interstitial space the shaman generally occupies in his or her society. By virtue of his or her transformation, the "shaman is a being of two worlds—of this world and the otherworld," effectively existing with one foot in the human world and the other in the world of the spirits.[48] The superhero similarly goes on to serve as a mediating figure, bridging the gap between different realms. Tony Stark, for his part, joins together the realms of humanity and technology. From *Iron Man* (2008) to *Iron Man 3* (2013), he embodies his name literally with a heart made of iron. Even after that point, his technical and scientific expertise is shown as without parallel, exceeding even Bruce Banner who (if his own remark is taken at face value) has seven doctorates.[49] It is Stark who not only invents the arc reactor, constantly upgrades his armor, and invents (however problematically) artificial intelligence, but also solves the problems inherent in time travel. Throughout the film series, Stark serves as the mediating figure between the realms of the human and the technological, living out the status suggested by his superhero name.

Other MCU figures operate similarly. Thor and Captain Marvel connect the sky to the Earth, or in the latter's case, more accurately space and Earth, as well as alien and human. As an earthling who has lived for a prolonged period among aliens, yet sided with Earth against those aliens, Carol Danvers is both, yet neither. As Thor has power over thunder and lightning, he represents the sky-earth bridge, but also bridges godliness and humanity, as his humility and romantic interests are gained primarily through his time on Earth. Bruce Banner, for his part, combines humanity with monstrosity, blending the ego and the id, to take a Freudian tack. As his line ("I'm always angry") prior to the climactic battle in *Marvel's The Avengers* makes clear, there is not as clean a line between the identities of "Hulk" and "Banner" as he would sometimes like to suggest. The one lurks constantly in the other, inhabiting the same space at once.[50]

Other examples abound throughout the MCU. Steve Rogers blends the soldier and civilian spheres of life, bringing the military into the humane and the humane into the military, as it were. He is also a person displaced in time: due to seventy years of suspended animation in the Arctic, Rogers is a man from the 1940s transplanted into the 2010s, and thus not wholly belonging to either. This fact is not lost on Rogers or others, as he is often referred to in *Marvel's The Avengers* as "old-fashioned" or, in the villain Loki's words "the man out of time."[51]

Otherwise, Stephen Strange moves between the earthly dimension and the multiple mystical domains of the universe, dealing with malign spirits entering the mundane world, and also sending his own spirit self on disembodied journeys.[52] As another similarity, further aligning the MCU's

Doctor Strange character with Indo-Tibetan imagery specifically, when he and his sorcerer colleagues cast spells, their hand gestures invariably create images like Tantric *maṇḍala*s, which are geometric figures meant to symbolize the esoteric connection between individual and the cosmos, and are often used to facilitate meditative efforts as well. For their parts, Scott Lang navigates the macro- and microverses, Clint Barton darts between the spheres of domestic and secret agent life, and T'Challa bridges Wakanda with the other nations of the world. A few members of the team assembled in *Guardians of the Galaxy* (2014) also exhibit this tendency, as Peter Quill comes from human/alien parentage, Rocket is a sentient humanoid-like animal, and Groot is a walking tree. Of these few, Rocket perhaps comes closest to the shamanic experience, having been taken years ago for repeated experimentation to create him in his present form. He describes his experience in this way: "I didn't ask to get made! I didn't ask to be torn apart and put back together over and over and turned into some little monster."[53] Rocket's description in that passage is eerily similar to the shamanic reports of abduction and dismemberment by outside, unearthly powers.

To be sure, each of the superheroes deals with their experiences differently, and the ways that they negotiate the blending of their respective categories and the realms they connect shifts over time in the MCU. This is especially true in the cases of Stark, Banner, Rogers, and Thor, who end up substantially revising and even resolving their divided personalities as a key part of the mythos' concluding episode, *Avengers: Endgame*, which we will investigate in detail in Chapter Six. At this point, though, it is enough to note that like the shaman, the superheroes of the MCU are shown as the extraordinary protectors of the rest of the less extraordinary world. While the shaman protects his or her community from disease and the incursions of malign spirits and demons, the superhero protects his or her community from all supernormal threats. For Doctor Strange's society of sorcerers, this means safeguarding the "natural law" and monitoring for "other-dimensional beings who threaten the universe."[54] In the case of Thor, it is a role inherited from his father Odin and more ancient Asgardians who, for instance when the Frost Giants attacked Earth, intervened so that "humanity would not have to face this threat alone."[55] In this same vein, Steve Rogers in particular and the Avengers in general, assume their roles to protect the weak from the abuses of the strong.

As both Eliade and Stutley recognize, the shaman derives powers and the ability to mediate worlds from the traumas he or she has endured: having healed, he or she can then heal others.[56] Looked at another way, though, the shamanic crisis and its tendency to split a person across two realms also results in considerable stress and strain. For the shaman, this can mean living a life in continual flux and peril to the soul. As Takinguchi

Naoko writes, "By definition the shaman is a liminal being. As a mediator, he is between this and the other world, his presence is betwixt and between the human and the supernatural."⁵⁷ For the superhero, as Clare Pitkethly makes clear, to take on this in-between status is a sentence of perpetual identity confusion: "Incorporating both sides of an opposition, the superhero embodies a paradox, or in other words, he [or she] becomes unsure of exactly what he [or she] actually *is*."⁵⁸

At the same time, it would be wrong to entirely remove choice from the equation as the MCU superhero's continued liminality is often directly related to a decision made to retain or further that status. After returning to the United States after his escape, Stark signals the change in his personality during an initial press conference:

> I had my eyes opened. I came to realize that I had more to offer this world than just making things that blow up. And that is why, effective immediately, I am shutting down the weapons manufacturing division of Stark Industries.⁵⁹

This new mentality leads to an almost obsessive drive to reclaim or destroy his misused technology, to the point where he tells his assistant, Pepper Potts, "There's the next mission, and nothing else."⁶⁰ Once his rival, Obadiah Stane, is defeated, however, and the illegal sale of his technology appears halted, at yet another press conference, Stark has the opportunity to use an alibi provided by SHIELD to explain away the extraordinary events of which he was part and go back to a normal life. Instead, he throws away the alibi and declares to the world, "The truth is, I am Iron Man."⁶¹ This acknowledgment, though, does not equate to complete acceptance. Using the arc reactor on his chest as a metaphor for the continuously liminal status he now bears, during *Marvel's The Avengers*, Stark admits the following: "This little circle of light is part of me now; it's not just armor. It's a terrible privilege."⁶²

We find something of the same sense with Bruce Banner in *The Incredible Hulk*. When pressed by Betty Ross, his former girlfriend and confidant, if he thinks his mind is still somehow in control of the Hulk, Banner replies, "I don't want to control it. I want to get rid of it."⁶³ Later, though, when an unethical scientist uses gamma radiation and gamma-infected blood to turn the soldier Emil Blonsky into the monstrous "Abomination," Banner realizes he is the only hope for stopping the beast's rampage. This time, Betty hesitates, and they briefly argue:

> BANNER: It's the only thing that can stop it. *I'm* the only thing that can stop it.
> BETTY: You think you can control it?
> BANNER: No, but maybe I can aim it.
> BETTY: This is too risky! It's insane!
> BANNER: I know, but I have to try. I'm sorry.⁶⁴

With that, in order to serve the greater good of defeating the Abomination, Banner willingly puts himself in a position to turn into the Hulk and seemingly embraces his liminal status. In a similar vein, though he has destroyed the Rainbow Bridge to save Jotunheim, cutting off access to Earth, Thor does not turn his back on that realm, instead standing with Heimdall and asking for news. Steve Rogers is faced with his own impossible situation when the bomber he has commandeered from the Red Skull can only be stopped by crashing it into the icy sea. To save countless lives, he chooses to sacrifice his own, or at least the life he has known, as the freezing conditions put him in suspended animation for seventy years.

In *Guardians of the Galaxy*, Peter Quill exhorts the rest of his group to become something more than the independent mercenaries each has been to that point. As he points out, this involves coming to terms with the trials they have already faced and accepting those yet to come:

I look around at us, you know what I see? Losers. I mean, like, folks who have lost stuff. And we have. Man, we have. All of us. Our homes, our families, normal lives. And, usually, life takes more than it gives, but not today. Today, it's given us something. It has given us a chance.[65]

In their own way, then, each superhero embraces and chooses the struggles and ordeals placed before them, internalizing and assenting to their liminal status, with all its difficulties, as the best way available to make the world a better place. For both the shaman and the superhero, therefore, it is perhaps the case that, to paraphrase Stan Lee's famous line in the early run of the *Spider-Man* comic series, "With great power comes great instability."[66] Another term we have seen for this instability, though, and all the difficulties connected with it, owing to van Gennep and Turner, is liminality, which is never wholly benign nor without risks. Turner tells us that, in relation to the rest of society, such individuals "appear as dangerous and anarchical, and have to be hedged around with prescriptions, prohibitions, and conditions."[67] Those who are in the liminal space or embody liminality, according to van Gennep "are outside society, and society has no power over them, especially since they are actually sacred and holy, and therefore untouchable and dangerous."[68] Drawing on both points, in his classic sociological study of religion, Émile Durkheim argued that, across world traditions, whatever is considered sacred, due to its unearthly power and potential to spread fluidly across boundaries, is ritually-separated from its profane surroundings. By extension, then, "sacred beings are, by definition, separate beings. They are characterized by a discontinuity between them and profane beings" out of a need to safeguard both worlds.[69] Eliade notes the same ambivalence in his studies, remarking that, across cultures, "the sacred attracts and repels, is useful and dangerous, brings death as well as immortality."[70]

A particular example of this within a shamanic tradition can be found in the Warao people of the Venezuelan Orinoco delta. The shamans of this society are divided into three specialties to interact with the ancestors, the forces of fertility, and the spirits of the underworld. Exerting control over these realms is obviously considered a great benefit to the larger community, but, in ways both unintentional and at times intentional, by interacting with these powers, the shaman can also bring down hardship and affliction. As reported by ethnographers, "each of these religious practitioners can be benevolent or malevolent, they can kill and they can cure sicknesses brought about by other shamans of their own type or by the powers of the deities with whom they communicate."[71]

The superhero, like these shamans, is a being of both great benefit but also great danger. By coming into contact with the sacred powers of the otherworld, the shaman or the superhero is him or herself a conduit for the sacred, which poses risks to the ordinary world. As we saw, for this reason, within his or her respective society the shaman is often demarcated on the fringes of the social order and communal space, invited in for regular rituals or when necessary for healings, but considered too dangerous to have regular contact with the people, given his or her connection to uncanny entities. Total seclusion is not possible for either the shaman or the superhero, however, as obviously they must have contact with the people they are charged with protecting. Just as liminality is never resolved entirely for the shaman in order for him or her to do the spiritual work that needs to be done, the ambiguity and identity conflict the MCU superheroes undergo is not settled until the mythic narrative concludes. Until then, the superhero, purely as a result of being a superhero and thus a liminal being, emanates danger and instability. He or she protects from harm, but also exudes peril; they can heal others, but also potentially hurt them. An exchange between Nick Fury and a member of his oversight council speaks to this very point:

> COUNCIL MEMBER: I don't think you understand what you started by letting the
>   Avengers loose on the world. They're dangerous.
> FURY: They surely are. The whole world knows it. Now all worlds know it.[72]

As we will see in later chapters of this book, succeeding episodes in the MCU mythos reveal this duality and play out this dynamic and its consequences again and again.

Finally, the superhero and the shamanic religious specialist are connected in one last respect: death. While the shaman achieves his or her status via a symbolic death, so too is each superhero's origin either a symbolic or a literal enactment of death. Furthermore, the shaman and the superhero both carry out the rest of their careers in a struggle against death, attempting to save lives and protect their communities. Indeed, this struggle occupies multiple levels in the MCU, for even as the superheroes fight against death in this mundane sense, the apotheosis of death (Thanos) is revealed in the post-credits of *Marvel's The Avengers* as the MCU's primary villain for its Phases One through Three (also known as "The Infinity Saga").[73]

Merely surviving the rite of passage and becoming a mediating figure, as we have discussed in this chapter, is not the only mythic challenge facing the superheroes in the MCU. The superheroes' latent ambiguity emerges in the MCU stories almost immediately after their origins in the form of the first antagonists they respectively face. Consistently these villains amplify, reflect, invert, or even stem from some aspect of the superheroes' darker sides. It is to the relationship between the superheroes and their villains, and the corresponding mythic and religious corollaries, which we turn in the next chapter.

Two

A Shadow Follows

The MCU Superheroes
versus Their Darker Selves

Whoever fights with monsters should see to it that he does not become one himself. And when you stare for a long time into an abyss, the abyss stares back into you.
—Friedrich Nietzsche, *Beyond Good and Evil*, p. 69

SOLDIER: *How you feeling, man?*
EMIL BLONSKY (THE ABOMINATION), PLAYED BY TIM ROTH: *Like a monster.*
—*The Incredible Hulk* (2008)

In addition to a spectacular origin, as part of their journey mythic heroes often face an antagonist, usually in the shape of a force of evil or a monster. We find this whether it is Odysseus encountering Polyphemus the bloodthirsty Cyclops, the Buddha contending with Māra, Jesus being tempted by Satan, Gilgamesh battling Humbaba, Hercules fighting the Hydra, or so on out of a countless number of examples. According to philosopher Paul Ricoeur, the centrality of the antagonist in the hero's story is due to the centrality of evil in life:

> Evil is part of the interhuman relationship, like language, tools, institutions … there is thus an anteriority of evil to itself, as if evil were that which precedes itself, that which each person finds and continues while fighting it, but beginning it in [their] turn. That is why in the Garden of Eden the serpent is already there; he is the other side of that which begins.[1]

The importance of the figure of evil or the monster in the world's mythologies means we should not be surprised that the role of villain looms large in the origin movies of the MCU, which take place primarily in Phase One, but also appear in Phases Two and Three of the franchise as well. As we will see in this chapter, the villain each hero faces is somehow reflective of the hero and fitted to the personality traits of the superhero in question. Some have seen this as a weak point of the MCU, *Game of Thrones* author George R.R. Martin among them:

> I am tired of the Marvel movie trope where the bad guy has the same powers as the hero. The Hulk fought the Abomination, who is just a bad Hulk. Spiderman fights Venom, who is just a bad Spiderman. Iron Man fights Iron Monger, a bad Iron Man. Yawn.[2]

Contrary to the boredom and laziness implied in Martin's "yawn" comment, from the perspective of Religious Studies, the symbolism and portrayal of a villain as the reflection or inversion of the hero, particularly in an origin story, makes a great deal of sense. That they often reflect aspects of the hero, particularly their negative qualities, is entirely in line with psychologist Carl Jung's archetypal theory of the "shadow-self." In Jung's estimation, all the facets of an individual's personality exist in the unconscious and the greatest journey one can undertake involves delving into this untapped repository. Within that realm, however, is "the shadow, which personifies everything negative that the subject refuses to acknowledge about [themselves] and yet is always thrusting itself upon him [or her] directly or indirectly."[3] During the journey, whether internal through self-examination or metaphorical in the hero's journey, a confrontation with the shadow is inevitable, as Jung further describes:

> Whoever goes to himself risks a confrontation with himself: the mirror does not flatter—it faithfully shows whatever looks into it; namely the face we never show to the world because we cover it up with the persona, the mask of the actor. But the mirror lies behind the mask and shows the true face. This confrontation is the first test of courage on the inner way, a test sufficient to frighten off most people, for the meeting with ourselves belongs to the more unpleasant things that can be avoided so long as we can project everything negative into the environment. But if we are able to see our own shadow and can bear knowing about it, then a small part of the problem has been solved.[4]

From this vantage we can see why it is perfectly logical—not to mention perfectly mythical—for, to paraphrase George R.R. Martin, the Hulk to fight a "bad Hulk" or Iron Man a "bad Iron Man": it is a representation of the hero struggling against his or her shadow-self, their flaws and negative aspects projected into a kind of dark twin. Indeed, this tendency has many mythic precedents. In Zurvanism, a subset of Zoroastrianism, Ohrmazd and Ahriman, the good and evil principles of the world, are considered twins, born from the same womb.[5] In certain Southeast European folklore traditions, God and Satan were considered brothers, perhaps stemming from the strands of much older Gnosticism in which Christ and Satan were brothers.[6] In India, the myths of the Buddha's contest with Māra, the god of death and desire who attempts to forestall Siddhartha Gautama's realization of awakening, have sometimes been characterized in this way as well: "Māra is the Buddha's devilish twin.... Māra is the self to Buddha's selflessness, the fear to Buddha's fearlessness, the death to Buddha's deathlessness."[7] As expressions of the good principle's shadow-self, the forces of malignancy haunt the hero's first, and subsequent, steps on the path.

How the form of the shadow-self is hypostasized and characterized in world mythology is also important and it is helpful here to consult Monster Theory, a subfield that crosses multiple cultural disciplines including Religious Studies. As scholars in that subfield have observed, the monster across cultures is often a "harbinger of category crisis," meaning that it represents a disruption of the perceived natural or cultural order, in both what it represents and the actions it takes. To this end, the monster is frequently represented as a grotesque mish-mash of body parts or hybridities, combined with violent tendencies or other excesses.[8] As an example, think of the Greek Chimera, which combines lion, goat, and snake, blurring natural categories just as it exhibits destructive habits. As David Gilmore summarizes it, "the monster is a metaphor for all that must be repudiated by the human spirit. It embodies the existential threat to social life, the chaos, atavism, and negativism that symbolize destructiveness and all other obstacles to order and progress."[9] In other words, though the symbol of the monster has served many purposes socially, culturally, and theologically, it can and frequently has been used to stand as an embodiment of the disordered negativity of the shadow-self, which the hero must defeat. This is precisely the role we see played by the monstrous villains of the MCU's origin stories. They are monstrous inversions of the heroes, dark amplifications of their worst flaws, greatest temptations, and most unseemly impulses. The villains of this portion of the MCU thus serve as multiple metaphors for how the superhero conquers himself, mastering the shadow inside.

However, an alert reader will note the similarity in description between the monster and concepts discussed in the previous chapter. As beings which frustrate and endanger categories, monsters can also be regarded as examples of the "in-between" or liminal, just as heroes themselves are. This at once cinches the bonds even tighter between the heroes and their villains and also lends credence to Timothy Beal's point that in mythology we often see "it takes a monster to kill a monster."[10] In this way, perhaps the MCU shows that heroes and villains simply occupy opposite extremes of liminality and the superheroes, as much as they attempt to conquer the shadow-self, never can fully escape its reach, just as they never can fully shake their in-between, unstable status. To an extent, we can see the villains the superheroes face in these stories as examples of the "dark shaman," the spiritual intermediary who uses his/her power to hurt and harm rather than heal. Indeed, throughout the following we will see that the thin line at times between the superhero and his/her shadow villain is composed primarily of the varying intentions that each brings to their powers.

Overall, the shadow-self villains we will examine in the MCU origin stories fall generally into three different categories, each one comporting to a vice or defect related to the superhero concerned. The first is greed, or the temptation to employ one's status, powers, and abilities for one's own gain, to hoard those abilities and their outcomes selfishly. Given, as described in the previous chapter, Tony Stark's past as a weapons-selling war-profiteer, it is fitting that his main adversary in *Iron Man* is Obadiah Stane, an older member of the Stark Corporation. When the viewers first meet Stane, he is portrayed as only concerned about profits and sales. Rather than see it as a significant technological breakthrough capable of bettering the world, to him the arc reactor is "a publicity stunt to make the hippies shut up."[11]

Gradually, though, Stane's more duplicitous nature comes to light. For instance, after Stark announces a cessation to weapons manufacturing, Stane colludes with the corporation's board of trustees to lock Stark out of the company. Prior to that, it is revealed that Stane had been making money selling weapons not only to the United States government, but also the country's enemies. Most seriously, the viewer discovers eventually that Stane conspired with the insurgents in Afghanistan to attempt to murder Stark in order to take full control of the company. Stane's betrayal comes to a head when he builds his own suit of armor in an attempt to usurp Stark's technology for sales around the world. As Stark lays paralyzed through a special neural device, Stane rips the miniature arc reactor from the superhero's chest, telling him he should be glad to have helped produce a "whole new generation of weapons." He then uses the device in his own massive suit, termed the "Iron Monger," which Stane describes as less "conservative" than Stark's version.[12]

When the viewer sees Stane's version, this description turns out to be accurate. The Iron Monger suit entirely dwarfs Stark's rendering; indeed, if the latter is inspired in color and sleekness by a sports car or hot rod, the Iron Monger is more like a grim bulldozer or a tank. Besides the repulsor rays of Iron Man's suit, the Iron Monger has missiles, chain machine guns, and rocket boosters, expressing Stane's violent and excessive nature. After first desperately finding an old chest piece to keep his heart beating, Stark uses his greater experience with the armor and the arc reactor to defeat Stane.

In the oversized stature of his Iron Monger armor and his goal of exploiting the technology to accumulate and hoard wealth, the character of Obadiah Stane plays into very old mythic tropes. David Gilmore, for instance, has noted how monsters are frequently shown across cultures "looming over smaller, weaker" humans, perhaps as a psychological

As Iron Man, Tony Stark (Robert Downey, Jr., top) battles the much larger Iron Monger (Jeff Bridges), created and piloted by Obadiah Stane. Their battle replicates the older mythic trope of the hero versus the giant. From *Iron Man* (2008).

(particularly Freudian) holdover of juvenile inferiority in the face of the father figure.[13] Marina Warner makes a similar point, arguing that the ogre and the giant in world mythology, which must be overcome at some point during the journey or adventure, represents the atavistic past that the hero has to conquer in order to usher in the future.[14] This makes a certain amount of sense as Stane was a contemporary of Stark's father and could be seen as the father figure needing to be overcome before Stark could complete his transformation into a new person. The Iron Monger's size would then stand in for the daunting and intimidating nature of Stark's past, both in familial but also strictly personal terms.

Size is not the only symbolic quality found in the Iron Monger, however, as his aggressive, acquisitive nature also stands out. These aspects, combined with his size, put the character in standing with monstrous figures of myth who destroy and also hoard all they encounter. As Watkins has observed, hoarding monsters (like the giant or the dragon) who keep wealth from circulating are common in societies where gift exchange is central to proper group relations.[15] In ancient Indian Vedic mythology, the massive serpent Vritra, whose Sanskrit name literally means "enclosed," held back the primordial waters and all other necessities for life. Only when the thunder god Indra destroyed the serpent could the world take shape.[16] Engaging the same theme, a Zulu tale describes an enormous, humpbacked monster that swallows people, animals, and even entire villages, growing larger and larger and more violent until a hero kills it and releases everything trapped inside.[17] A Basotho story similarly deals with a "huge shapeless thing" roaming about, swallowing every living creature and thing of value until a magical hero cuts it open, freeing those imprisoned.[18]

The template of the violent, hoarding monster is not only found in India and Africa. In a story from the Salish of Montana, the trickster Coyote hears of a giant who consumes all in his path. Unknowingly, Coyote walks into the beast's mouth, meeting all the people and animals the giant has swallowed. From the inside, Coyote stabs the monster's heart and it vomits up everything it has trapped.[19] One can also see the dragon of the Anglo-Saxon epic poem *Beowulf* occupying this role as well, being referred to as the "hoard-watcher" for the vast store of gold it jealously keeps, so much so that it spreads devastation when a single goblet is removed.[20]

As interpreted by Warner, again drawing on Freud, these overly large and disgustingly appetitive ogres, giants, dragons, and other monsters "correspond to the ungovernable Id," which represents desire gone wrong, ill-directed, and grown out of proportion. These monsters' voraciousness, size, and violence signify the strength of the Id's drive, and their frequently obtuse, bumbling nature and "vulnerability to the cleverness of human wits" stand for the intellect's ability to triumph over these lower forces.[21] In *Iron Man*, Stane is characterized the same way as a greedy, Id-driven, violent accumulator. He refers to Stark as his "golden goose" for producing so many money-making inventions, obsesses over stock prices, and makes several attempts to discover what Stark's new project involves. The excess, in weaponry and size, of the Iron Monger is thus an extension of the violent, hoarding mentality of Stane. Just as Vritra, Beowulf's dragon, and the consuming monsters of African and Native American mythology are portrayed as potentially entrapping the entire world if not stopped, we are left with the impression that if Iron Man does not defeat Iron Monger, Stane will spread copies of his armor throughout the world, reaping huge amounts of wealth while the planet is consumed in war. Also, to Warner's point, Stark is shown as more clever and intelligent than Stane, who primarily relies on brute force. During their battle, Stark employs his knowledge that the iron suits are vulnerable to icing at high altitudes, deploys flares to disrupt the Iron Monger suit's visual display, then uses his technical expertise to damage the wiring that controls Stane's weapons-targeting systems. Overall, in ways similar to the hero's triumph over the ogre or the giant in world mythology, Stark defeats Stane through his greater intelligence and wit.

Iron Monger's symbolism operates at another level as well, since Stane's overriding concern with money and war-profiteering mirrors Stark's own personality at the beginning of the film. He too lives in excess, maintaining a hangar of sports cars, gambling, drinking, and engaging in meaningless sex. He shows no regard for the consequences of his weapons sales, even joking, when a reporter calls him the "merchant of death," that "that's not bad." His Mark I armor, the first version he fashioned in the Afghan cavern, also bears slight resemblance to the Iron Monger suit in its metallic gray design and intent for intimidation. Even Stark's more elegant red and gold suit frightens motorists during the fight with Iron Monger, causing one family to scream in terror as he looks into their windshield. Besides excess, Iron Man and Iron Monger also overlap, at least somewhat initially, in causing fear.

On this point, the Micmaq of the Canadian Atlantic coast have a story of the culture hero Glooscap facing a monstrous rival chief "so huge that if one stood at his feet, one could not see his head." This horrible being had dammed all the rivers, hoarding the drinkable water for itself, and swallowed up countless living things. In order to overcome him, Glooscap grows twelve feet tall, paints his face fierce colors, and contorts his features into a snarl, terrifying all he encounters on his way to fight the giant chief. At the battle, he cuts the rival chief open, letting loose mighty streams of water.[22] As Beal has observed, this may be a case of needing a monster to kill a monster, and it bears some similarity to Stark's situation: to overcome Stane/Iron Monger, he must be the Iron Man, which is not as frightful as the Iron Monger, but is still disconcerting and unsettling to the crowds of bystanders, at least in his initial appearances.

By representing greed and the unrestrained violence of war, Iron Monger is thus the perfect villain for Stark, standing in for the "merchant of death" shadow-self he has strived to shed and exorcise since becoming Iron Man. Like Iron Monger, the *Ant-Man* villain "Yellowjacket" is obsessed with profit, even through fueling warfare, and is equally unbalanced mentally and morally. Decades before the events of the film, the viewer learns that the scientist Hank Pym has discovered particles that, through use with a special suit, can allow a person to shrink in size and retain full physical strength. Through this technology, Pym becomes the "Ant-Man," so called because he is the approximate size of an ant, but also because he can communicate with and, to an extent, control the behavior of ants. He takes on a pupil, Darren Cross, but comes to regret it. Pym later describes their relationship this way: "I thought I saw something in him. The son I never had, perhaps. He was brilliant, but as we became close, he began to suspect that I wasn't telling him everything ... he became obsessed with recreating my formula. But I wouldn't help him. So he conspired against me and he voted me out of my own company."[23] Yet again, we have a father figure versus a son, coming into conflict over technology and capitalistic interests, although the relationship is flipped: here it is the father figure who has moral concerns about the quasi-son, as is revealed during a conversation between the two later in the film:

> CROSS: What did you see in me?
> PYM: I don't know what you mean.
> CROSS: All those years ago, you picked me. What did you see?
> PYM: I saw myself.
> CROSS: Then why did you push me away?
> PYM: Because I saw too much of myself.[24]

Pym's instinct to recoil at Cross's obsessive, even reckless, appetite for technological advancement shows that he recognizes how his protégé exhibits aspects of his shadow-self, though his actions have lasting consequences. In control of the company, Cross is able to recreate the formula and make arrangements to sell it to the highest bidder, even the fascist terrorist organization Hydra, for amounts in the billions of dollars. Combined with the monopoly on the fuel required to run the suits using the formula, Cross anticipates becoming a very powerful and very rich person.[25]

Interestingly, this makes him the exact opposite of Scott Lang, whom Pym has chosen over Cross to take on the mantle of Ant-Man. Lang has just gotten out of prison for fraud against his former company. Even though it is portrayed as an act of rebellion against a corrupt employer and some even admire his actions, Lang's behavior has permanently damaged his life and he cannot find work due to his criminal record. This prevents him from seeing his daughter, who lives with his ex-wife and her husband. Described by Cross disdainfully as nothing but a "martyr who took on the system and paid the price," Lang nevertheless has the good intentions and moral fiber Cross lacks, and thereby gains Pym's coveted mentorship. In a moment of resentment, Cross suggests that Pym was drawn to Lang as both share a past in which rash actions endangered a relationship with a daughter, Lang through his criminal acts and Pym through his secretive behavior following the death of his wife. Outbursts like this create the semblance of a kind of sibling rivalry, then, with Cross as the materially successful but morally faulty "brother," and Lang as the "prodigal son" who has failed in some aspects of his life, but longs to do good in the world.

The distinctions between the characters of Lang and Cross are further refined by their respective Ant-Man and Yellowjacket suits. Since both control shrinking technology and manipulate size, they represent an inherent instability and insecurity in both individual's lives and, to a degree their personalities: Lang is attempting to overcome a criminal past and Cross is mercurial and violent in his temperament. While the Ant-Man suit, save for a conical portion on the mask, conforms entirely to the shape of the human body, the Yellowjacket version possesses glowing yellow eyes and a mouth and, in addition to the wearer's own arms and legs, four prong-like stingers

Darren Cross' Yellowjacket (Corey Stoll) displays the bodily deformation (multiple appendages and glowing eyes) common in monsters across cultures. From *Ant-Man* (2015).

that shoot disintegration rays. Cross's design is thus much more militaristic and violent than Pym's and renders his body as more misshapen. By blending insect and human features, in Jeffrey Cohen's words, the Yellowjacket suit can be categorized as monstrous since it is "a form suspended between forms that threatens to smash distinctions."[26] At one point in the film, as Cross holds Lang's daughter Cassie hostage, she asks him, "Are you a monster?" He replies, "Do I look like a monster?" In response, she screams, providing answer enough from her and the audience's perspective.[27]

The glowing eyes, together with the stingers, also connect to the thesis of Paul Trout's work in *Deadly Powers*. In that book, Trout argues that some forms (such as prominent or glowing eyes, stingers, fangs, claws, etc.) are found cross-culturally in representations of monsters because they evoke the attributes of saber-tooth cats, hawks, snakes, and other animals that would have hunted our evolutionary ancestors.[28] The predatory analogy is apt for the representation of Yellowjacket, and to describe Cross's actions in the film. Whether it is opportunistically pouncing on Pym's company, preying on his ideas, or later hunting down Lang's daughter, Cross is portrayed as an amoral predator only concerned with safeguarding his own interests. In this way, he is also a fitting villain for Pym and Lang, as each of those characters have also been guilty in the past of putting their own interests ahead of others. In the case of Pym, it was research over a relationship with his daughter, Hope. For Lang, it was defrauding his company, which made a point to the corrupt bosses, but severely impacted his own family. Cross' incessant self-interest serves as the foil and shadow-self to both Pym and Lang.

Continuing with the theme of predation, we find the "Vulture" suit in *Spider-Man: Homecoming* (2017) represented in a fashion similar to the Yellowjacket. As a combination of human and raptor bird, its wearer, Adrian Toomes, possesses hovering rocket wings, piercing goggle eyes, and lacerating metal claws for feet. At one point, a character in the film describes Toomes in his Vulture suit as "a psychopath dressed as a demon," while Peter Parker, after their first encounter recalls him, "swoop[ing] down, like a monster."[29] Interestingly, Toomes thinks of himself as a working class person who deserves to get ahead and has rationalized the steps he has taken through that credo. Early in the film, his salvage business is crippled when government officials confiscate the scrap and other materials Toomes has collected for resale from the debris left-over after Loki's Chitauri army invaded New York in *Marvel's The Avengers*. The government misses one load, though, and Toomes holds onto it, saying, "This is our last chance to get what's ours." He and his cohorts go on to use the alien materials to make powerful weapons they sell for high prices on the black market. Toomes' justification through his working-class pretense surfaces during a confrontation with the film's hero, Peter Parker ("Spider-Man"):

> TOOMES: Peter, you're young. You don't understand how the world works.
> PARKER: Yeah, but I understand that selling weapons to criminals is wrong!
> TOOMES: How do you think your buddy Stark paid for that tower or any of his little toys? Those people, Pete, those people up there, the rich and the powerful, they do whatever they want. Guys like us, like you and me ... they don't care about us. We build their roads and we fight their wars and everything. They don't care about us. We have to pick up after them. We have to eat their table scraps. That's how it is. I know you know what I'm talking about, Peter.[30]

Toomes' appeal and his attempt to draw Parker into his rationalization, even onto his side, hides two facts: his work is not as honest as a construction worker or a soldier and he also is no longer working class, as his illegal dealing in weapons has made him quite wealthy. His attempt at an avuncular demeanor is also belied by a brutal streak, which surfaces quickly when he kills a member of the gang who threatened to reveal the true nature of the business to Toomes' family. Later, Toomes threatens Parker the same way:

> Peter, nothing is more important than family. You saved my daughter's life, and I could never forget something like that, so I'll give you one chance. You ready? You walk through those doors, you forget any of this happened. And don't you ever, ever interfere with my business again. Cause if you do, I'll kill you and everyone you love. I'll kill you dead. That's what I'll do to protect my family.[31]

His twisted notion of family values aside, Toomes' real concern lies obviously with maintaining his lifestyle, income, and reputation, which Parker threatens through his actions as Spider-Man. To undercut his motivation, Toomes tries to pull Parker into his way of thinking, even to make compromises or effect deals with him. Besides the inherent monstrosity of the Vulture suit, Toomes' penchant to tempt Parker puts his character into resemblance with other figures of world mythologies and religions. In the Indian Buddhist tradition, prior to becoming the "Buddha," Siddhartha Gautama is accosted by Māra, who challenges his quest as wrong-headed and ill-fitting for someone of his ancestry. As Gautama sits meditating under the Bodhi tree, Māra says to him, "Follow the dharma [duty] that is your own, abandon the dharma [duty] of awakening. By subduing the world with arrows and rituals you will attain Indra's realm. To travel along that path brings fame … asceticism brings ignominy to one born in a line of royalty."[32] Rather than truly having Gautama's best interests at heart, Māra, of course, is primarily interested in sidetracking Gautama's practice and preventing him from achieving Buddhahood, which would threaten the god's control over the realm of death and desire. Here he offers a tempting alternative more in line with worldly rather than spiritual success.

In a Pāli Buddhist text, the *Mārasamyutta*, Māra takes several opportunities to similarly proposition the Buddha, this time regarding ways his powers have caused him to neglect things of this world or could provide him with wealth. On one occasion, he tells the Buddha, "One who has sons delights in sons, one who has cattle delights in cattle. Acquisitions truly are a man's delight, without acquisitions one does not delight," suggesting that one should forego the practice of the Buddhist path in order to experience the pleasures of these worldly things.[33] Later in the text, Māra tries to plant the seed of acquisition and worldliness in the Buddha's mind another way, pointing out that a person possessing the Buddha's rarified powers "need only resolve that the Himalayas, the king of mountains, should become gold, and it would turn to gold."[34]

The Buddha rebuffs these (and other) temptations and threats by Māra, seeing through them as stratagems to compromise his practice and enmesh him in a worldly, appetitive existence. In a chillingly similar way, Toomes appeals to sensibilities he hopes to find or instill in Parker about the inherent value of acquiring wealth and how his path of heroism as Spider-Man is an affront to worldly values. Just as Māra attempts to muddle and dissuade the Buddha from a path that threatens the established order, Toomes connives to sidetrack Parker from threatening his villainous activities.

Within the Christian gospel tradition, we find another parallel in stories of Satan's temptation of Jesus in the desert. Appearing primarily in *Matthew* and *Luke*, Satan first tells the presumably hungry Jesus that "if you are the Son of God, command that these stones become loaves of bread." Later, he tells Jesus he could demonstrate his godly powers by throwing himself from a parapet to be caught by angels. Finally, he shows Jesus all the kingdoms of the world, promising them and all their riches in exchange for his worship. Jesus refuses each bargain, seeing them for what they are: temptations to misuse his status and power for personal, worldly gain.[35]

These are bargains Toomes has made with himself, however, and then passes on to Parker, who is actually a very logical superhero to expect to be tempted by them. At one point, in fact, he is sorely tempted to don his Spider-Man suit to impress a girl at a party. Though not told in the MCU, as a standard part of the Spider-Man origin story, after acquiring his powers, Parker used his abilities at first to make money in carnivals and wrestling matches. When a manager cheated him out of a payment, Parker stood by while the man was robbed. Later, the same robber killed Parker's beloved Uncle Ben, leading him to adopt the famous "with great power comes great responsibility" ethos.[36] Toomes voices the same temptation and represents Parker's older, shadow-self impulse to use his great luck and great powers to amass great wealth, all out of a smug self-justification that he deserves it. In his guise as the "Vulture," Toomes stands for what Parker (and Gautama and Jesus, for that matter) would have become if he had not chosen a different path as Spider-Man, which he articulates in the following way: "When you can do the things I can, but you don't, and then the bad things happen ... they happen because of you."[37] Parker is able to arrive at that more enlightened, heroic ethic by resisting and repulsing the kinds of shadow-self temptations that Toomes' Vulture represents.

Iron Monger, Yellowjacket, and Vulture thus represent the selfishness and greed that Iron Man, Ant-Man, and Spider-Man have long dealt with as aspects of their own personalities, and their defeat of the villains expresses their willingness to confront these shadow-self projections. The form of the projection, of course, changes in correspondence to the darker side of the superhero(es) in question. For instance, in the cases of the Hulk and Captain America, these figures are defined by their relationship to strength and power, making it perfectly logical that the villains they would face represent the temptation to revel in or abuse strength and power. Taking the Hulk first, we find him paired against Emil Blonsky, who becomes the "Abomination" in *The Incredible Hulk*. A British Special Forces officer called in by General Ross to hunt Bruce Banner, Blonsky first sees Banner transform into the Hulk when they have cornered him inside the Brazilian bottling factory in which he had been working and hiding. While the rest of the military team is terrified, Blonsky exhibits a kind of attraction to the sheer power that he saw: "Something big hit us! It threw a forklift truck like it was a softball. It was the most powerful thing I've ever seen."[38] As an aging soldier almost in his forties, he feels the vigor of youth slipping away, and with the sight of the Hulk, he glimpses strength the likes of which he did not know was possible. Sympathetic to Blonsky's desires since he, too, has plans to harness the military potential of the Hulk, General Ross arranges for Blonsky to receive doses of an experimental replica of the super-soldier serum. Though his stamina, agility, and recuperative abilities improve, Blonsky also begins to mutate, his skin growing sallow and his backbone protruding into spine-like plates. Noticing his condition, a fellow soldier even asks, "How you feeling, man?" to which Blonsky replies, almost with revelry, "Like a monster."[39]

He gets his chance to fully realize that assertion when he confronts Dr. Stearns, a professor working with Banner in an attempt to control the Hulk's transformations. Stearns had taken samples of Banner's blood for experimentation and Blonsky, aware of his knowledge about the Hulk, holds the professor at gunpoint, making a desperate demand: "I want what you got out of Banner. I want that. I need that. Make me that."[40] Stearns complies and through the combination of the serum, Banner's blood, and gamma radiation, Blonsky becomes the gigantic, deformed "Abomination." Covered in scales, horns, and other protuberances, the enormous beast rampages through New York, only being brought to a halt after a brutal battle with the Hulk.

As a creature of raw power-lust, rage, and deformity, the Abomination stands in the mode of ancient monster mythology, resembling creatures such as *Beowulf*'s "Grendel." He too was considered deformed—harboring scales, spikes, spurs, and "barbs like steel"—and was large enough in size to require four men to lift his head.[41] Like the Abomination, he marauds and kills for the joy of it, ripping people apart as a monument to his unbelievable strength. Outside of *Beowulf*, within Greek mythology, the Minotaur, the scourge of Minos' labyrinth, and Polyphemus, the horrid Cyclops who

Portrayed with horns, a ridged back, and other deformities, The Abomination (Tim Roth) showcases classic monstrous characteristics. From *The Incredible Hulk* (2008).

waylays and kills members of Odysseus' crew, would also fit this template of the oversized, misshapen monster using its strength and power to debased, brutal ends.[42] In Mesopotamian myth, Humbaba, the guardian of the Cedar Forest whom Gilgamesh and Enkidu challenge, also fits this template. He is described as having teeth that are "knife-sharp and stick out like tusks" and a face "blood-smeared" and like "a lion's," that can also turn into a "thousand nightmares."[43] When this horrid appearance does not dissuade Gilgamesh and Enkidu from their attack, Humbaba "let out a deafening cry, his roar boomed forth like a blast of thunder, he stamped and the ground burst open, his steps split the mountains of Lebanon, the clouds turned black."[44] It is only with the divine help of the god Shamash that the heroes triumph over the beast.

The difference in the mythologies mentioned above is that, while in *Beowulf* and the Greek stories a human protagonist is summoned to stop the beast, both Gilgamesh and Enkidu are not quite human. The former is part god and has, until just before the events of the epic, horridly oppressed his subjects in Uruk. Enkidu, on the other hand, is part animal and a newcomer to the concept of civilization. Separately, human/god and human/animal, respectively, each is a category-problem and arguably monstrous; together, they make each other more human. As quasi-monstrous beings with strength befitting that status, they are a logical choice to oppose the monstrosity of Humbaba. Following this same ancient, mythic reasoning, it is the Hulk, himself a monster, who is the only one capable of defeating the monstrous Abomination. The Hulk's own monstrosity is effectively choreographed in the film's earlier sequence revealing Banner's transformation in the bottling factory. At first, his presence in the dark factory is indicated only by people disappearing, being dragged screaming into the shadows. Then, his own roars and growls emerge, along with glimpses of a gigantic shape, then a foot, and then a hand. Finally, his full face appears out of the steam and smoke, startling the viewer and impressing upon him or her the size and ferocity of the creature, perhaps not unlike how the monster of a horror movie would be revealed.[45]

That Banner himself feels that the Hulk is a monster appears multiple times in the MCU, and was discussed in the previous chapter. It is for this reason that he is reluctant to transform, except when there is no other choice, such as when the Avengers face Hydra, Loki's Chitauri army, and when he alone must stop the Abomination. As Black Widow puts it later in the franchise, he spends his life "avoiding a fight because he knows he'll win," implying that, in the process of winning, the monstrosity of the Hulk will produce collateral damage or, like Blonsky, he may come to enjoy flexing his gamma-powered muscles.[46] In fact, with the Abomination shown as initially stronger, the Hulk can only triumph by tapping even further and deeper into rage and hatred, which is triggered when the fight imperils Banner's love interest, Betty Ross. At the end of the battle, when the Hulk holds the Abomination by a steel chain around the neck, he appears ready to indulge those feelings and kill his adversary. Before doing so, however, he relents, showing that despite their numerous overlaps, the Hulk and the Abomination exist in an inverse relationship: the monstrous Abomination has always been inside the human Blonsky, but the humanizing Banner has always been inside the monstrous Hulk. It is only by putting the Abomination and the Hulk in conflict that this contrast comes to the fore.

Also defined by an obsession with power, though not necessarily of the physical kind entirely, is the Captain America villain the "Red Skull." As the scientist Abraham Erskine describes to Steve Rogers, the Red Skull was once known as Johann Schmidt when he was a member of Hitler's inner circle and demanded a dose of a very early version of the super-soldier serum. The serum then turned Schmidt into a scarred man whose barren, reddened, and skull-like face gave rise to his fearsome new name. The reason, Erskine explains to Rogers, is because "the serum amplifies everything that is inside, so good becomes great, bad becomes worse."[47] Schmidt's ambitious, tyrannical impulses are thus propelled into full megalomania through the serum, leading him to steal the object known as the "Tesseract," a source of almost limitless power with which he can make weapons to conquer the world.

To oppose the Red Skull, Erskine selects the physically feeble Steve Rogers, arguing that it is precisely this frailty that will make him the perfect anti-fascist counterpart: "Because the strong man who has known power all his life may lose respect for that power, but a weak man knows the value of strength and knows compassion."[48] Armed with this deeper knowledge of the true worth and aim of power, as Captain America, Rogers confronts the Red Skull multiple times and on each occasion these differences come to light in their banter. In the Red Skull's view, the power he already possesses as well as what he seeks is his right, as he tells Rogers: "You could have the power of the gods! Yet, you wear a flag on your chest and fight a battle of nations!"[49] Besides transcending nations and gods, in his own mind, the Red Skull also believes he has surpassed the need for humanity: "You are deluded, Captain. You pretend to be a simple soldier, but you are just afraid to admit that we have left humanity behind. Unlike you, I embrace it proudly, without fear!"[50] By contrast, Rogers remains entirely grounded in his former identity, though enhanced with the physical prowess (and beyond) that he lacked previously. While the Red Skull craves power as an end in itself, Captain America aspires to strength as a means to do good. For this reason, Schmidt was utterly transformed by the serum, while Rogers remains in many ways the person he was prior to the experiment. This difference is amply demonstrated in the exchange below:

> RED SKULL: [Erskine] resented my genius and tried to deny me what was rightfully mine, but he gave you everything. So, what made you so special?
> STEVE ROGERS: Nothing. I'm just a kid from Brooklyn.[51]

Their outer appearances reflecting their inner constitutions, these two "super-soldiers" represent two very different philosophies of power: one good-natured and orderly, the other twisted and tainted. The Red Skull embodies Erskine's warning of what happens when a person abuses power and thus serves as a potent caution that Rogers carries forward for the rest of his career as Captain America, allowing him to remain on-guard against this shadow-self tendency.

Yet a third villain from the MCU origin films fits into this category of abuse of power, though more loosely than the Abomination or the Red Skull. Serving as the principal menace in *Guardians of the Galaxy*, the Kree warlord Ronan "the Accuser" harbors an intense hatred for the people of the planet of Xandar. While holding a Xandarian captive, Ronan makes the following declaration about his intentions toward those people, as well as how he is perceived by his fellow Kree and the rest of the galaxy:

> They call me "terrorist," "radical," and "zealot" because I obey the ancient laws of the Kree and punish the people who do not. Because I do not forgive your people for taking the life of my father, and his father, and his father before him. One thousand years of war between us will not be forgotten … you Xandarians and your culture are a disease. I will cure it![52]

With those words, Ronan brutally executes his helpless Xandarian prisoner with a hammer blow to the head, sending his blood pouring across a ceremonial structure. Otherwise, we learn that Ronan, inspired by his hatred of the Xandarians, is rampaging throughout the galaxy, destroying their outposts and slaughtering their people, including children. His ultimate goal, the viewer discovers, is to procure an object called "the Orb" for Thanos of Titan who will, in exchange, use his vast military forces to wipe out Xandar. However, tired of being condescended to by Thanos, Ronan eventually takes the Orb for himself. When the object is revealed to be the Infinity Gem known as the "Power Stone," Ronan intends to use it to annihilate Xandar.

Though little of the Kree religion (if such an establishment exists in the MCU) is discussed or portrayed in the film, Ronan's rhetoric coincides with religiously-fueled extremism and violence, particularly as those phenomena have been delineated by scholars in Religious Studies. Primarily focusing on Christianity and Islam, Charles Kimball cites rigid exclusivism and the tendency to "elevate the teachings and beliefs of their traditions to the level of *absolute* truth claims," which we see in ample measure in the character of Ronan, as the basis for religiously-based violence.[53] One of the leading scholars of religion and violence, Mark Juergensmeyer, suggests that certain elements are usually present in a religious tradition or movement that spark a turn to violence, including demonization of rival groups, a sense of duality or war on a cosmic scale, a feeling of marginality, and the theatrical desire to enact their beliefs on a grand scale.[54] Importantly, these elements can and do occur across religious traditions around the world, including Christianity and Islam, but also Hinduism, Buddhism, Judaism and other groups.[55] Even in the brief introduction to Ronan's character, we see these factors in his beliefs as well, as he has demonized the Xandarians, sees conflict with them as an endless war, has been marginalized even by the Kree authorities, and will settle for nothing less than the obliteration of the planet of Xandar and the extermination of its people.

In opposition to this, both literally and figuratively, stand the Guardians of the Galaxy. Whereas Ronan is obsessed with his own visions of law, order, and purity, the Guardians of the Galaxy, as a group, break laws, defy order, and (as discussed in the previous chapter) occupy liminal statuses that frustrate purity. Ronan, as his title "Accuser" implies, practices harsh judgment, especially of difference, which he sees as the crime of the Xandarians: their culture is different from the Kree's and thus must be extirpated. This push toward homogeneity and sameness is even illustrated in the zombie-like soldiers Ronan employs, who are necrotized creatures without any marks of distinction or individual will. By contrast, each of the Guardians of the Galaxy is strikingly unique, including a human/alien hybrid, a cybernetically-enhanced raccoon, and a sentient tree. Over the course of the film, the Guardians of the Galaxy grow to accept one another as friends and even family, pledging to oppose Ronan together on that basis, as Gamora tells the group: "I have lived most of my life surrounded by my enemies. I will be grateful to die among my friends."[56] While Ronan divides the universe into groups of strict allies and enemies, espousing an us-versus-them view, the Guardians of the Galaxy pull the different and eccentric into their orbit, accepting them as friends and perhaps even more. This is most touchingly exhibited in a scene near the end of the film when Groot, the tree-being whose vocabulary to that point has consisted only of the phrase "I am Groot," extends his body around the other Guardians of the Galaxy to protect them as their spaceship crashes. His reason for doing so, he tells the others, is "*We* are Groot."[57] Ronan's hatred of the different and the foreign renders him an obvious villain for a group to whom there is no otherness, even to the point of seeing others as an extension of oneself.

The third and final category of shadow-self villains we will consider in this chapter are those animated by a desire for revenge. As opposed to the villains acting out of greed or lust for power, these figures instead pursue a cause connected to a personal trauma. Despite the seeming righteousness of their actions or ambitions, they are usually blind or inured to the chaos and destruction their simpleminded pursuit of justice has unleashed. At times in world mythology, the monsters acting out of revenge are not given the opportunity to voice their own grievances, but the circumstances are usually plain. In Ovid's *Metamorphoses*, there is Medusa, once a strikingly beautiful woman with splendid hair, who was raped by Neptune (Poseidon) in the temple of Minerva (Athena). For supposedly causing this transgression, Minerva turns Medusa into a monster with snakes for hair, who from then on uses her fearsome appearance to turn all who gaze upon her to stone.[58] The monster Scylla was created in a similar tale of woe, as the sorceress Circe, in a fit of jealousy, turned her into a grotesque monster. *The Odyssey* describes her as a serpent with "twelve legs, all writhing, dangling down and six long swaying necks, a hideous head on each, each head barbed with a triple row of fangs, armed to the hilt with black death."[59] Unable to vent her anger on the one truly responsible, like Medusa, Scylla instead feasts on passing sailors. As a final example, Grendel's mother also silently, but wrathfully, after "brooding over her wrongs," takes vengeance for the death of her son upon the occupants of Heorot.[60]

There are also those figures in myth and religion who are far from wordless when it comes to the perceived wrongs visited upon them, but are instead almost eloquent enough to convince the reader that they are in fact the true hero of the tale. Perhaps the most famous of this typology comes in John Milton's retelling of the fall of Satan (and then humanity) in *Paradise Lost*. Meant as an epic of Christianity in the mold of the Classical world, Milton's work deftly portrays the warped thinking that leads Satan to position himself as a valiant rebel against an omnipotent tyrant, fighting bravely for freedom against impossible odds. Yet, festering underneath this seemingly lofty goal, is an obviously hateful and vengeful spirit, as the following lines make clear: "his doom / reserved him to more wrath, for now the thought / both of lost happiness and lasting pain / torments him."[61] Satan turns this sadness and anger into defiance as he addresses his defeated followers in the pits of their new abode, Hell:

> In dubious battle on the plains of Heav'n / we shook His throne. What though the field be lost? / All is not lost: th' unconquerable will / and study of revenge, immortal hate / and courage never to submit or yield / and what is else not to be overcome? That glory never shall His wrath or might extort from me: to bow and sue for grace / with suppliant knee and deify His pow'r....[62]

Though clearly the weaker and deficient party in the struggle, Satan signals an absolute refusal to surrender, flying in the face of what any clear line of logic would dictate. In his twisted imagination, Satan tries to cast the defeat of the rebel angels and their fall into Hell as a noble victory of the spirit. Rather than reassess his situation, he hardens his view further and brings along those who surround him to the same perspective. His vanity and pride blind him to the true horrors of their new surroundings as the once luminous angels, who floated on wings of light, begin now to buzz about like debauched flies around a murky hive.[63]

In the origin stories of the MCU, three villains fit this mythic model of the at-times sympathetic, but also deluded and self-deceiving monster. First, in *Doctor Strange* we meet the sorcerer Kaecilius who has rebelled against the Ancient One's teaching, seeing her as a hypocrite for drawing energy from the Dark Dimension, even as she forbids others to experiment with the same ritual. Another of the Ancient One's apprentices, Karl Mordo, describes Kaecilius and his background this way: "When he first came to us, he'd lost everyone he ever loved. He was a grieving, broken man searching for answers in the mystic arts. A brilliant student, but he was proud, headstrong. He questioned the Ancient One and rejected her teaching."[64] In his combination of stubbornness, intelligence, and arrogance, Kaecilius mirrors Strange, who also came to the Ancient One in the depths of grief, thinking his professional life was finished, and went on to repeatedly challenge her over the content and pacing of her teachings.

However, the depth of Kaecilius' pain over his lost family, and the delusional thinking to which it has driven him, push the two characters apart. Kaecilius' twisted logic and Strange's different perspective emerge during a comparatively lengthy exchange following a fight between the two:

> KAECILIUS: All things age. All things die. In the end, the sun burns out…. But the Dark Dimension is a place beyond time … the world doesn't have to die, Doctor. It can take its place [in the Dark Dimension] as part of the one. We can all live forever. People think in terms of good and evil when time really is the true enemy of all. Time kills everything.
> STRANGE: What about the people *you* killed?
> KAECILIUS: Tiny. Momentary specks in an indifferent universe. Humanity longs for the eternal, for a world beyond time…. Time is an insult. Death is an insult. Doctor, we don't seek to rule the world, we seek to save it.[65]

So mired in anguish and enraged by the Ancient One's perceived slights, Kaecilius has rationalized murdering other sorcerers, as well as opening the world to Dormammu, the ruler of the Dark Dimension. This final act would mean enslaving the planet in a state of living death that Kaecilius' damaged psyche has mistaken for eternal life. Like other monsters, Kaecilius' disordered intentions and mind are mirrored in a scarred body, as the dark rituals he and his followers perform scar their flesh and leave them with charred, blackened eyes. These facts are not lost on Strange, who notes the parallel as he rejects Kaecilius' philosophy: "No, I mean, come on. Look at your face! Dormammu made you a murderer. Just how good can his kingdom be?"[66]

In addition to their intelligence and stubbornness, Kaecilius and Strange share a selfish outlook. Though he claims pulling the Earth into the Dark Dimension is for the eternal life of all humanity, in truth, Kaecilius only wants an end to his own misery and hurt. Though this was precisely Strange's view at the beginning of the film, where he was only concerned with securing enough knowledge to heal his crippled hands and restore his lost stature and prestige, by the conclusion he has grown past both his self-centeredness and his previous conception of pain. After Kaecilius destroys the final protective sanctum on Earth, the only way Strange can forestall the planet's destruction is to lock himself and Dormammu in a time-loop where the Dark Lord kills him over and over again. This also imprisons the Dark Lord, but he first attempts to threaten Strange:

> DORMAMMU: You will spend eternity dying.
> STRANGE: Yes, but everyone on Earth will live.
> DORMAMMU: You will suffer!
> STRANGE: Pain's an old friend.[67]

Unwilling to remain locked in the loop with Strange, Dormammu betrays Kaecilius, whose still juvenile view of his suffering leads, ironically, to eternal torment. Strange's own journey as a sorcerer, hero, and person, thus comes more into relief with the vengeful, agonized shadow-self figure of Kaecilius alongside him.

Just as Kaecilius' motivation to escape death is understandable on a certain level, N'Jadaka, also known as "Killmonger," in *Black Panther* also possess a compelling and sympathetic backstory. Back in the early 1990s, we learn that Prince N'Jobu served as a Wakandan spy in Oakland, California. Angered by the racial injustice rife in the United States, he conspired to smuggle advanced Wakandan weaponry around the country to foment revolution. His brother, King T'Chaka, arrived to arrest him and, when N'Jobu resisted, was forced to kill him. With an American woman, N'Jobu had had a young son, named N'Jadaka, who was left behind in Oakland.

Years later, T'Chaka's own son T'Challa becomes king and N'Jadaka has successfully plotted his way back to Wakanda. There he confronts the royal court with his father's same disdain for the kingdom's lack of action on racial injustice: "Y'all sitting up here comfortable. Looks good. About two billion people all the over world look like us but their lives are a lot harder. Wakanda has the tools to liberate them all."[68] The matter turns far more personal, though, as N'Jadaka turns to the new king: "You ain't the son of a king, you the son of a murderer!" Having recently learned of his father's morally questionable actions, T'Challa suspects the true identity of this intruder, but fears what disruption will result from revealing these family sins and secrets. As a result, he first tries to sweep the matter under the rug by asking that royal guards take N'Jadaka away. Before that can happen, N'Jadaka's identity is exposed and his demand for ceremonial combat over the right to the throne cannot be refused.

At the ritual, N'Jadaka's seething, obsessive desire for revenge ripples through every action, especially when he declares the violent, blood-soaked lengths he has gone to in order to fight T'Challa, someone he has never even met previously: "I spent my entire life waiting for this moment. I trained, I lied, I killed, just to get here. I killed in America, Afghanistan, Iraq. I took the lives of my own brothers and sisters on this continent. All this death, just so I could kill you."[69] Like Kaecilius, N'Jadaka's single-minded hatred has blinded him to the horrors he has committed, even as he wears them proudly on his body. While Kaecilius' eyes are burned away and blackened, N'Jadaka has scarified his body with one subcutaneous bump for each life taken. When he removes his armored vest and shirt prior to the ritual combat, the viewer sees that every centimeter of his chest and arms is covered in these ghoulish decorations, monstrifying his body into a monument to violence and murder.

The fight is a study in contrasts as the hate-fueled N'Jadaka easily, and brutally, beats the denial-burdened T'Challa, casting him over the edge of the waterfall cliff to an apparent death. In an artful cinematic moment, when N'Jadaka later takes his first steps into the throne room as the new king, the film moves in slow motion and the image is inverted, slowly spinning back into regular orientation, depicting graphically how the moral and social order has been overturned by the momentary triumph of vengeance and rage.[70] Announcing his first orders as king, N'Jadaka's words have a similarly disorienting impact, for he wishes to use Wakanda's weapons and armies to "kill those in power, their children, and anyone else who takes their side … the world's gonna start over, and this time we're on top."[71]

Meanwhile, before this campaign of violence can be enacted, T'Challa, as we discussed in the previous chapter, has actually survived and is given another dose of the heart-shaped herb. Under its influence, he has a second vision of his father. This time, he confronts T'Chaka, in front of all the other ancestors present, demanding to know why he abandoned N'Jadaka as a boy, and also isolated Wakanda for so long. When T'Chaka's answers do not satisfy him, T'Challa's moral indignation finally boils over:

T'CHALLA: Why didn't you bring the boy home?
T'CHAKA: He was the truth I chose to omit.
T'CHALLA: You were wrong to abandon him.
T'CHAKA: I chose my people. I chose Wakanda. Our future depended on—
T'CHALLA: You were wrong! All of you were wrong! To turn your back on the rest

of the world? We let the fear of our discovery stop us from doing what is right. No more. I cannot stay here with you. I cannot rest while [N'Jadaka] sits on the throne. He is a monster of our own making…. I must right these wrongs.[72]

Newly empowered, both morally and once more as Black Panther, T'Challa returns to face N'Jadaka, who now also has Black Panther strength and a suit with identical abilities. They engage in a ferocious fight, pausing only briefly for the following exchange:

> T'CHALLA: You want to see us become like the people you hate so much. Divide and conquer the land as they did…. You have become them. You will destroy the world, Wakanda included.
> N'JADAKA: The world took everything from me! Everything I ever loved! But I'm going to get even![73]

Revealingly, in the heat of the moment, when the battle has boiled down to the two characters' most fundamental motivations, N'Jadaka refers not to global economic disparities or systemic racial oppression, as real as those are, but rather his own personal trauma as a child. Earlier in the film, when N'Jadaka has his own vision after receiving the heart-shaped herb, he also sees his father, but greets him not as an adult, but as a boy, the same age he was when his father died. This suggests that, in every way except physically, N'Jadaka has remained a wounded, angry, frightened boy from that day forward, seeking to share his pain with the rest of the world by making it hurt as well.

T'Challa defeats N'Jadaka, leaving him grievously, though not mortally, wounded and suggests it is not too late to heal him, perhaps of his spiritual as well as physical injuries. Riven with hate, N'Jadaka does not even consider the offer, saying instead, "Why, so you can just lock me up? No. Just bury me in the ocean with my ancestors that jumped from the ships because they knew death was better than bondage."[74] This declaration once again elevates N'Jadaka's complaint to the level of mass racial oppression, but in many ways it is still a mask for his own personal hurt, as the boy who has never gotten over his father's death. In evoking grandiosity to cover pride and using eloquence to make a fundamentally mistaken and twisted cause seem acceptable, N'Jadaka's words resemble the prideful sentiments of Milton's aforementioned portrayal of Satan. Especially pertinent are Satan's words when he persuades the fallen angels that, having lost heaven, they should be glad to accept their lot in Hell:

> Farewell, happy fields / where joy forever dwells! Hail horrors, hail / Infernal world! And thou, profoundest Hell, / Receive thy new possessor, one who brings / a mind not to be changed by place or time! / The mind is its own place and in itself / can make a Heaven of Hell; a Hell of Heaven. / What matter where, if I be still the same…. Better to reign in Hell than serve in Heaven![75]

On one level, Satan's words are inspirational, speaking to the power of self-determination and triumph over one's adverse circumstances. This interpretation evaporates, however, with knowledge of the context—Satan and his followers have manufactured this circumstance themselves through unremitting, unrepentant pride. N'Jadaka's comment also contains the admirable theme of defiance in the face of oppression, yet he also has let his pride and hurt drown out his reason. In contrast, though he too was blinded by self-serving pride in his father's supposed infallibility, by virtue of the encounter with N'Jadaka, T'Challa sheds that defect, and then stands as a more just king, and a better person. In this battle of rival Black Panthers, N'Jadaka thus represented the myopia of revenge and pride that T'Challa needed to conquer before truly becoming king.

Despite the importance of N'Jadaka and Kaecilius in their respective stories, the most important villain in the entire first phase of the MCU is Loki. First seen in *Thor*, the immediate contrast between Loki and his (adoptive) brother Thor is clear: Loki is thin, dark-haired, intelligent, and wields magic, whereas Thor is muscular, blonde, physical, and accomplishes his goals with his fists. The sibling rivalry between the two surfaces early and, from a certain viewpoint, Loki is justified in his resentment since his true Jotunheim parentage was kept secret, rendering vain any hopes he had for the crown, as Thor was favored from their youth. These experiences poison Loki's outlook and he sets out, through more devious and violent means, to establish himself as ruler of Asgard.

While all the previous villains discussed display their mental monstrosity with corresponding physical deformity, Loki's misshapenness surfaces instead through his ability and proclivity to shape-shift. "The monster's body," Jeffrey Cohen writes, "is both corporeal and incorporeal; its threat is its propensity to shift."[76] In the Christian tradition, Satan and other demons were considered able to change shape at will, assuming whatever form was necessary to suit their needs.[77] In Buddhism, Māra is similarly considered a shape-shifter, taking on different guises to trick or frighten the Buddha and his followers.[78] The monster's lack of a set, dependable form underscores its chaotic, disordered nature. Its potential capacity to be anything and anywhere also communicates the anxiety created by the presence of such a being. In Loki's case in the MCU, the ability to shape-shift highlights his cunning, manipulative, and deceitful personality, as well as the instability of his temperament.

In *Thor*, as discussed in the previous chapter, Loki's scheme to solidify his hold on Asgard's throne involves killing Thor while he is vulnerable on Earth, then annihilating Jotunheim, presumably out of self-loathing for his true ancestry. After this plot fails, he falls into exile himself, coming into the service of Thanos in *Marvel's The Avengers*. While Thanos' servant "the Other" complains that Loki's "ambition is little and born of childish need," he and the Titan make a deal: Loki will procure the Tesseract for Thanos in exchange for an army to conquer and rule Earth.[79] This army, called the "Chitauri," embodies classic models of monstrosity. First, their point of origin—teleported from outer space to New York—evokes Freud's concept of the *unheimlich*, the "uncanny," or that which intrudes upon the interior from the exterior. Beal argues that this notion of *unheimlich* is central to the category of the monster, and his words apply easily to the case of the Chitauri: "Monsters are in the world, but not of the world … they invade one's sense of personal, social, or cosmic order and security."[80] They are, literally, space invaders, having invaded from space and intruded upon human space, representing something fundamentally other breaking into a once familiar world. The Chitauri, to add Cohen's perspective, can thus be seen, like so many monsters before, as "an incorporation of the outside, the Beyond—of all those loci that are rhetorically placed as distant and distinct."[81]

Beyond their uncanny cosmic origin, the army is also physically monstrous. A mish-mash of organic and technological components, the Chitauri are neither fully humanoid nor fully machine. When their masks are removed, their eyes and teeth bulge grotesquely, reminding one of Paul Trout's point on predatory symbolism in mythic monsters.[82] They are also supported by category-collapsing beasts (called "Leviathans," bringing to mind the chaos-producing sea monsters of the Bible) as large as skyscrapers that resemble armor-plated whales, but possess iron jaws and fly through the air.

The horrid army conjured by Loki in *Marvel's The Avengers* has mythic parallels with other beings who have marshaled terrifying hosts, at times also in service of claiming a throne. In the ancient Babylonian myth *Enuma Elish,* the sea dragon Tiamat, after the assassination of her consort Apsu, launches an invasion of the godly realm at the head of a frightful host: "she bore giant snakes, sharp of tooth and unsparing of fang; she filled their bodies with venom instead of blood … she stationed a horned serpent, a demon, a rabid dog, a scorpion man, a fish man, and a bull man."[83] In Buddhist mythology, after Siddhartha Gautama resists his initial temptations, Māra resorts to physical violence to prevent the sage from becoming the Buddha, which would threaten the god's rule over the realm of desire and death. He summons a misshapen legion of creatures, "some with faces of boars, fish, horses, donkeys, and camels, some of tigers, bears, lions, and elephants, some with one eye, some with many mouths, some with three heads, some with tusks, some armed with talons, some with skulls as faces, some with colossal mouths."[84] To these specific examples, we can add the more general descriptions collected by Jeffrey Burton Russell of medieval

Christian myth and folklore of Satan and his demons as having "human bodies, but animal features, such as lizard skin, apelike heads, and paws."[85]

In all these cases, whether Tiamat, Māra, or Satan, the monstrous army represents the disorder beneath the pretense, that the desire to rule is not based on justice, but violence and fear. Loki's Chitauri perform the same function, though updated for the twenty-first century as armor-plated, cybernetic beasts from another galaxy. However, just as Tiamat is no match for the thunder god Marduk and Gautama's meditation dispels all of Māra's attacks, the assembled Avengers repel Loki's army and leave him bruised and battered for his efforts.

In addition to his army's attack serving as the forming reason for the Avengers, Loki also serves as the foil for Thor, whose initial childishness and ruthlessness (discussed last chapter) find a mirror in his adoptive brother. Having painfully divested himself of these flaws on Earth, he can quickly recognize Loki's perverted approach to leadership:

> THOR: You imagine yourself better than humans?
> LOKI: Well … yes.
> THOR: Then a throne would suit you ill.[86]

In this contest of prince versus prince, Thor can identify the character defects that once marred his own approach to the world.

As we have seen throughout this chapter, the pattern of the superhero's confrontation with his shadow-self is recurrent in numerous MCU origin stories. They face a part of themselves that they must conquer, often, as Jung would point out regarding the shadow-self, the darkest part, the part they would most wish to hide from the world. The triumph over the villain representing the shadow-self then heralds the superhero's accession to greater self-understanding and moral clarity. Also uniting these stories were the common categories of greed, abuse of power, and revenge that the villains shared, not to mention their participation in classic monster symbolism through their misshapen, hybrid forms.

Importantly, while the monstrous villain is thus a liminal figure, so too are the superheroes. Even after defeating their respective shadows, this liminality does not disappear for any of them. To a degree, the disorder, instability, and conflict in their careers only seems to increase, as the inchoate Avengers spend nearly as much time battling one another as they do Loki's army. Indeed, if it is not Thor fighting Iron Man, leveling a forest, or Thor and Hulk destroying a hangar as they rampage against one another, Iron Man and Captain America bicker and argue incessantly. On the very premise of the Avengers, Banner is as blunt as he is seemingly correct: "Are we a team? No, we're a chemical mixture that makes chaos. We're a time bomb."[87] With the uncertainty and danger associated with the liminal status inherent in the superhero, the kind of explosive outcome Banner warns against seems inevitable, meaning that perhaps the greatest threat is not the villains the superheroes face, but themselves.

At this point in the MCU, the superheroes' position is reminiscent of a Tlingit story about a cannibal giant and the hero sworn to destroy him. Stalking the giant for days on end, the hero finally found him and, after employing a crafty plan, killed him. To make sure the giant was dead, he cut up the body and burned it to ashes. Out of nowhere, the giant's voice said, "Though I'm dead, though you killed me, I'm going to keep eating you and all the other humans in the world forever." The ashes from the fire then turned into tiny specks—the first mosquitoes, biting and sucking human blood ever since.[88]

Like this Tlingit story, though the MCU superheroes appear triumphant, their problems have in fact only dispersed and multiplied. In the next chapter, we will see how, latent even in their apparent victories against their shadow-selves, the seeds of impurity, infiltration, and corruption have been planted, nurtured by their own category-defying statuses.

THREE

Impurity and Pollution in the MCU's Phase Two

Sacred rules are thus merely rules hedging divinity off, and uncleanness is the two way danger of contact with the divinity.
    —Mary Douglas, *Purity and Danger*, p. 8

Hydra grew right under your nose and no one noticed.
    —Steve Rogers ("Captain America"), played by Chris Evans, *Captain America: The Winter Soldier* (2014)

After the triumph of defeating their shadow-selves and uniting as the Avengers to repel Loki's alien hordes, the superheroes next assemble during the film entitled *Avengers: Age of Ultron*, which comes near the end of the MCU narrative's Phase Two. While the roster of superheroes has grown by this point to include the twins Wanda and Pietro Maximoff (who have powers of telekinesis and hyper-speed, respectively) and the cybernetic Vision, this chapter in the mythos is marked far less by growth and success than by chaos and confusion. Rather than defeat an external threat in an unambiguously righteous struggle, instead the Avengers face Ultron, a menace they themselves have created, and along the way must come to terms with the damage they have caused. This crisis of character and mission is such that, prior to the climactic confrontation with Ultron, Captain America tells his comrades, "Ultron thinks we're monsters, that we're what's wrong with the world. This isn't just about beating him—it's about whether he's right."[1]

The story of how the MCU mythos arrives at this point of tension begins with elements already present in Phase One, and has roots in the religious symbolism of pollution, impurity, and contagion. From *Leviticus* in the Hebrew Bible to the *Dharma Sūtras* of Hinduism, from Polynesia to the Mediterranean, purity rules form a central aspect of the ethical and ritual codes of most religious traditions around the world. Expansively understood, purity can and has referred across these different traditions to regulations and prohibitions regarding ritual practices, mental objects, diet, social interactions, and funerary issues, among other realms. To the extent that they do or do not abide by the codes or understandings relative to their traditions, individuals can thus be regarded as pure or impure mentally, morally, and physically, covering all the spheres that humans inhabit. Often expressed ritually and in everyday practices, purity codes are also enacted and reinforced through mythic narratives that detail the urgency of such prohibitions, frequently by describing the harsh consequences for an individual or a group running afoul of the prescribed behavior. Observing the universal presence of purity concerns in world myths and rituals, Paul Ricoeur notes, "Dread of the impure and rites of purification are in the background of all our feelings and behaviors."[2]

In the work *Purity and Danger*, anthropologist Mary Douglas has written perhaps the most definitive study on purity concerns, arguing that fears of contamination and pollution—whether moral, mental, or physical—stem from a culture's system of classification. According to Douglas, impurity can come from anything considered "dirty" and dirt is defined simply as "matter out of place."[3] Those anomalous entities and states that resist classification in the dominant system—that are, in other words, "out of place"—are regarded as pollution and in need of avoidance or regulation. As Douglas puts it, "pollution behavior is the reaction which condemns any object or idea likely to confuse or contradict cherished classifications."[4] From this perspective, Douglas argues, we can understand the dietary and moral prohibitions in a text like *Leviticus*: since the foods considered unclean and the actions deemed impure do not fall neatly into a given category, they are somehow incomplete and disordered, and holiness for the Hebrews was connected to completeness and orderliness.[5]

As discussed in the previous chapters, the MCU firmly positions its superheroes as liminal figures who are precisely the kind of anomalous, category-confusing characters Douglas discusses as heralding pollution concerns. As Douglas explains, echoing the words of van Gennep and Turner, "Danger lies in transitional states, simply because transition is neither one state nor the next, it is undefinable. The person who must pass from one to another is himself a danger and emanates danger to others."[6] Outside of anthropology, Julia Kristeva makes a similar assertion in the realm of philosophy when defining the roots of personal experiences of horror or, in her terminology, "abjection." "It is thus not lack of cleanliness or health that causes abjection," she writes, "but what disturbs identity, system, [and] order. [And] what does not respect borders, positions, [and] rules. [It is] the in-between, the ambiguous, [and] the composite."[7] In other words, purity codes, despite their rhetoric to the contrary, are not aimed at purity in terms of cleanliness, but purity in terms of classificatory order, and perceive with horror and label as polluting those things which frustrate categories.

As we saw, though the superheroes are not monsters in the same way as their shadow-selves, by virtue of their origin and realm-spanning natures, they are perpetually in the kind of transitional states that resist easy categorization, and thus radiate impurity and generate danger. By remaining within the fabric of society while still embodying liminality, they violate the prohibition, noted by Durkheim and mentioned in Chapter One, that the sacred and sacred beings must be separated due to their contagious and potentially destabilizing power.[8] Importantly, then, the persistence of these liminal states constitutes danger for others as well, as the chaos and impurity they represent is liable to heighten instability around them.

Employing multiple metaphorical devices for the concepts of impurity and pollution, Phase Two of the MCU is primarily the portion of the mythic narrative that deals with these themes. With the superheroes established through origin stories set mostly in Phase One, Phase Two thus focuses on the subsequent complications that arise for the superheroes. To a degree, this is consistent with a stereotypical three-act narrative structure: setup, confrontation, and resolution. According to this narrative structure, then, within a trilogy (or in the case of the MCU, a trilogy of Phases), the second part would thus be the portion where the complication would logically occur. The origin of this narrative structure is open to debate, with some tracing it back to Aristotle's *Poetics*, while others argue there is evidence that Aristotle was merely observing the structure of the dramas of his time rather than making recommendations on what form stories should take.[9] At any rate, this tripartite form is one found across cultures, and frequently in popular culture, with examples such as the *Star Wars* trilogy (where *The Empire Strikes Back* demonstrates a downturn for the heroes) and the *Lord of the Rings* (with the volume *The Two Towers* separating the Fellowship of the Ring and putting their respective parties into dire situations and jeopardy).

On that note, non-MCU superhero films in recent decades have tended to an extent to show a similar pattern, for instance the Spider-Man films of the early 2000s. In those movies, the first volume depicted Peter Parker's origin as "Spider-Man," while the sequel *Spider-Man 2* showed his difficulties and disenchantment with the role. In *Spider-Man 3* he comes to terms with his identity, but only after defeating an evil alien symbiote that literally infects and pollutes his mind and body.[10] Certain DC-oriented films have been structured similarly, including Christopher Nolan's "Batman" trilogy, where Bruce Wayne triumphantly becomes Batman in *Batman Begins*, struggles against the disruptive and disorienting attacks of the Joker in *The Dark Knight*, and resolves the disjunction between his Bruce

Wayne and Batman personalities in the third and concluding volume, *The Dark Knight Rises*.[11] Though it is not a full trilogy, the DC film *Batman v. Superman: Dawn of Justice*, shows many of these same elements, with Superman (on the heels of embracing his powers in the preceding film *Man of Steel*) encountering uncertainty regarding the exact nature of his obligations to humanity, as well as battling the horrific monster Doomsday, created from the contaminated biochemical mixture of human blood and a Kryptonian corpse.[12]

It is notable in the foregoing how many of these complications faced by heroes centered on contamination and pollution of some sort. For our purposes in this chapter, what is significant is that the MCU's intermediate Phase Two both employs the structure of the darker middle act (noted above as fraught with new complications and downturns for the heroes) as well as, befitting the religious imagery we have seen in the films to this point, evokes the themes of impurity, pollution, and contagion to communicate those new complications and dangers. Looking at Phase One's *Iron Man 2*, which constitutes the MCU's first sequel of any kind, helpfully illuminates the identity issues and connected pollution themes that appear more prominently in films later in the larger narrative. Following closely on the events of *Iron Man*, Stark enjoys even greater celebrity status and in many ways seems to have fallen back into his sexist, narcissistic, and self-destructive tendencies. In reality, this behavior masks deeper troubles pervading his life. For one, his technology has been copied by Ivan Vanko, the son of a former rival of his father. More pressingly, though, palladium (the element powering his chest piece) is slowly poisoning him. Stark's artificial intelligence succinctly outlines his dilemma in the following way: "It appears your continued use of the Iron Man suit is accelerating your condition. Unfortunately, the device that is keeping you alive is also killing you."[13] Read from our theoretical vantage, by lingering in his liminal status as the "Iron Man," an amalgam of machine/human, Stark is corrupting his own body, polluting it with a toxic element. The film graphically depicts this contamination by showing black lines progressing ever outward from the plate in Stark's chest to his skin, veins, arms, and eventually his neck. Meanwhile, as Stark faces that crisis, Vanko attacks him, first with arc reactor–powered whips on a race track, then later through a host of robotic automatons manufactured by industry rival Justin Hammer. In the course of this latter assault, Vanko is able to infiltrate and co-opt the programming of the "War Machine" suit, piloted by Stark's friend James Rhodes. Although Stark and Rhodes ultimately prevail against Vanko and Hammer, with Stark even creating a new element to fuel his chest plate without the toxic side effects, the elements of pollution are present on multiple levels. Whether it is the poisonous palladium running loose in Stark's

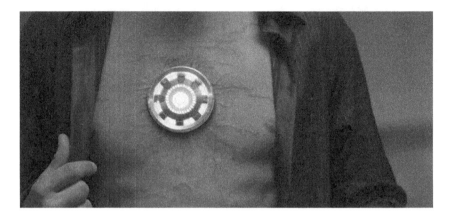

Tony Stark (Robert Downey, Jr.) suffers from poisoning by Palladium, the element powering his chest reactor. This shows the troubling impurity connected to his condition as a liminal superhero. From *Iron Man 2* (2010).

veins or his technology running loose on the world market, contamination and contagion exist at the heart of the confrontations Iron Man faces in the follow-up to his origin story.

Other sequels placed much later in the MCU mythos partly echo these themes. For instance, in Phase Three's *Ant-Man and the Wasp* (the sequel to *Ant-Man*), the struggle to maintain control over Pym's technology and keep it from proliferating forms a central concern. "Ghost," the primary villain of the film, is also revealed to be a young woman adversely affected by Pym's quantum technology, doomed to a painful life in which her body continuously phases in and out of solidity.[14] In *Guardians of the Galaxy: Volume 2*, Peter Quill unknowingly aids his father "Ego" in energizing a myriad of spores planted across the universe, which, when activated, will grow to infect and consume reality as we know it, subsuming all life into Ego's control and presence.[15] Though not technically a sequel, though it follows the preceding MCU films, *Marvel's The Avengers* possesses aspects of this theme as well with Loki's ability, through his mind-gem-powered staff, to take over the minds of Clint Barton and Erik Selvig.[16] These films thus highly evoke the sense of disorder, inconstancy, and contamination that is central, according to the thought of those such as Douglas and Kristeva, to the cross-cultural concept of pollution.

The most prominent and structurally consistent examples of the impurity theme in the larger MCU myth, however, occur in a triad of films in Phase Two, all of them sequentially and narratively setting the stage for the chaos and confusion already discussed as a focal point in the culminating *Avengers: Age of Ultron*. The films *Iron Man 3*, *Thor: The Dark World*, and *Captain America: The Winter Soldier* together form a parallel structure and study in impurity/pollution symbolism that is critical to our understanding of the MCU's larger religious and mythic imagery.

To fully understand the complexity and multi-faceted nature of that imagery, we should first look at other examples of how world religions have described the perils of pollution and contamination in rituals and mythologies. In the tradition of Hinduism, for instance, purity has had a prominent place since ancient times, with standards of cleanliness regarding diet, marriage, and dealing with the deceased, not to mention a regimented social stratification, all codified through ancient texts such as the Vedas and the *Dharma Sūtras*.[17] As these texts explain, the consequences for violating these prohibitions are dire. For example, those who have divulged the secrets of the Vedas to lower classes will be cast out from the social order.[18] Likewise, adultery or sexual intercourse with a member of another class can result in rebirth as a member of that class, or, during the current lifetime, grievous physical punishments.[19] Additionally, even eating food considered impure, such as that prepared by the member of a lower class, can result in an inauspicious rebirth, even in the form of an unclean animal, such as a pig or a dog.[20]

Within Hindu mythic narratives, it is demonstrated time and again that even the gods are not immune to these rules. In the previous chapter, we briefly discussed the Vedic myth of Indra, the thunder god, destroying the monstrous snake Vritra. Even this seemingly justified violence, through the shedding of blood, constitutes a polluting act and Indra must purify himself through ritual fires and auspicious sacrifices before he has expiated this moral stain.[21]

Even more frequently associated with transgressive practices is the god Śiva. Throughout the massive mythological corpuses known as the *Purāṇas*, Śiva is a boundary-defying, liminal figure, at once renouncer and householder, celibate ascetic and erotic force, all as a means of showing the unity of usually opposed elements.[22] Despite this totality, Śiva is shown as quick to anger at times and thus not above the possibility of impurity. In one version of a famous myth, Śiva becomes enraged at the creator god Brahmā and lops off one of the deity's five heads. As punishment for this breach of conduct, Śiva is cursed to have the skull of the severed head adhere to his hand, so the defilement of his act literally sticks to him until he makes ritual amends.[23]

One famous Hindu myth showing the dangers of escalating liminality also involves Śiva but is primarily concerned with the origin of the god Gaṇeśa, the elephant-headed deity of auspicious beginnings and remover (and also placer) of obstacles. Found in several *Purāṇas*, the story relates how the goddess Pārvatī, lonely while her husband Śiva engages in a lengthy meditative retreat, uses the dirt from her body to create Gaṇeśa.

Seeing the beautiful boy she has fashioned from this dirt, she sends him to guard her doorway while she bathes. Śiva then returns home and, enraged at being blocked from his own home, beheads the boy. Pārvatī is understandably distraught and, to calm her, Śiva replaces the lost head with an elephant's. Thereafter, in keeping with his physical hybridity, Gaṇeśa is known for guarding the liminal space of thresholds, as well as overseeing the in-between notion of beginnings and endings. Importantly, neither Gaṇeśa, nor Pārvatī, nor Śiva are in themselves considered by Hindus as deities of pollution, but the story illustrates how an act born of impurity (that is, from an impure substance, namely the dirt of Pārvatī's body) has a ripple effect of pollution and further liminal consequences. As Paul Courtright puts it, "in making Gaṇeśa—the one born of her own impurity—her guardian, [Pārvatī] puts him in jeopardy and makes him vulnerable to Śiva's inevitable conquest."[24] Going further, we see in the story that even Śiva's conquest is not the end of the difficulties, for the violence against Gaṇeśa must be atoned for, all showing the cascading, rippling effect that can occur when dealing with impure substances.

Elsewhere in South Asia, in Buddhist Theravāda traditions, impurity is likewise seen as having dangerous ramifications if allowed to persist. Within the Theravāda, impurity is more often referred to as an inner state of defilement (*kilesa* in the Pāli language) of the mind depending on the state of its attachment to the three poisons of greed, lust, and hatred. In addition to the focus of the *sangha*, or Buddhist community, on the individual's cleansing of these traits, the monastic organization is considered a "field of merit" for the surrounding community, who gain good karma from donating to the monastery. If members of the *sangha* abide in or persist with the impurity of defilements of greed, lust, or hatred in their minds, however, it contaminates the whole, nullifying the community's donations and potentially undermining the entire relationship between the monastic and lay groups.[25]

In China, a similar dynamic was believed to obtain between individual and communal purity. From the Daoist perspective, all existence was grounded in the shared being of the formless Dao, and as a result, "the people's own lives are parts of the larger body … and those bodies will either fall ill or be in a healthy state according to the knowledge about the purifying heart," or, in other words, the Dao.[26] Correspondingly, if an individual or individuals violate cultural purity norms, such as by mishandling bodily fluids, touching corpses, or being sexually licentious, they open themselves up to chaotic circumstances such as visitations by liminal creatures such as ghosts (who blur the boundary between life and death) or fox spirits (shapeshifters who dwell on the margins of wilderness and civilization).[27] What is worse, as Chinese mythology and folklore warns, once a crack is formed in the purity order by one person, not only will that polluted person be plagued by these beings, their influence will spread out to afflict and contaminate others in that person's immediate familial and, eventually, communal circle.[28] For instance, in one well-known story, a farmer noticed a fox travelling in and out of his stores of hay. He followed the fox, who he found could speak and assume human shapes, and the two became friends. The fox spirit began to frequent the farmer's house as well, speaking to his wife and children occasionally. One night, when the farmer accompanied the fox to a tavern, he asked why the spirit did not speak to any of the other patrons. The fox replied that he could only approach those whose virtue was somehow blighted, causing the farmer to realize that he himself must somehow be thus tainted. He then made a resolution to live a better life, for the sake of himself and his family, causing the fox spirit to disappear at that very moment.[29]

Owing to its strong emphasis on cosmic dualism, Persian and Iranian Zoroastrianism has also had a long tradition of concerns regarding purity and corruption. Drawn from the distinction between the ultimate good of god (Ahura Mazda) and the corrupting forces of evil (led by Angra Mainyu), life, fire, water, and vegetation are seen as agents of purity, while elements associated with decay, such as insects (particularly flies) and corpses, are seen as vectors of destruction capable of spreading their pollution to what is otherwise clean. In keeping with this interpretation, in traditional Zoroastrianism, to bury a corpse (an impure element) in the earth (a pure element) is considered sinful as it contaminates a realm of goodness with the impurity of evil. Instead, corpses were to be left on the outskirts of a settled area in tall, raised structures, called *dakhma* or "Towers of Silence," for the carrion to pick clean and thus render pure.[30]

In the eastern Mediterranean, ancient Judaism showed similar tendencies, articulating throughout the Hebrew Bible how certain animals, foods, bodily emissions, diseases, and sexual behaviors can render one "unclean."[31] What is more, these states can transfer from one individual to infect the rest of the group, as is made clear by the following excerpt from *Numbers*: "The Lord said to Moses, 'Order the Israelites to expel from camp everyone with a scaly infection, and everyone suffering from a discharge, and everyone who has become unclean by contact with a corpse…. You shall expel them from the camp so that they do not defile their camp.'"[32] Similarly, in an instance recounted in *Leviticus*, those around a man who had taken the Lord's name in vain were said to be tainted merely by being present to hear the blasphemy and must purify themselves.[33] On an even greater scale, there is a sense in the Hebrew Bible that human transgression is especially dangerous to the Temple, nullifying the efficacy of rituals conducted there, and can even go on to pollute the very land itself, causing damage that can only be repaired by expelling those responsible.[34]

Within the mythic narratives of the Hebrew Bible, the figure of David serves as an interesting example of how even a highly placed individual is still subject to purity laws and punishments if those codes are broken. According to those stories, David first gained fame as the one who defeated Goliath, a powerful and imposing warrior among the Philistines, a deadly enemy of the Israelites.[35] Later, after he becomes king, David begins to exploit his position, indulging his lust by committing adultery with Bath-sheba and arranging for her husband to be killed.[36] The myth describes that, as punishment for David's extramarital and homicidal transgressions, the child born of his union with Bathsheba will die, despite the King's pleas and protests to the contrary.[37]

As one last prominent example, purity was a constant concern for the ancient Greeks, who undertook small and large scale purification rit-uals on a daily basis, involving regulation of exterior behaviors, such as blood-shedding, bathing, sexual intercourse, and also inner states, includ-ing the piety of one's thoughts.[38] This concern took on similar dimensions to the cultures discussed previously, as described by Linda-Marie Gün-ther: "the differentiation between 'pure' and 'impure' in the cults of the Greeks played a major part in the process of collective identity, as who-ever caused impurity in the sacred site … was expelled—until purity was restored—from the cultic community."[39] In addition to the cultic and com-munal realm, the Greek preoccupation with the impact of impurity is also especially prevalent in the mythic realm, and in no more poignant instance than Sophocles' tragedy *Oedipus*. Sophocles bases his play on preexisting material and starts the action after events with which the audience would already be familiar, namely Oedipus' heroic actions in defeating the Sphinx, a category-blurring creature with the face of a woman, an eagle's wings, and a lion's body. The Sphinx had tormented the city of Thebes and, as a reward for his triumph, Oedipus becomes its new king and marries the widowed Queen, Jocasta, having four children with her.

Later, a plague strikes Thebes and the oracle declares that the affliction will only be lifted when the murderer of Laius, the former king and Jocas-ta's previous husband, is brought to justice. Using language that potently evokes purity imagery and the cross-cultural impulse to separate out pol-lution, the oracle commands the citizens of Thebes to "drive the corrup-tion from the land, harbor it no longer, past all cure, don't nurse it in your soil—root it out!"[40] What Oedipus (and Jocasta) do not suspect is that he is the very murderer of whom the oracle speaks, having been born to Laius and Jocasta, but cast out as an infant due to another prophecy that he would kill his father and marry his mother. He survived, however, and made his way back to Thebes to unknowingly fulfill that very forecast. Though a hero for destroying the monstrous Sphinx, over the course of the play Oedipus discovers that he has become an impure monster himself through the crimes of patricide and incest. Indeed, just as the Sphinx breaks classificatory rules through its haphazard collection of body parts, Oedipus blurs and challenges socially-accepted categories, both for himself and the children he fathers. As the blind seer Tiresias puts it during the climax of the play, Oedipus is "brother and father both to the children he embraces, to his mother, son and husband both—he sowed the loins his father sowed, he spilled his father's blood!"[41] A gory amalgam of the crimes of incest and patricide, Tiresias' lines not so subtly invoke the fluids involved with both acts, all set against the background of the plague defiling Thebes, which represents the rippling outward of Oedipus' contamination to impact the entire community. Although Jocasta commits suicide and Oedipus blinds himself prior to going into exile, the pollution created by their acts does not end there, for their sons Eteocles and Polynices go to war over the throne, eventually also embroiling their daughter Antigone in a cycle of violence and chaos.

A pattern emerges from this brief cross-cultural survey of concepts of impurity and pollution in world religions and mythologies. First, whether it is Oedipus, Śiva, or the fox spirit, liminal entities are dangerous. This danger, if left unchecked, can produce situations of impurity which are liable to spread, first to those nearest the liminal individual, then the society at large. This potentially imperils entire social institutions, such as, drawing on our examples above, the Buddhist *sangha*, the Jewish Temple, or the whole city of Thebes. Given the nearly universal nature of these codes and patterns around the world, it is not surprising to see similarities to aspects of the MCU mythology. Particularly, the MCU's pollution themes appear most strongly in the Phase Two films, which represent the period following the superheroes' introduction, when they have already been introduced as liminal figures, and begin to explore the consequences of their existence.

As mentioned before, the primary films this period covers include *Iron Man 3*, *Thor: The Dark World*, *Captain America: The Winter Soldier*, and *Avengers: Age of Ultron*. The first film in this series, *Iron Man 3*, is set in the aftermath of *Marvel's The Avengers* and the battle in New York with Loki's invading army. The inciting events for the film, however, come years in the past when Stark, at a conference in Switzerland in 1999, encounters two different scientists, Maya Hansen and Aldrich Killian. He treats both with characteristic egotism and callousness, seeing Hansen primarily as a brief sexual fling and Killian, who fawns over Stark and begs for a chance to collaborate with him, as an opportunity for mockery. Stark tells the limping, visibly disabled Killian to wait out in the cold on the rooftop,

Aldrich Killian (Guy Pearce), co-inventor of the Extremis virus, shows its contaminating effects on the human body. From *Iron Man 3* (2013).

never intending to meet with him. Back in the movie's present day, Stark suffers from panic attacks and insomnia following his experiences in *Marvel's The Avengers*. These afflictions distract him as threats begin to mount, namely a mysterious terrorist figure called "the Mandarin" who has seemingly orchestrated multiple bombings across the world, and a new biological technology called "Extremis" created by Hansen and Killian. The latter invention is composed of a virus that activates the brain's regenerative powers, allowing people to regrow limbs and heal deformities, as well as gain strength and heat-generating powers. Those who receive too high a dose or whose bodies reject the virus, however, burn alive from the inside out, literally exploding. The fortunate ones who tolerate the Extremis virus are thereafter marked by traces of bright red and orange throbbing under their eyes and skin.

In actuality, it is Killian who is behind the masquerade of the Mandarin and the explosions are victims of Extremis positioned to look like terrorist bombings. When Stark's friend Happy Hogan is injured in one of these explosions, he rashly challenges the supposed Mandarin, giving out the address of his mansion in Malibu. Reminiscent of Odysseus's disastrously foolhardy boast to Polyphemus—in which, in the wake of blinding the monstrous Cyclops, Odysseus could not resist bragging of the deed by declaring his true name and city of origin, allowing Polyphemus to know exactly who to tell his father (the god Poseidon) to target in revenge—Stark's bravado is just as costly as Killian's attack helicopters find the mansion and blast it to ruins with rockets and missiles.[42] As Stark works to track down his attackers, Killian kidnaps Pepper Potts, injects her with the

Extremis virus, and moves forward with his larger plan, which involves attempting to kill the President of the United States and replacing him with the Extremis-supporting Vice-President.[43]

From this synopsis, it is clear that several aspects of the film correspond to the multivalent nature of the religious and mythic pollution codes and imagery discussed earlier. First, it is Stark's own immoral actions toward Killian and Hansen that earn their enmity and drive them to later employ Extremis against him. As Stark even admits in the opening and closing of the film, "We create our own demons."[44] Extremis itself, as a virus that once injected into the body remakes and taints it, is a very literal impurity and corruption. Not incidentally, with Stark's girlfriend Potts being subjected to the virus, as well as his friend Hogan's injury in an Extremis explosion and his mansion's destruction, we see how the impurity and pollution generated by Stark and his Iron Man career has affected those around him. Indeed, with Killian's plot imperiling the President, the entire country is put at risk. This clearly mirrors how Jewish, Greek, Buddhist, and other traditions observed that the impure status of one individual ripples outward to affect an entire community, like the epicenter of an earthquake shudders off waves of aftershocks.

Thor's dilemma in *Thor: The Dark World* is of even greater scope as the entire fabric of the universe's reality hangs in the balance. In the film's prologue, the audience learns of the Dark Elves, who come from the primordial darkness antecedent to the beginning of the universe. They are led by Malekith, who seeks to use the "Aether—an ancient force of infinite destruction" to return all existence to a state of inert darkness. Thus described, Malekith and his Dark Elves are analogues of the Vedic Vritra, Babylonian Tiamat, and Egyptian Apophis, the monstrous chaos dragons who all sought to swallow civilization, the Earth, and all the universe into their gaping maws, extinguishing all life.[45]

These Dark Elves reenter Thor's time during an extremely rare alignment of the cosmic realms, called a "convergence," which thins the boundaries between dimensions and planes of existence. His love interest Jane Foster, during one of her searches for Thor, stumbles into one of these converging areas and is transported to another realm where she encounters the holding chamber for the Aether. Portrayed as a viscous, pulsating, reddish-black liquid, the Aether invades Foster's body, pulsing red and black in her veins. She becomes ill and seeing her condition, Thor carries her to Asgard where healers diagnose the Aether as an "infection" in her body that is "ever-changing, seek[ing] out host bodies, drawing strength from their life-force."[46] As we saw in the previous chapter, this kind of predatory, vampiric instability is the very definition of monstrosity, and in this case, also of pollution. In addition to having brought the Aether and its

impurity into Asgard, Thor has also violated the realm's laws by bringing Foster, a human, into their midst. His father Odin is particularly dis-
pleased on this latter point, declaring, "She does not belong in Asgard any
more than a goat belongs at a banquet table."[47] As if consciously channel-
ing Douglas' definition of impurity as "matter out of place," the weakening
of walls between realms, the infectious presence of the Aether, and Foster's
unwelcome intrusion into Asgard all serve to render nearly the entire universe as "dirty."

While he cannot control the convergence, Thor is directly responsible for the presence of the Aether and Foster in Asgard and his actions
have dire consequences. Drawn to the Aether, Malekith and his reawakened Dark Elves infiltrate Asgard in invisible, undetectable ships, as well
as an agent disguised as a prisoner in the kingdom's dungeon. They smash
into the palace itself, destroying the ceremonial throne, rampaging through
the halls, and killing Thor's mother, Frigga. Though the Dark Elves are
unable to retrieve the Aether, their attack motivates Thor to leave Asgard
to hunt them down, which entails disobeying Odin, fighting an entou-
rage of guards, and committing treason by releasing from prison Loki, the
only one who knows of a pathway to the Dark Elf realm. As the convergence increases in intensity, the Aether is extracted from a sickening Foster, Loki is seemingly killed by the Dark Elves, and, when the walls between
realms are virtually non-existent, Thor finally defeats Malekith. Along the
way, though, the chaos spread by the Aether, the convergence, and Thor's
own actions have pulled the order of Asgardian society apart. Indeed, without Thor's knowledge, Loki has actually survived (or actively faked his own
death; it is not clear from the events of the film), used a magic spell to cast
out Odin, and employed his shape-shifting abilities to assume the king's
form in order to rule over Asgard.

In *Captain America: The Winter Soldier*, Steve Rogers faces a situation of similar personal and global upheaval, although the pollution
and contamination involved in this situation is of a more metaphorical nature. Early in the film, Rogers is informed that SHIELD has begun a
massive buildup of armed forces, constructing three heavily weaponized
heli-carriers, purportedly for use in deterrence of hostile groups. Following
an assassination attempt on Director Nick Fury, Rogers allies with Natasha Romanoff to investigate these developments, eventually uncovering a
secret SHIELD bunker. In that installation, they discover a hidden room
filled with computers and data tapes containing the uploaded consciousness of Arnim Zola, a scientist who worked with the Red Skull during the
Second World War. Zola describes how, following the Second World War,
SHIELD recruited him and other Hydra officers into their ranks. From
there, the Hydra personnel recruited others, and Zola brags "the new Hydra

grew, a beautiful parasite within SHIELD," where "for seventy years we have been secretly feeding crises and reaping war."[48] The newly constructed, heavily-armed heli-carriers are thus part of a Hydra plot within SHIELD to target potential dissidents around the globe, stamp out all resistance, and impose their fascist order on the entire world. The SHIELD that Rogers and Romanoff thought they were serving has in fact been infected to its core by the very enemies they believed they were fighting.

As if this were not discomfiting enough, during the course of a later battle with Hydra agents posing as members of SHIELD, Rogers discovers that their chief assassin is none other than his childhood friend James Buchanan "Bucky" Barnes. Believed to have been killed during a battle with Hydra during the Second World War, Barnes was instead taken captive by the organization, experimented upon, mentally-altered and conditioned, and placed in cryogenic suspended animation to be reawakened only for killing assignments. Wearing a black mask and a metal, robotic appendage in place of an arm severed by Hydra scientists, Barnes is now known as the "Winter Soldier." In the face of these mounting threats, Rogers, Romanoff, Fury, and their new ally Sam Wilson (who takes on the guise of the "Falcon" via a military grade rocket glider jet-pack), come together to defeat the Winter Soldier and prevent Hydra from executing its plan. In the process, though, the three heli-carriers are destroyed and crash into the Triskelion, the SHIELD headquarters, utterly devastating it. In the end, Rogers is left wondering about his place in the world.

Together, the three films construct a thematically-unified discourse on purity that parallels the concerns we have seen appearing in mythologies and religions across the world. First, in each case an obviously corrupting influence has intruded into the superhero's respective domain. The Extremis virus and the Aether particularly meet standard pollution notions that we saw in Jewish, Greek, and Chinese understandings of bodily contamination: both represent pathogenic kinds of substances or fluids that invade or compromise the physical form and even spread to impact others. In the case of Hydra, this is certainly corruption in at least a metaphorical sense, as an outside force worms its way into an institution, sullying first the host organization and then reaching out with its tentacles into world affairs. This type of pollution is consistent with the more institutional orthodoxy outlook on purity found, as we discussed earlier, in the Buddhist monastic setting or even the ancient Jewish Temple priesthood, who both saw differences in mental outlook as blights upon their traditions, and thus a kind of potential contamination.[49]

Besides merely experiencing and witnessing the pollution, each superhero bears a degree of responsibility. Stark, through his mistreatment of Killian and Hansen, sets in motion the events that lead to the existence of the Extremis virus. Thor does not create the Aether, but he brings the Aether-infected Jane Foster into Asgard, which in turn leads to the Dark Elves' attack. Steve Rogers may be the least culpable, but he and Romanoff still go about their assignments for SHIELD largely oblivious to its aberrant behavior. By straddling established classificatory categories, whether it be disparate time-periods in the case of Captain America, human and machine for Iron Man, or human/divine and earth/sky for Thor, the superheroes are each magnets for potential crisis as their interstitial status weakens the dividing walls of the social systems around them. Like Śiva or Oedipus, their inherently liminal status attracts instability to them, specifically in the form of impurity, rendering them the center of a veritable whirlpool of at least potential for pollution. On this very point, Mary Douglas argues, "A polluting person is always in the wrong. He has developed some wrong condition or simply crossed some line which should not have been crossed and this displacement unleashes danger for someone."[50]

Douglas' words are especially appropriate when we consider the impact of these superheroes' actions on those within their immediate circle of influence. In *Iron Man 3*, Stark's friend Happy Hogan is badly injured when an Extremis victim explodes and his girlfriend Pepper Potts is taken captive and infected with the virus. In *Thor: The Dark World*, not only is Jane Foster forced to become the vessel for the Aether, his friend Dr. Erik Selvig becomes deranged, his mother is killed by the Dark Elves, and the throne is left (unbeknownst to Thor at the time) in the hands of the deceptive and duplicitous Loki. Finally, in *Captain America: The Winter Soldier*, it is none other than Rogers' closest friend "Bucky" who is Hydra's most ruthless and powerful assassin, but only due to the mind-altering treatment of which he has been a subject, which in itself certainly constitutes a kind of pollution of the brain. At every turn in this triad of films, someone close to the superheroes, whether dear friend, family member, or loved one, is wounded, sickened, killed, or otherwise contaminated. In the myths we examined, as well as others around the world, those closest to the liminal or impure figure similarly suffer ill effects. Oedipus may have been the patricide, but Jocasta and his children are implicated in his incest, and thus are also made to suffer. Śiva's absence from the home leaves Pārvatī feeling neglected, leading to her creation of Gaṇeśa from the impurity of her body, which in turn leads to the boy's decapitation upon Śiva's return. In Chinese folklore and myths of ghosts and fox spirits, the one in violation of morality and purity standards may be the one who first attracts these entities through their impropriety, but the effects soon spread to the rest of his or her family when the beings plague them as well. We find this same phenomenon amid Native American and Southeast Asian tribal groups, as well: supernatural danger emanates from the individual in violation of the purity norms and it is only a matter of time until those in the immediate vicinity are likewise tainted. For an especially enlightening example in the Southeast Asian context, there is the phenomena of spirits (called "Lulik") who target people who have transgressed the social norms, then go on to afflict those individual's family members one after another.[51] These MCU films operate in the same manner, showing that to be adjacent or akin to the superheroes' liminality is to be in jeopardy and at risk of pollution.

Furthermore, in each case the pollution heralds an atmosphere of abject confusion. For a lengthy stretch of time in *Iron Man 3*, Stark (and the governmental and military authorities) believe that the culprit of the explosions is the mysterious Mandarin, but this is merely a sham character to mask Killian. Thor himself contributes to such an environment in *Thor: The Dark World* by insisting on his own insubordinate plan to fight the Dark Elves, enlisting his Asgardian comrades to fight against other Asgardian soldiers while he absconds with Foster and his brother Loki. Finally, uncertainty and paranoia permeate *Captain America: The Winter Soldier*, as Rogers discovers Fury had planted listening devices throughout his apartment and assigned an undercover agent to surveil him from the room next door. Based on this, Rogers does not know who to trust and in the film's conclusion can only declare, to those still possibly loyal to SHIELD's founding principles, that Hydra agents "could be standing right next to you."[52] All of this confusion proceeds from systems that have been knocked out of joint and classifications moved out of place: friend is mixed with foe and clean is mixed (to borrow Douglas' imagery again) with dirty. Arguably, the source of the dirt in most of these cases is the superheroes themselves.

Finally, as we saw in our discussion of other mythic and religious traditions, if left unaddressed, impurity can potentially undermine entire social institutions. In the ritual purity schemes of ancient Judaism, if pollution or sin was not purged it could ripple outward to defile the Temple or even the very land itself. Likewise, in Chinese Imperial thought, the regent's right to rule could weaken and falter if plagued by broken social codes, as the supporting mandates from the heavenly realm were withdrawn. Additionally, we saw that the mental defilements of even one monk in a Theravāda Buddhist monastery could negatively impact the entire *sangha*'s merit-making relationship. The same situation obtains in the MCU as the impurity instigated by the superheroes spreads outward, building to greater and greater devastation. For Stark, besides the threats to his closest loved ones, his mansion is destroyed by Extremis agents and Killian's ultimate plot grows to threaten the President of the United States. In Thor's case, Asgard itself is attacked, the palace is badly damaged, and the realm's dungeons are emptied. For Rogers, as a result of the response he coordinates to counter Hydra's infiltration and operation, SHIELD collapses as a coherent organization, both institutionally and physically, as its Triskelion headquarters is reduced to rubble. In all these cases, then, an institution is threatened, undermined, or even destroyed due to a defiling influence, as symbolized by the destruction of previously stable or iconic locations, such as Stark's mansion, Asgard's palace, or the Triskelion. From this, we are left to conclude that, as is consistent with the legacy of world religious traditions, once pollution and contamination have progressed beyond a certain point, remediation is impossible and only ruin can purge the influence.

Rather than resolve the superheroes' purity dilemmas, these films instead only highlight their growing intensity, and the concerns with pollution reach a crescendo in *Avengers: Age of Ultron*, the second Avengers film and the penultimate entry in the MCU myth's Phase Two. This film builds on and, as we will see, in many ways culminates the themes of contamination and moral confusion threaded throughout Phase Two's preceding entries. Indeed, Joss Whedon, the writer and director of *Avengers: Age of Ultron*, expressed in this way the extent to which the film delved into the problematic nature of the superheroes: "'Strong but damaged by power' describes every person in this movie … it may, in fact, describe what the movie is about. You know, the more power that we have, the less human we are."[53] In the film, the eponymous "Ultron" is an artificial intelligence created by Tony Stark with the assistance of Bruce Banner, based on their own research and plans, but also raw materials and schematics salvaged from a destroyed Hydra base. Stark's purported objective with Ultron's creation is to establish a powerful defensive system to hold off future alien attacks, such as the Chitauri's in the first *Avengers*. This, to use Whedon's phrase, is his "damage," which was hinted at in *Iron Man 3*: a deep-seated paranoia about threats to the planet and the inability of the Avengers to contain them. His hubris once again surfaces, however, as he refuses to consult his teammates, knowing they would object. Instead, he is intent on creating Ultron, which will establish, he believes, "peace in our time."[54]

Beyond the uneasy historical context of that phrase (i.e., Neville Chamberlain's disastrous appeasement of Adolf Hitler), there is reason within the narrative context of the MCU to view such a statement with suspicion. If we recall, in *Marvel's The Avengers*, when he first appeared, Loki also promised peace, to which Nick Fury replied, presciently, "Yeah, you say peace. I kind of think you mean the other thing."[55] Just as Loki is revealed to have a twisted sense of peace founded on his own myopic, egotistically-based morality, Stark's perspective is also skewed and his invention results in anything but peace.

Indeed, within mere seconds of Ultron achieving consciousness, he exhibits a marked malevolence and animosity. Recognizing his commission as a "global peace-keeping" program, Ultron begins scanning history files and current events. Based on this, he determines that the Avengers in particular, and humanity in general, are the greatest threat to global peace. As the Avengers hold a party and jest about whether any of them besides Thor is worthy to lift his hammer, Ultron makes his first appearance and interjects, "No, how could you be worthy? You're all killers…. There's only one path to peace: the Avengers' extinction."[56] From there, using his computer interfaces, Ultron infiltrates all the Avengers' files, surveillance footage, and spreads across the Internet. Using automation, he begins making nearly countless duplicates of himself. Along the way, Ultron also finds allies, namely the Maximoff twins Pietro and Wanda, who gained powers through Hydra's human experimentation. Holding a grudge against Stark for manufacturing weapons used in a war in their native Sokovia, the Maximoffs initially share Ultron's hatred of the Avengers.

As Ultron enacts his plan to destroy humanity by plunging the city of Sokovia into the earth like a meteor, he comes into conflict multiple times with the Avengers. During these encounters, Wanda Maximoff uses her mental powers to force the Avengers to view nightmare visions particular to their own inner demons. Romanoff relives her brutal training and sterilization, Rogers sees the World War II homecoming he can never have, and Thor sees himself and fellow Asgardians in the realm of Hel. As Thor's lightning power bursts out of control, killing his own people, a blind Heimdall grabs him, saying, "You're a destroyer, Thor Odinson. See where your power leads?"[57] Most calamitous, Wanda Maximoff is able to use her powers to turn Banner into an entirely berserk version of the Hulk who rampages through a city, only subdued after a destructive battle with Stark's Iron Man.

As a result, each of the Avengers starts to harbor doubts about the nature of their abilities and begins to wonder about their own status in terms reminiscent of the topics we discussed in the previous chapter: have their powers tainted them to the point that they have become monsters? The term and the rhetoric around it are repeated by multiple characters throughout the middle portion of the film. Romanoff, for instance, tells Banner, "You think you're the only monster on this team?" Later, Stark, also to Banner, uses the same term, but, with surprisingly little shame given his role as Ultron's creator, sees it as an affirmative: "We're mad scientists, buddy. We're monsters. We gotta own it." Even the newest Avenger, the "Vision," created through an amalgamation of Stark's J.A.R.V.I.S. computer program, Ultron's vibranium-engineered body, and the cosmic Mind Stone, wonders aloud, "Maybe I am a monster. I don't think I'd know if I were one." The Avengers' uncertainty about whether their powers and liminal, category-breaking statuses have finally tipped them over the fine line from heroism to monstrosity leads to Rogers' line, quoted at the beginning of this chapter: "Ultron thinks we're monsters, that we're what's wrong with the world. This isn't just about beating him—it's about whether he's right."[58]

In the face of this challenge, the Avengers resolve to purify the world of Ultron's proliferating presence. With the help of the Maximoffs, who change sides when they learn Ultron wants to wipe out all humanity, and the newly-created Vision, they prepare for this very task. As stated by the Vision, "[Ultron's] pain will roll over the earth. So he must be destroyed. Every form he's built, every trace of his presence on the net."[59] In other words, like a bacteria, a virus, or any other contaminant or impurity, Ultron must be completely purged for the world to be safe again. In the course of a ferocious final battle in Sokovia, the Avengers succeed, but not without destroying the city they were intending to protect and losing Pietro Maximoff, whom Ultron kills.

In many ways, this film is the culmination of the purity themes found in the preceding Phase Two episodes in the MCU narrative. Ultron, between his propensity to infiltrate and proliferate uncontrollably, fits the mold of a dangerously polluting or contaminating influence. Additionally, just as the superheroes were to an extent responsible for the damage caused by the Extremis virus, the Aether, and Hydra, the Avengers are to blame for Ultron. Stark and Banner created Ultron and, through their arrogance and hubris, refused to consult with the rest of the Avengers team. Like Oedipus or Śiva, whose quick tempers and pride create cascades of purity problems, the two superheroes set in motion the chain of events that led to the pollution of their team and put the safety of the entire world at stake. On this point, Ultron's observation that "everyone creates the thing they dread," seems pertinent to the actions of the MCU superheroes and their mythic antecedents: due to their liminal status, their actions in the world cannot help but be ambiguous to a greater or lesser extent.

That ambiguity marks much of *Avengers: Age of Ultron* as the superheroes spend much of their time, once again, fighting with one another, erasing or at least complicating any clear delineation of moral purity that they might once have possessed. Besides the Maximoffs' battles with the Avengers, as mentioned above, under Wanda Maximoff's influence Banner becomes an exceptionally savage version of the Hulk, brought to heel only when Stark dons an even more massive version of his armor. In the process, a large portion of the city of Johannesburg in South Africa is demolished, raising questions about the Hulk, namely if, as Banner later claims regarding this incident, "the world has finally seen the real Hulk."[60] The tension does not even end there, as Stark, Banner, and Barton fight with Rogers and the Maximoffs over the propriety of creating the Vision, smashing the Avengers' lab along the way. Shortly after joining the Avengers, Wanda Maximoff remarks, "Ultron can't tell the difference between destroying the world and saving it. Where do you think he gets that from?"[61] Though directed at Tony Stark, Ultron's primary creator, the statement could be applied just as easily to the entire Avengers and, by extension, the whole contingent of MCU superheroes who routinely, especially in these Phase Two films, cause almost as much damage as they prevent. Though the Avengers and other MCU superheroes, as discussed in the previous chapter, do distinguish themselves from their villainous counterparts by their intention to protect humanity and overcome their lower "shadow-selves," it is still undeniable that the Avengers were directly responsible for Ultron's existence. Within the realm of world religions and myths, this kind of transgression of purity would call for penance, expiation, and sacrifice, which the Avengers accomplish partly through annihilating each and every copy of Ultron, but the price is usually of a personal nature as well. For instance, Oedipus blinds himself and goes into exile, Śiva bears the severed head of Brahmā, and David suffers the loss of a child, all to balance out their lapses in purity. The Avengers similarly suffer a loss, in the person of Wanda Maximoff's brother, Pietro, who had joined the group as "Quicksilver." In a sense, then, Pietro Maximoff's death could be seen as the price paid by the Avengers in blood, a kind of sacrifice for the sake of purity that they must make to atone for having created Ultron.

Avengers: Age of Ultron thus culminates the pollution and impurity themes we see at work in the MCU's myth's Phase Two. In this section of the mythos, we have found at work Mary Douglas' thesis about the dangers impurity has traditionally been seen to pose for societies. In her words, "Society is subject to external and internal pressures; that which is not with it, part of it, and subject to its laws is potentially against it."[62] As liminal beings, the MCU superheroes flout the laws of ordinary society in terms of classification and thus of purity. Rather than increase order, the presence of such beings, world mythologies have shown, instead leads to chaos, which the Phase Two films exhibit in abundance. The consequences for the defilement of order, as we see with Pietro Maximoff and others who perish during this period of the MCU, can be harsh, but are hardly unexpected, as observed by Paul Ricoeur: "Suffering is the price for the violation of order; suffering is to satisfy the claim of purity for revenge."[63]

The MCU myth, however, does not show the superheroes as being unaware of the pollution and chaos of which they are the epicenter. Besides Rogers' challenge to his team to show Ultron, as well as the rest of the world, that they are not monsters, at the end of *Captain America: The Winter Soldier*, Romanoff, in a combination of contrition and defiance, addresses a congressional committee with words that, by the end of Phase Two, could apply to the entire roster of the MCU's superheroes. When questioned as to why she and the other superheroes should not be imprisoned for the devastation wrought by the battle with Hydra, as well as the intelligence and information breaches, she answers, "Because you need us. Yes, the world is a vulnerable place, and yes, we help make it that way. But we're also the ones best qualified to defend it."[64]

Acknowledging that, at best, their liminality as super-powered individuals is a double-edged sword, Romanoff still argues that their role as defenders of society should be maintained. In this we can see, as described in Chapter Two, the tension produced in any culture by the presence of the religious virtuoso, like the shaman (whose template most closely matches the MCU figures), who is in constant contact with sacred and supernatural powers. The community needs and depends on their ability to mediate with otherworldly powers, but when brought too close into the midst of society, their abilities can create the very chaos they seek to dispel. Like an electrical power line, they bring valuable energy, but, if the boundaries or rules are not observed, also harbor the danger of electrocution.

At this point, the progression of the larger narrative of the MCU starts to come somewhat into focus. After acquiring their powers in the origin story, the superheroes each, through their more altruistic choices and greater strength of character, overcome the villains who represent their shadow-selves. However, they cannot entirely overcome their liminal nature and, like shamans or other religious virtuosos who dwell on the fringes of society due to their proximity to the hazardous powers of the sacred, also radiate danger and the potential to upset the careful balance between purity and impurity. The MCU Phase Two shows the consequences of the superheroes' continuing liminality with the tilt into themes of impurity. As the MCU mythos progresses into its next episodes, rather than seeing the issues raised in Phase Two resolved, in Phase Three the threads of society and the connections between the Avengers and other superheroes become even more frayed. While the corruption was symbolized by the villainous likes of Aldrich Killian, Malekith, Hydra, and Ultron in Phase Two, in Phase Three, the superheroes instead either turn on one another or must contend with threats even closer to home. As we will see, during this next Phase, superhero will fight superhero, family will turn on family, and confusion will reign at times over who even is a hero or a villain. These episodes of the MCU and their mythical-religious symbolism and parallels are the subject of the next chapter.

FOUR

Families Divided

Internecine and Intergenerational War in the MCU[1]

When brothers are split, a quarrel is sure.
—*The Mahābhārata: The Book of the Assembly Hall,*
translated by J.A.B. van Buitenen, p. 124

TONY STARK ("IRON MAN"): *I'm trying to keep you from
tearing the Avengers apart!*
STEVE ROGERS ("CAPTAIN AMERICA"): *You did that when
you signed* [the Sokovian Accords].
—*Captain America: Civil War* (2016)

In her essay on the Greek epic *Iliad*, philosopher Simone Weil wrote, "In wielding their power, they never suspect that the consequences of their actions will afflict them in turn."[2] Though intended to describe the actions of the warriors in Homer's classic poem, Weil's observation could just as easily be applied to the superheroes in the films of Phase Three of the MCU mythology. Building on the Phase Two events that dealt with the perils of impurity and pollution, the Phase Three films have at their root the continuing reverberations of the superheroes' inherent liminal status. In this series of episodes in the larger MCU narrative, instead of the intrusion of alien and external contaminating foes, the superheroes fight instead with a long-lost sibling, a cousin, a father or father-figures, an abusive adoptive family, and, in the most pointed and poignant case, each other.

The threats the superheroes face in Phase Three are thus of a more internal, even intimate variety, suggesting an intensification and escalation of the problems caused by the ambiguities of their powers and statuses. At its lowest point, when they combat one another, the sobering and startling opening words of the *Iliad* itself are appropriate to express the rancor that emerges: "Rage—Goddess, sing the rage of Peleus' son Achilles, murderous, doomed, that cost the Achaeans countless losses,

85

hurling down to the House of Death so many sturdy souls."[3] Once violence of this intra-communal, internecine sort is loosed, it can become self-sustaining and difficult to contain, as scholar of sacrificial rituals René Girard has noted: "When differences come unhinged they are generally identified as the cause of those rivalries for which they are also the stake.... As in the case of sacrificial rituals, when they no longer serve as a dam against violence, they serve to swell the flood."[4] In these cases, the superhero-versus-superhero battles seem to indicate a society that is falling apart and the triumph of the destructive impulses behind their supernormal, sacred-mediating powers.

In other cases, however, the Phase Three films show the superheroes reacting to their familial or internal enemy in ways that represent attempts to redefine or renew themselves, as well as reconcile with others, though the process is never without trauma, scarring, or the loss of something held dear. Still, these more hopeful aspects of Phase Three show the MCU mythos moving toward the possibility of the superheroes being able to deal constructively with their liminal status. All along the way, the episodes in this Phase resonate with and parallel religious concepts and mythic narratives from around the world that also articulate and cope with situations of familial division, confusion, and strife.

As the first film in Phase Three, *Captain America: Civil War* powerfully sets this tone. It is also one of the MCU movies with a direct primary source from Marvel comics, namely the 2007 graphic novel limited series, *Civil War*. In that work, after a group of irresponsible young superheroes cause an explosion that kills hundreds of school-children, the United States government forces super-powered individuals to either register with the authorities to be supervised by law enforcement or be treated as vigilante criminals. As a debate ensues between the need for security versus the potential loss of civil liberties, Iron Man leads the pro-registration forces and Captain America organizes an anti-registration contingent, setting the stage for a brutal showdown between the two superhero factions. Given its inciting incident of a tragic loss of life and the proceeding debate on the needs of the state versus the freedom of individuals, the graphic novel series is an obvious parallel to the events of 9/11 and the subsequent political situation in the United States.[5]

Aside from the primary fault-line and point of conflict being situated also between Iron Man and Captain America, the events and intent of the film *Captain America: Civil War* deviate substantially from the graphic novel series. As opposed to a charged political statement, the MCU film instead tells a more personal story of tension and animosity developing, then exploding, between superheroes who have become like family to one another. As Anthony Russo, one of the directors of the film, explained at the time of its release, "We were trying to tell the story of a family falling apart. The tragic end of the story is that the family is divided."[6] In some ways, though, this particular family has always been divided, as we have seen Tony Stark and Steve Rogers bicker and argue in *Marvel's The Avengers* and even briefly fight physically in *Avengers: Age of Ultron*. Tension has always seethed just under the surface between not only those two figures, but the entire superhero contingent of the MCU who exhibit the tendency to engage in violence upon first meeting one another. This pattern is seen, for instance, in the Stark/Thor and Thor/Hulk battles in *Marvel's The Avengers* and recurs in other smaller skirmishes, such as the brief scuffle between Sam Wilson ("Falcon") and Scott Lang ("Ant-Man") in *Ant-Man* and the fisticuffs that ensue when a contingent of the Guardians of the Galaxy first meets Tony Stark, Peter Parker, and Doctor Strange in *Avengers: Infinity War*. Altogether, these incidents suggest that whenever super-powered beings are brought together, their instability leads them to violence. In the wake of the further destabilizing events of the preceding Phase Two, the stage is thus set in Phase Three for potential cataclysm.

Events do not start at this high pitch in *Captain America: Civil War*, however, but instead slowly escalate. The film begins with a flashback to Siberia in 1991, where the Winter Soldier is re-awakened from his cryogenic sleep to steal packets of experimental super-soldier serum. In the present day, Steve Rogers leads a portion of his new group of Avengers—composed of Black Widow (Natasha Romanoff), Scarlet Witch (Wanda Maximoff), and Falcon (Sam Wilson)—after former Hydra agent Brock Rumlow, who is in Lagos, Nigeria attempting to steal a biological weapon. When cornered by Rogers, Rumlow detonates explosives strapped to his body in the hope of killing them both. Instead, Maximoff uses her telekinetic powers to hurl him upwards, but unfortunately he lands against a building, killing numerous innocent bystanders.

General Thunderbolt Ross, the Hulk-hunting military officer from *The Incredible Hulk* who is now Secretary of State, arrives with Tony Stark at Avengers headquarters to deliver an ultimatum: in the wake of the destruction in Lagos, New York, Sokovia, and other locations, the superheroes must either sign the "Sokovia Accords," which puts them under the direction and jurisdiction of a United Nations panel, or cease their activities. In connection to the previous chapter, the ambivalence toward the superheroes is clear and Secretary Ross's description of them points to their own position as potentially polluting agents. Specifically, he identifies their propensity to spread danger and cross international borders without regard for the law as reasons the Accords are necessary. In other words, like a polluting agent, they need to be contained.

The proposal immediately splits the Avengers into factions. Wilson and Rhodes, another new Avenger in his "War Machine" armored guise, take opposing sides, against and for the agreement, respectively. The android Vision puts the matter more philosophically, and mathematically, in the following dialogue:

> VISION: In the eight years since Mr. Stark announced himself as "Iron Man," the number of known enhanced persons has grown exponentially. During the same period, the number of potentially world-ending events has risen at a commensurate rate.
> ROGERS: Are you saying it's our fault?
> VISION: I'm saying there may be a causality. Our very strength invites challenge. Challenge incites conflict. And conflict breeds catastrophe.[7]

The Vision's reasoning is a testimony to the Avengers' dawning realization of their own inherently liminal nature and the dangers it can create. Within the context of the argument, Stark pounces on that point and declares, "We need to be put in check. If we can't accept limits, if we're boundary-less, we're no better than the bad guys."[8] What both Stark and Vision do not appear to comprehend, though, is that, as we saw in the previous chapters through the work of van Gennep, Turner, and Durkheim, beings who have come into contact with the sacred (or superpowers, in the vernacular of the MCU) are not easily bounded or limited. Without complete separation, the contagious and otherworldly power of the sacred is still liable to spill over into the mundane world through its intermediary figures, the superheroes in this case. Whether the Accord would provide an adequate boundary is unknown, but Steve Rogers disagrees with any level of oversight, undoubtedly due to his growing distrust of overarching institutions in the wake of Hydra's infiltration of SHIELD. "If we sign this," he argues, "we surrender our right to choose. What if this panel sends us somewhere we don't think we should go? What if there's somewhere we need to go and they won't let us? We may not be perfect, but the safest hands are still our own."[9]

Both sides thus make compelling arguments and the audience clearly is meant to see each viewpoint as worthy. At this stage, the superheroes also still hold one another in obvious regard, treating each other with respect and even affection. Later, after signing the Sokovia Accord herself, Romanoff visits Rogers and entreats him to do so as well. Saying, "Staying together is more important than how we stay together," she then even embraces him.[10] As the Russos intended, these superheroes who will soon face off on the battlefield act initially with great respect toward each other, as one would expect from members of a family.

Though they eventually reach the heights of bloody madness, the ancient Greek *Iliad*, the Hindu *Mahābhārata*, and the Irish *Táin Bó Cúailgne* also go to great lengths to show the original esteem or even affinity that obtains between combatants in the respective wars they describe. In the *Iliad*, despite the enmity between the Trojans and the Greeks, the poet certainly works to provide an evenhanded portrayal of the struggle, providing regular windows into the common humanity of the warriors.[11] For instance, the imposing Greek hero Achilles bemoans the very need to fight, wondering why they have even engaged in this war, as "it was not Trojan spearmen who brought me here to fight. The Trojans never did me damage, not in the least."[12] Across the battlefield, on the opposing Trojan side, the reader is given one of the more poignant moments of the epic as Hector, Troy's greatest fighter, approaches his wife Andromache and their young son, Astyanax. The boy becomes frightened of his father's helmet and armor, and when they are removed, he holds the child, but sees the tears streaking his wife's face. "Why so much grief for me?" he asks, although he already knows the answer all too well: should he and the Trojan army be defeated (which they will be), upon his death, Andromache will be enslaved and Astyanax murdered.[13]

This common humanity on both sides works its way onto the battlefield, as experienced between Hector and the Greek Ajax. When a duel between the two lasts into dusk, they agree to a truce and Hector even makes a further proposal: "Come let us give each other gifts, unforgettable gifts, so any man may say, Trojan soldier or Argive, 'First they fought with heart-devouring hatred, then they parted bound by pacts of friendship.'"[14] Through these moments the complex personalities of the figures involved in the war are illuminated and Homer shows the shared humanity on each side, allowing the reader to identify with both groups.[15]

The great Hindu epic *Mahābhārata* communicates much the same message. Composed during a period of tremendous social change and upheaval in India, the *Mahābhārata* tells the story of a terrible war between two factions of the same family.[16] The Pāṇḍavas and Kauravas become deadly enemies over who possesses the legitimate claim to the throne of the kingdom. Though in some ways the perspective of the epic favors the Pāṇḍavas and their claim since the Kauravas deceive them out of their birthright and heap multiple humiliations and dangers upon them, moral ambiguity still abounds, as we will see in greater detail later on, and each side is treated with both admiration and admonition.[17] In the outer frame of the narrative, where the King Janamejaya has asked the priest Vyāsa to relate the story to him, he asks, "How did that breach arise between these men of untroubled deeds?"[18] Suggesting that both sides are of "untroubled deeds," i.e., morally venerable, places the eventual battle between the Pāṇḍavas and Kauravas on a relatively level ethical field. Even Kuntī, the mother of the five Pāṇḍava brothers, laments the strife that has divided the family, crying out in distress, "Accursed be the wealth for the sake of which there will be great carnage and slaughter of kinsmen, for there will only be defeat in this family war ... for the dispossessed it is better to die, for there is no victory in the killing of kin."[19]

The Pāṇḍavas themselves feel the same way, becoming painfully conflicted as war draws close. The eldest of the five brothers, Yudhiṣṭhira, who even stands to become king should they triumph, mourns for the relationships that will be torn asunder. Foreseeing "the killing of men who ought not to be killed," he bemoans, "How can war be waged with men we may not kill? How can we win if we must kill our teachers and elders?"[20] In spite of the wrongs the Kauravas have visited on the Pāṇḍavas, they are still regarded as noble due to their positions and interrelations. For this reason, the legendary Pāṇḍava archer Arjuna famously hesitates just prior to the beginning of the battle on the plains of Kurukṣetra. This episode in the *Mahābhārata*, called the *Bhagavad Gītā*, involves the god Krishna, who is serving as the archer's charioteer, counseling Arjuna through this moral crisis. In its early passages, the *Bhagavad Gītā* captures Arjuna's grief over the coming battle: "Krishna, I see all my family poised for war, my limbs falter and my mouth goes dry.... I see no good to come from killing my family in battle."[21]

Across the world, the Irish *Táin Bó Cúailgne* (abbreviated often as "the *Táin*") strikes the same chords. Telling the tale of a war between the lands of Ulster and Connacht, incited when the latter invades the former to acquire a legendary bull, the great warrior Cúchulainn single-handedly defends Ulster for a time against the Connacht army. He slays fighters by the tens and hundreds until they negotiate a deal whereby one fighter from the Connacht side will face Cúchulainn each day. He continues his string of victories until Connacht sends a warrior named Ferdia, who is Cúchulainn's foster brother. "I swear I don't want this meeting," Cúchulainn says mournfully, "not because I fear him, but because I love him so much."[22] Trained in the same arts of war by the same teachers, their skills are even and the two fighters battle for days on end. At the conclusion of one such bout, even though the outcome of their struggle is still undetermined, their affection for one another shines through: "they came up to each other and each put his arm around the other's neck and gave him three kisses."[23]

Altogether, the *Iliad*, the *Mahābhārata*, and the *Táin* create an atmosphere that *Captain America: Civil War* replicates. Prior to (or even during, in the case of the *Táin*) the heinous conflicts that each epic recounts, the moral equivalency, common humanity, and relatability of the combatants is established, showing that what follows is a struggle not between heroes and monsters, but, far more tragically, between heroes and heroes. In *Captain America: Civil War*, we can see this in the deferential, even playful interactions between the superheroes, but also their motivations for their respective positions. Stark is motivated early in the film to favor sign-ing the agreement after he is confronted by a mother whose son died as a bystander to the Avengers' battle with Ultron in Sokovia. While Stark has experienced what can occur with an excess of power, Rogers, who saw what Hydra nearly accomplished through SHIELD, has experienced what can occur with power in the wrong hands. Both sides are supportable and understandable, making the eventual conflict ambiguous.

Furthermore, each epic depicts the combatants as interconnected, even as family members in the cases of the *Mahābhārata* and the *Táin*. The Avengers as well are shown as a close-knit, family-like unit, with affection for one another that is reinforced by their common mission, but also the mundane situations that arise from living in the same space. Maximoff must regularly reprimand Vision for entering her room unannounced, for instance, and Stark complains (with obvious humor) about household maintenance: "Who's putting coffee grounds in the sink? Am I running a bed-and-breakfast for a biker gang?"[24] As in the other world myths, this level of comradery only elevates the coming calamity when these figures, who clearly care for one another, are torn apart and set against one another.

As a final point, each myth also shows that the coming conflict is inevitable. Fate figures prominently in two of the epics, as the gods have foreordained the Trojan War in the *Iliad* and "smitten the minds" of the Kauravas and Pāṇḍavas.[25] Though the concept of fate is not invoked literally in *Captain America: Civil War*, the trajectory of the Phases One and Two towards Phase Three, as evidenced in Vision's observation quoted previ-ously, is an escalation of violence from the external to the internal, increas-ing in intensity. Despite the tantalizing mirage that the superheroes' affinity for one another could help them avoid conflict, like the epic figures before them, war is inevitable. All that is required is an incident to set the strife in motion and create an avalanche of rancor and revenge.

In the case of *Captain America: Civil War*, the incitement is an explo-sion targeting the Vienna building in which the Sokovian Accords are being ratified. Seemingly set off by Bucky Barnes, the "Winter Soldier," the blast kills King T'Chaka of Wakanda, setting his son T'Challa on the path to become the next king. The incident also sets T'Challa on another path: revenge. As Romanoff tries to console him that a task force will find Barnes, T'Challa reacts bluntly: "Don't bother, Ms. Romanoff. I'll kill him myself."[26] The cycle of revenge actually begins earlier in the film, as Rumlow's moti-vation for luring Captain America to Lagos is to gain retribution for the injuries he suffered in *Captain America: Winter Soldier*. When he loses his fight with Captain America and detonates his explosives, Wanda Maxi-moff sends him into the building with innocent bystanders, which sets the Accords in motion, in turn leading to the bombing and T'Challa's desire to exact a toll for the loss of his father. The roots of revenge thus extend back to the beginning of the film, and beyond, into Phase Two and even Phase One.

To save his friend from this deepening, widening spiral of retaliation, Rogers finds Barnes and protects him from both the police and T'Challa, though they are all eventually apprehended. When Barnes escapes from custody, Rogers and Wilson follow him and a new interpretation of events emerges: a man named Helmut Zemo planted the bomb in Vienna and, using the Hydra code words and conditioning, released Barnes from the holding cell, putatively to learn where other "Winter Soldiers" are being held in storage in Siberia. Barnes, Wilson, and Rogers assume Zemo plans to use these other soldiers as a personal army of terrorists and to stop him they assemble a group of superheroes who have not signed the Sokovian Accords, including Maximoff, Clint Barton ("Hawkeye"), and Scott Lang ("Ant-Man"). Meanwhile, Stark—who is still fuming and hurt that Rogers will not sign the Accords, if only as a way of keeping the Avengers together—creates his own team, composed of Romanoff, the Vision, Rhodes, T'Challa (as "Black Panther"), and newcomer Peter Parker (as "Spider-Man").

The two sides are destined to come into conflict, like Achilles and Hector, the Kauravas and Pāṇḍavas, or Cúchulainn and Ferdia, to the eventual anguish of all. The site of their first skirmish is the Leipzig airport, where Rogers and his team aim to gain transport to Siberia. Confronting them, Stark accuses Rogers (as quoted at the beginning of this chapter) of tearing the Avengers apart, only to have the charge turned back around on him. When the fighting begins, both sides initially act with reserve, even at times behaving in a jovial manner. Spider-Man, for instance, when trading punches with Barnes, remarks, "You've got a metal arm? That's awesome, dude!"[27] Lest we think this tone is purely a function of Parker's age, elsewhere Romanoff and Barton similarly joke with one another as they grapple, the former asking, "We're still friends, right?" with the latter replying, with a smile, "Depends on how hard you hit me."[28]

Even in the midst of this levity, bruises and contusions abound until one of their number is seriously wounded. As Rogers and Barnes fly off in the Avengers' Quinjet, Wilson covers their escape by escorting them in his Falcon jetpack. Vision attempts to hit Wilson with an energy blast, but instead strikes Rhodes, destroying his reactor cell. Without power, Rhodes plummets to the ground, incurring an injury to his spine that leaves him paralyzed. Seeing his close friend lying unconscious, Stark angrily blasts Wilson with a repulsor ray, knocking him out as well, and adding to the accelerating cycle of revenge. Referring to his earlier remarks to the group, Vision turns to Maximoff and declares, "It is as I said: catastrophe."[29]

At this point in the film, the seeds of revenge have sprouted and now begin to show their ugly fruit, which will fully mature at the conclusion. For a preview of what that will look like, we need go no further than the myths referenced earlier. In the *Iliad*, as Achilles remains in his tent due to a dispute with the Greek leader Agamemnon, his close friend Patroclus fights in his stead to defend the Greek ships. Hector kills Patroclus, strips his body, and goes so far as to put his heel on Patroclus' chest.[30] Hearing of his friend's death, Achilles becomes enraged, acquires new armor, and reenters the war, ravenous for vengeance. He is described after that point as, "like inhuman fire raging on through the mountain gorges ... like a frenzied god of battle trampling all he killed and the earth ran black with blood."[31]

Though he slays hosts of Trojans, Achilles' real target is Hector, who initially flees around the city walls from his pursuer. He offers Achilles a pact that whoever wins will return the body of the vanquished unspoiled to his family. Achilles scoffs, "Don't talk to me of pacts. There are no binding oaths between men and lions—wolves and lambs can enjoy no meeting of the minds—they are all bent on hating each other to the death. So with you and me."[32] In quite vivid terms, this remark shows the extent to which his lust for revenge has dehumanized Achilles, where he thinks solely along the lines of animal impulses, of the violence of predator and prey rather than the shared dignity of the fellow solider. After delivering the killing stroke to Hector, Achilles even taunts his victim with the threat of cannibalism: "Would to god my rage, my fury would drive me now to hack your flesh away and eat you raw."[33] He proceeds to hook the body to his chariot, dragging Hector's corpse around and around in the dust, mutilating it over and over, leading the gods to call him "that man without a shred of decency in his heart."[34]

In the *Mahābhārata*, motivated by the desire for revenge against the Kauravas, the Pāṇḍava brothers are similarly driven to disregard rules of decency and commit acts of shameless brutality. As Alf Hiltebeitel notes, "the *Mahābhārata* war is the scene of numerous acts the text does not hesitate to call sins. Nearly all are committed on the Pāṇḍava side."[35] When his son Abhimanyu is killed, Arjuna finds the man responsible and decapitates him with an arrow, sending the head into that man's father's lap, to make him grieve for his son as well.[36] Bhīma, another Pāṇḍava brother, fulfills earlier vows to avenge the humiliation of their wife Draupadī at the hands of the Kauravas, particularly Duḥśāsana and Duryodhana. The former he dismembers and beats to death with his own arm and the latter he crushes with a club blow to the groin.[37] In order to defeat the venerable Kauravas Bhīṣma and Droṇa, once teachers of the Pāṇḍavas, the brothers resort to the underhanded tactics of lying and using human shields.[38] Finally, Arjuna entirely disobeys the Indian warrior code of conduct by showering a mortal enemy, Karṇa (who we will discuss in more detail later in the chapter), with arrows when he is defenseless, having dropped his weapons to remove a chariot wheel mired in the battlefield mud.[39] As Ruth Katz has observed regarding all these events, "All [the Pāṇḍava's] ultimately effective actions in the war are opposed to the Indian rules of warrior chivalry."[40] Blinded by their rage and desire for revenge, the Pāṇḍavas quickly forget the veneration they once held for their kin among the Kauravas, succumbing with startling, even horrifying, effect to the power of violence.

We observe this kind of behavior also in the *Táin*, where Cúchulainn, upon hearing of Connacht forces killing a troop of Ulster soldiers, undergoes a so-called "warp spasm." As described, this phenomenon appears to be a berserker rage or, in the parlance of the MCU, a "Hulk-out" of sorts. The "spasm," we are told,

> made him into a monstrous thing, hideous and shapeless, unheard of. His shanks and joints, every knuckle and ankle and organ from head to foot shook like a tree…. He squeezed one eye narrower than the eye of a needle; he opened the other wider than the mouth of a goblet. He bared his jaws to the ear; he peeled back his lips to the eye teeth till his gullet showed … on his head the temple skin stretched to the nape of his neck … malignant mists and spirits flickered red in the vaporous cloud that rose boiling above his head.[41]

Even though Ferdia is his adopted brother, in the course of their duel, as tempers rise higher and higher, something of the same spasm comes over Cúchulainn and, after being stabbed in the chest, he uses a special spear to impale his friend/enemy. Feeling wronged, Ferdia cries, "You have killed me unfairly. By way of deceit, no good can come."[42] Overwhelmed first by rage and then by loss, Cúchulainn picks up his slain brother's body, clasps him in his arms, and grieves for the pointless war that brought them both to this end.

Across all these myths, then, once the cycle of violence and revenge is engaged, the earlier moments of humanity and interconnection are wiped away, with only carnage left in their wake. Just as it is destined that Achilles and Hector are to collide, the Pāṇḍavas and Kauravas are to strive in war, and Cúchulainn and Ferdia are to clash, so Iron Man and Captain America, Tony Stark and Steve Rogers, are magnetically drawn to battle in *Captain America: Civil War*, subject to the same irresistible forces of vengeance and anger. During a respite after the confrontation at the Leipzig airport, Stark learns of Rogers' discovery about Zemo and begins to reconsider his position. Joining Barnes and Rogers in Siberia, they discover instead that all the other Winter Soldiers are dead. Zemo, who has been waiting for them, unveils his real plan: to incite civil war among the Avengers. It is revealed that Zemo himself is also acting out of revenge for the deaths of his father, wife, and son during the Avengers' battle with Ultron in Sokovia. "You lost someone," Rogers says, trying to empathize, perhaps somewhat like Hector with Achilles, and Zemo responds with Achilles' negativity: "I lost everyone. And so will you."[43] At that, he plays the video of Barnes stealing the super-soldier serum in 1991—from Stark's mother and father, whom he has savagely murdered.

Though Stark realizes that Barnes was under the mental influence of Hydra, he pays no mind to that fact, transforming into the very image of vengeful rage, like Achilles, Arjuna, and Cúchulainn before him. Shaking with anger, he interrogates Rogers:

> STARK: Did you know?
> ROGERS: I didn't know it was him.
> STARK: Don't bullshit me, Rogers. Did you know?!
> ROGERS: Yes.

At that response, Stark viciously attacks both men. Rogers defends Barnes and the fighting grows increasingly ferocious and uncontrolled as Stark uses rockets and repulsor rays to attempt to kill the man who murdered his parents. "This isn't going to change what happened," Rogers says, trying to reason with Stark, who will not be dissuaded, replying, "I don't care. He killed my mom."[44] Later, Rogers tries again, telling him, "I'm sorry, Tony. You know I wouldn't do this if I had any other choice, but he's my friend," to which Stark responds, "So was I," with the past tense emphasized.[45] These brief exchanges place this MCU film in close company with the *Iliad*, the *Mahābhārata*, and the *Táin*: Achilles kills Hector for the sake of revenge for his friend Patroclus, Arjuna and the other Pāṇḍavas commit atrocities to avenge their fallen family members, and Cúchulainn and Ferdia, brothers and friends, are forced to fight to the death. If, according to the oft-quoted aphorism, "all politics is local," then these myths work together to show that "all war is personal." By embracing this ancient mythic theme, *Captain America: Civil War* emotionally depicts the dissolution of a superhero fraternity.

As the fight continues, Barnes attempts to escape via the shaft of the base's missile silo, but Stark pulls him back and all three fall into the concrete basement of the facility, a move that symbolizes how they have descended from the higher realm of heroism into the lower world of violence. In this pit, Stark severs Barnes' metal arm with a repulsor blast from his chest, then beats Rogers until his former friend falls to his knees, dripping blood. As a sign of how far their relationship has degenerated, Rogers responds to Stark's calls to give up by remarking, "I could do this all day," a quip he notably used previously as a retort to a back-alley bully and the Red Skull himself.[46] When Stark's attention is briefly turned, Rogers grabs his one-time friend, hurls him to the ground, then uses his shield to smash his helmet and arc-reactor, ending the battle.

In a rupture of their previous alliance, Captain America (Chris Evans, left) and Iron Man (Robert Downey, Jr.) battle, pitting superhero against superhero in ways reminiscent of epic battles between the likes of Arjuna and Karna or Achilles and Hector. From *Captain America: Civil War* (2016).

Meanwhile, above ground, T'Challa, who has also found his way to Siberia, confronts Zemo and learns the truth that Barnes was not responsible for his father, T'Chaka's death. "This is all you wanted?" he demands of Zemo. "To seem them tear each other apart? Vengeance has consumed you."[47] From the foregoing, we can see that it has consumed Stark, Rogers, and Barnes, as well. Simone Weil's words on the *Iliad* are appropriate here: "Such is the character of force. Its power to transform human beings into things is twofold and operates on two fronts; in equal but different ways, it petrifies the souls of those who undergo it and those who ply it."[48] Once the horrors of violence and revenge are released, they inevitably draw in Stark, Rogers, Barnes, and all those around them.

Adding to the tragedy is the sense of pointlessness to the entire conflict, for they have all been manipulated into fighting one another. Through the fog of revenge, confusion reigns in the entire film, whether it is Stark initially viewing Rogers as the cause of strife due to the Accords, T'Challa wrongly blaming Barnes for T'Chaka's death, Vision accidentally hitting and crippling Rhodes, Rogers believing in the plot of a group of secret assassins, or Stark attempting to kill Barnes, a man who was under mind-control. In the end, everyone's motivations prove false or suspect and their actions ultimately come to naught.

Similarly, in the *Iliad*, Achilles has no illusions about what the final outcome of the Trojan War will be for him or most of the other fighters, regardless of their allegiance. In a chilling speech, he undermines and even derides the entire Greek heroic code: "What lasting thanks in the long run for warring with our enemies, on and on, no end? One and the same lot for the man who hangs back and the man who battles hard. The same honor waits for the coward and the brave. They both go down to death."[49] Those who know the events of the story of the Trojan War beyond what is recounted in the *Iliad* realize the frightful accuracy of Achilles' pronouncement: shortly after Hector's funeral, he too is killed.

For the *Mahābhārata*, the results are similar, as only the five Pāṇḍava brothers are left alive, with their own allies and the entire Kaurava contingent slaughtered. There is, then, at the end of the war, no real kingdom left to rule and a whole segment of Indian society, the warrior class, has been washed away in a tide of blood. The *Táin* as well comes to a disastrous end as the sought-after Ulster bull and a Connacht bull kill each other. After more carnage, both armies withdraw, with neither side gaining what it wanted. Medb, one of the leaders of the Connacht side, appropriately comments, "We have had shame and shambles here today."[50]

So it is also with the superheroes in the MCU. At the conclusion of *Captain America: Civil War*, Stark, Rogers, and Barnes are all alive, but broken and covered in blood. The defining symbol of each—the arc reactor, the shield, and a metal arm—are either shattered or abandoned, reflecting the amount of damage they have done to one another and the frayed state of their relationships. Again, as Weil writes about the effect of such paroxysms of violence, "conquerors and conquered are brothers in the same misery, each a heartache to the other."[51] The real winner, in the *Iliad*, the *Mahābhārata*, the *Táin*, or *Captain America: Civil War*, is not any of the heroes or superheroes involved, but, as Girard would predict, violence itself. "Inevitably," he argues, "the moment comes when violence can only be countered by more violence. Whether we fail or succeed in our effort to subdue it, the real victor is always violence."[52]

Evoking these tropes, *Captain America: Civil War* thus shows the state of the superheroes' world and situation as the mythos enters its Phase Three: increasing inner tensions that have unraveled into a spiral of intra-communal violence where superhero fights superhero. Owing to the superheroes' inherent liminality, in the trajectory of the larger narrative, there is a certain logical or natural progression, as the seeds for this outcome had been planted in earlier portions of the mythos. For example, in Phase One, when Steve Rogers became Captain America, Bucky Barnes was drawn into battle at his side, only to be captured and turned into the Winter Soldier in Phase Two, who then faces Stark's wrath in Phase Three. Parallel trajectories could be mapped for most of the other MCU characters demonstrating what led them to this point in the story, where close relationships have begun to unravel, but as we saw in Chapter One, it all leads back to the same primary cause: their abilities are founded on a betwixt and between status, which confers power but also volatility. Put in the language of religion and mythology, they have been touched by the sacred, and contact with the sacred confers danger, on the individual as well as others surrounding them.

Yet, despite the pain of the rift that occurs in *Captain America: Civil War*, signs of hope do appear. In the film, Stark and Rogers both reveal a growing awareness of the instability of their superhero status—Stark responds with the call for oversight and Rogers seriously reconsiders his "Captain America" persona, as evidenced when he relinquishes the emblematic shield at the movie's conclusion. Most touchingly, the film ends with a letter Rogers has penned to Stark, which reads in part,

> We all need family. The Avengers are yours, maybe more so than mine.... I know I hurt you, Tony. I guess I thought by not telling you about your parents I was sparing you, but I can see now that I was really sparing myself, and I'm sorry. Hopefully one day you can understand. I wish we agreed on the Accords, I really do. I know you're doing what you believe in, and that's all any of us can do. That's all any of us should. So no matter what, I promise you, if you need us ... if you need me ... I'll be there.[53]

While the old order has come apart, within the sentiments Rogers communicates to Stark is the hope for a new order to take its place, for the previous relationships to be reformed on a different foundation. Loss is thus juxtaposed with the potential and the hope for a new beginning. In this same way, loss and renewal, trauma and revival coincide in other films of Phase Three, especially *Black Panther*, *Thor: Ragnarok*, *Guardians of the Galaxy Vol. 2*, and *Captain Marvel*. Like *Captain America: Civil War*, the process of pain and rejuvenation comes about through a struggle with an individual disturbingly close in relation to the superhero.

Starting with *Black Panther*, it is first most helpful to revisit the character of N'Jadaka, especially his similarity to the Indian epic figure of Karṇa, whom we briefly encountered above. In Chapter Two we saw that N'Jadaka, the "Killmonger," serves as T'Challa's shadow-self, a rival "Black Panther" of dark impulses. He is also T'Challa's cousin, making the conflict a familial one. When we consider that the cousins were also separated by circumstances beyond their control, the T'Challa/N'Jadaka rivalry comes to resemble the *Mahābhārata*'s feud between the characters Arjuna/Karṇa. If we recall, in the early 1990s King T'Chaka killed N'Jadaka's father and left the boy behind in the United States, cut off from his Wakandan birthright. He grew up bitter and resentful, angry over the racial discrimination and oppression he faced and the apathy of the people in Wakanda who have allowed it to happen. In Karṇa's case, his life, as Alf Hiltebeitel labels it, has also always been "disjointed."[54] His mother, Kuntī, became pregnant with him through the use of a mantra that allowed her to have children with the gods. In Karṇa's case, it is the god of the sun, Sūrya, who is his father. Unwed at the time and fearful of the shame of bearing a child without a husband, Kuntī abandons Karṇa soon after his birth and he is adopted by low-caste parents. This status follows Karṇa and, despite his obvious martial skill, owing to his adoptive background, he is denied the honor and recognition he believes is his due. When he meets the other Pāṇḍavas, who are in actuality his half-brothers through Kuntī, there is immediate antipathy with Arjuna, who is his equal in fighting stature but has had the advantage of legitimate caste birth and receives the associated accolades and acclaim. The Kauravas take advantage of this situation, recruiting Karṇa to their cause.

On the eve of the war, however, Kuntī and the god Krishna intervene in an attempt to bring Karṇa over to the Pāṇḍava side. Krishna tells Karṇa of his true parentage and that the Pāṇḍavas are fated to win. This means that, if he joins them, as the eldest brother he would be king. As tempting as this would be to most, in light of the way he was treated by his birth mother, Karṇa does not even consider the proposal, responding angrily, "Kuntī cast me out as though I had been stillborn.... Adhiratha [his adoptive father] thinks of me as his son and my love demands that I think of him as my father ... neither joy nor fear nor all of the earth nor piles of gold can make me a traitor to my word."[55] It is then Kuntī's turn to try to persuade him, appealing to his sense of eternal duty, that it is wrong to fight his brothers and that if he joined with them, especially Arjuna, they would be unbeatable. Again, Karṇa refuses: "The irreparable wrong you have done me by casting me out has destroyed the name and fame I could have had," he argues. Further, in his eyes, to turn away from the Kauravas on the brink of war would be cowardice and a betrayal of those who have taken him into their confidence and treated him with honor and respect.[56]

Parallels to the story of N'Jadaka stand out immediately. Both rightly consider themselves prisoner to circumstances outside their control, abandoned as children and subject subsequently to racial or caste discrimination, respectively. Just as N'Jadaka's fury against racial oppression has its noble qualities, Karṇa's refusal to abandon comrades who aided him in a time of need is also admirable. The two figures also share an innate hatred for an individual—T'Challa and Arjuna, respectively—born into the rank and privilege they covet, making it a lifelong mission to balance the scales by killing that person.

For both characters, there is also a darker emotion lingering under the surface of what at first appear to be understandable motivations. In N'Jadaka's case, we saw in Chapter Two that he holds and harbors pain from his childhood trauma of losing his father and uses racial oppression as a cover for waging genocidal wars that will make the rest of the world share his hurt. With Karṇa, it is a prideful, all-consuming concern for prestige and fame that leads him to disregard moral choices at critical points. During the battle, when his chariot wheel is caught in the mud, he calls out

T'Challa (Chadwick Boseman, left) battles long-lost cousin N'Jadaka (Michael B. Jordan) for the right to rule Wakanda. From *Black Panther* (2018).

to Arjuna that the rules of honorable combat demand a ceasefire in such a situation. Krishna, though, as Arjuna's charioteer, reacts with scorn, listing all of Karṇa's transgressions against honorable conduct, including contributing to the Kaurava's theft of the kingdom, looking on while the Kauravas cheated during a pivotal dice game, and reviling and humiliating the Pāṇḍavas' wife, Draupadī. "Where did your dharma [eternal duty and right conduct] go then?" Krishna pointedly accuses, before adding, "Those who are debased blame fate, not their own misdeeds."[57] At that point, Arjuna delivers the killing shot. Like Karṇa, N'Jadaka used his circumstances as justification for a long list of sins, and became blind to the fact that his own actions, after a certain point, also contributed to the state of his life.

As we have seen, those sins, which include countless murders, multiply when N'Jadaka infiltrates Wakanda and proceeds to exact a terrible toll on that land. Besides almost fatally beating T'Challa, this long-lost son of Wakanda kills the high priest Zuri, threatens the other members of the royal family, burns the entire stock of sacred heart-shaped herb, and sets the country on the path to war with the rest of the world. Besides nearly killing T'Challa, all of these actions throw his world into chaos, from cutting off his connection to the elders (Zuri's death) to truncating the line of future Black Panthers (destroying the heart-shaped herb).

Based on this, one would expect that once T'Challa overcomes

N'Jadaka he would act mercilessly and disdainfully toward an enemy that has cost him so much. On the contrary, after T'Challa has wounded and subdued N'Jadaka, he takes the fallen "Killmonger" to a cavern opening to see a Wakandan sunset, a natural spectacle which he had been curious about since childhood, but, due to being left behind in the United States, had never seen. As an interesting parallel touch, when Karṇa dies, the *Mahābhārata* says that the universe takes note and honors this person who had some nobility and, perhaps if given the chance, could have been even greater: the earth shakes, the sky rumbles, winds blow, and streams stop flowing.[58]

In this way, T'Challa distinguishes himself morally from Arjuna, who does not seem able or willing to separate the good from the bad in Karṇa's character and merely sees him as someone who must be destroyed. Rather than simply let N'Jadaka die, T'Challa offers to heal him and let him live in Wakanda, which in some ways resembles the offer from Krishna and Kuntī that Karṇa join his brothers and be a part of their kingdom. Both make prideful refusals that are not without a sense of dignity, but nevertheless still show that neither one can transcend their own feelings of hurt and grievance.

For T'Challa, however, the entire confrontation with N'Jadaka has been a lesson in doing just that, though the process began earlier during the events of *Captain America: Civil War*. Towards the end of the film, during his encounter with Zemo, T'Challa sees the corrosive effects of vengeance all around him and swears, "I am done letting [vengeance] consume me."[59] Building on that sentiment, T'Challa reacts to the challenges N'Jadaka represents, not to mention the sufferings he engenders, by repudiating the secrecy of his father, revising Wakanda's entire foreign policy, and showing his cousin mercy and kindness, though he certainly would have received neither if the situation had been reversed.

In *Thor: Ragnarok*, Thor finds himself in a comparable situation, although in this case, he faces a mysterious, long-lost sister. Troubled by dreams of the fire-demon Surtur destroying Asgard, Thor defeats the monster in his own realm and takes his enchanted crown back to Asgard. There he discovers Loki is still alive and masquerading as Odin. When the two brothers find Odin on Earth, he is near death, but before he dies he tells the brothers of their previously unknown sister, Hela. "Her violent impulses grew beyond my control," Odin explains, "I couldn't stop her, so I imprisoned her. She draws her strength from Asgard and once she gets there her power will be limitless."[60] As Odin perishes, Hela appears and orders Thor and Loki to kneel. When Thor resists, she smashes his hammer, Mjolnir, into pieces with one hand. Chasing them through the Bifrost bridge back to Asgard, she hurls them off on another trajectory, where they land on the planet Sakaar. Meanwhile, Hela takes control of Asgard and amasses an army of undead warriors.

On Sakaar, Thor and Loki acquire new allies, such as the Asgardian exile Valkyrie and the Hulk, who has been on the planet since the events of *Avengers: Age of Ultron*. After some travails, they return to Asgard, but Hela is far too strong. Brimming with anger that Odin cast her aside when he wearied of war and produced another heir (Thor), she ruthlessly overpowers Thor and cuts out one of his eyes, mocking his now closer resemblance to Odin, who also lost an eye in battle. As she holds him down and repeatedly stabs him, Thor has a vision in which he speaks to his deceased father.

> THOR: She's too strong. Without my hammer, I can't—
> ODIN: Are you Thor, "god of hammers?" That hammer was to help you control your power, focus it. It was never your source of strength.
> THOR: It's too late. She has taken over Asgard.
> ODIN: Asgard is not a place, it's a people…. Asgard is where our people stand, and right now our people need you.
> THOR: I'm not as strong as you.
> ODIN: No, you're stronger.[61]

In light of this vision, there is a connection we can make between Thor's experiences and the Norse mythology of Scandinavia. In those stories, Odin loses his eye not in battle, but as a sacrifice in exchange for greater wisdom, sometimes as part of a narrative that includes him hanging on the World Tree, Yggdrasill. Importantly, those myths do not involve Thor becoming similarly scarred, so the MCU's decision to have the son mirror the father in such a manner stands out all the more as this myth's attempt to align the two symbolically and have Odin, in some ways, become the vehicle for Thor's larger insights into his personality and abilities. Indeed, after Thor's partial blinding and then vision of his father, he conjures a massive burst of electricity, without any need for his hammer.[62]

The lightning strike, however, as powerful as it is, does not destroy Hela. Realizing that the only way to defeat her is to cause the very thing he had seen in his nightmares, Thor and his allies evacuate the people of Asgard onto a Sakaarian spaceship while Loki puts Surtur's crown into the Asgardian Eternal Flame. Growing to mammoth proportions, Surtur springs back to life and destroys Asgard in a torrent of flames, wiping out Hela and himself in the process. Thor, Loki, and the other refugees watch the realm explode as they drift away into space.

Like T'Challa, Thor must develop strength he did not know he previously possessed, as well as consider his homeland in new ways. Both suffer the loss of a father and then discover unsavory truths about that father while contending with a powerful, vindictive, and previously unknown family member. The consequences for Thor are arguably more severe, as in addition to the death of his father, he loses his hammer, Mjolnir—a pillar of his previous identity—and his homeland of Asgard is obliterated, reducing his people to refugees. Yet, even in the midst of this upheaval, Thor looks ahead to the potential of a new identity, accepting the throne for his people and even reconciling with his brother Loki.

Aside from the lateral generational conflict of cousins and siblings, Phase Three of the MCU myth also delves into the ancient religious narrative of father versus son and older versus younger, themes which have a rich history in stories from around the world. One famous example is found in Egypt, where the god Set (also spelled "Seth") kills his brother Osiris to claim the throne, but Osiris' son, Horus later challenges him. After a brutal series of battles in which Horus loses an eye and Set is partially dismembered, nephew overthrows uncle to become king. While there are other crucial themes in this narrative that we will delve into in later chapters, one aspect of the story relevant here is that the older generation is shown as acquisitive and greedily clutching for power, while the younger is shown as a potential threat, combined with themes of just versus unjust kingship.[63] In China, there is the story of Huang Di, the Yellow Emperor, who also faces a challenge by his nephew, but in this case, the moral weight is reversed. In the past, when the realms of the earth were first apportioned, the Fire Emperor of the South (Huang Di's half-brother) rebelled and after a calamitous battle, Huang Di prevailed.[64] Years later, the Fire Emperor's son Chi You assembled a horrid army of goblins and marched against his uncle. After a back-and-forth war, Huang Di defeated the army and restored stability to the land, though he was forced to execute his nephew.[65]

In the Persian epic *Shahnama* ("Book of Kings"), the older generation also perceives the younger as a threat and ultimately triumphs, but in this instance a tragic case of mistaken identity lies at the heart of the conflict. This epic relates the mythic history of Persia and centers largely around the deeds of Rustam (also spelled "Rostam"), an almost superhumanly powerful warrior. During his adventures, Rustam marries a young woman in a remote part of the country and conceives a son before leaving to pursue further journeys. The boy, named Suhrab (also spelled "Sohrab") grows up to tales of his father's exploits and receives a signet from his mother as proof of his paternity. Political intrigue conspires to place father and son at the heads of opposing armies and they inevitably face off in single combat. After a hard-fought struggle, Rustam throws Suhrab down and delivers a fatal sword wound. Suhrab cries out that his father, Rustam, will avenge him, and when the father sees the signet, he realizes the awful truth of what he has done.[66]

Elsewhere, it is the younger generation that wins the upper hand. In a Yoruba myth, during an ancient war between the gods, the God of Iron turns on his father, the King of Men, in order to bring about peace. As the war had embroiled all of the earth, the God of Iron justified the overthrow as the only way to save humanity. Disappointed in his son, the King of Men chose spitefully to sink forever into the soil, taking with him a bag full of wisdom and tools meant for humanity, but which would now languish deep beneath the ground.[67]

Another obvious example of ongoing intergenerational strife comes from Greek mythology. As told in Hesiod's *Theogony*, the universe started in chaos, but Ouranos (sky) and Gaia (earth) brought forth children, the youngest of whom was Kronos. Mother and son conspired to kill Ouranos, who had painfully trapped other children inside Gaia, and armed with a sickle, Kronos castrates and overthrows his father. Mindful that he too could be banished by a son, Kronos swallows all the children his wife Rhea bears, but she hides away Zeus, who in time repeats the pattern by casting his father down, making him regurgitate Hades, Poseidon, and most of the other Olympians in the process. With this past history, Zeus remains constantly wary of any future progeny of his own.[68]

The worldwide prevalence of such myths of intergenerational conflict points to the expression of a deep-seated human truth or need.[69] In a certain sense, we can see the stories as positing, as some scholars have argued, that "conflict permeates every level of the cosmos, even family life."[70] From this point of view, there is also a strong political element, as the Egyptian Pharaohs, Greek city states, and warring Chinese dynasties undoubtedly experienced high levels of court intrigue, where fathers, sons, uncles, and nephews would quickly turn on one another when questions of succession arose. Interpreted this way, these myths merely speak to brute political realities in these ancient lands.

As true as that may be, it is also the case that, from a base biological level, the younger generation inevitably replaces the older or at least struggles to do so. As Jan Bremmer has argued regarding the Oedipus myth, "it is a social principle of universal validity: for society to go on, sons must (destroy) replace their fathers."[71] Bremmer's comment can be seen as an expression of the biological reality or, from a more philosophical angle, as the quest of youths to define themselves and forge an identity, either in harmony or contrast to their forbears. At times, as the preceding myths express, the cost of this transformation of self-discovery is blood. For instance, at every turn in the *Theogony*, the new gods can only come into being after the defeat of the old order. As a more psychologically-themed example, Suhrab can know himself (as can Rustam, for that matter) only after father and son clash in battle, which reveals their true relationship. Likewise, in the Yoruba story, though the King of Men's bag of wisdom would have accelerated the development of human culture, by casting his father out and sparing the ongoing violence, the God of Iron actually gives humanity a greater boon: the power of self-determination to discover wisdom and culture on their own, without depending on an outside entity to define it for them.

Many of these ideas are present already in *Black Panther* and *Thor: Ragnarok*. N'Jadaka and Hela are both the products of cycles of violence propagated by the heads of respective families. Thus, when T'Challa and Thor battle these villains, it is in some ways a proxy fight with their own fathers, T'Chaka and Odin. Indeed, Thor especially has had a tempestuous relationship with his father, beginning with his banishment in Phase One and continuing into Phase Two with his insurrection against Odin's plans for fighting the Dark Elves. In Phase Three, through suffering the removal of his eye—which Hela even remarks makes him look more like his father—Thor equals Odin, then surpasses him by destroying Hela, something which his father was unable to accomplish. For T'Challa, his relationship with his father is more reverent, at least until he discovers the secrets T'Chaka has kept and the sacrifices he has made to preserve Wakanda's isolationism. With these actions exposed and their obvious linkage to the circumstances that created N'Jadaka, T'Challa, as explored in previous chapters, must grow past his fawning, naïve view of his father to create his own vision of Wakanda and the role of its king. To be sure, the torturous clashes that ensue in the Phase Three films are about overcoming the challenges that N'Jadaka and Hela represent, but an important aspect of each of those challenges is the legacy of T'Chaka and Odin. Only through taking the painful step of transcending their own fathers, as well as defeating N'Jadaka and Hela, do the two superheroes achieve victory and new insights into their own identities.

Picking up on these same ancient mythic themes, *Guardians of the Galaxy: Volume 2* and *Spider-Man: Homecoming* are also predicated on conflict with the father figure as a prerequisite for growth and self-determination. Beginning with the former, clues about Peter Quill's mysterious father occur throughout the original *Guardians of the Galaxy*, from bio-scans showing he is a never-before-seen hybrid of human and alien to, most personally, his mother's remark to him, just before her death, "You're so like your Daddy. You even look like him. And he was an angel composed out of pure light."[72] This suggests that Quill's father is a majestic being, but Yondu, a member of the "Ravager" clan (a loose group of space pirates) who took Quill from Earth as a boy, refers to this mysterious father as a "jackass."[73]

When the viewer meets Quill's father in *Guardians of the Galaxy: Volume 2*, the former seems more appropriate at first. He appears riding on the back of a spaceship and, to save the Guardians, wipes out an entire armada of fighter sentries. Eventually, the audience discovers that he is a powerful being called "Ego" who belongs to a class of beings known as "Celestials" who have existed almost since the beginning of the universe and possess nearly god-like abilities. To underscore Ego's quasi-divine status, the song "My Sweet Lord" by George Harrison plays as Quill, Gamora, and Drax travel to Ego's planet. As events unfold, Ego turns out to be the planet itself, which is able to generate humanoid-sized and -shaped forms through the immense amounts of energy it generates from a brain-like core. Though Ego feigns affection for Quill's mother and Quill himself, even making overtures at becoming a true father, the celestial being has sinister ulterior motives. Since the early days of the universe, Ego traveled from one end of existence to the other, planting spores of himself that, with enough power, will grow and absorb all life into himself. Calling this plan his "Expansion," Ego required another Celestial to generate the necessary energy. For this reason, he set about fathering children throughout the universe to pro-duce one capable of aiding in this Expansion. Only Quill had the sufficient power and, disappointed with his other progeny, Ego killed them, leaving their skeletons in a mass grave within the planet. On the same note, Ego confesses that in order to avoid mortal entanglements, he created the can-cer that killed Quill's mother.

Enraged at this revelation, Quill blasts Ego's humanoid body to pieces, but the planet easily rebuilds it and takes him prisoner, callously crushing his Walkman tape player. An outdated or, even in the time when it was cur-rent technology, minor possession to most people, the Walkman has potent significance to Quill, as it represents his link to his human nature and, more emotionally, his mother. Ego's move to destroy it denotes an obvious bid to extirpate his son's humanity and render him inured to emotion. When the other Guardians arrive, they free Quill and join him in an attempt to destroy the brain at the center of the world, which is the only way Ego can die. The planet summons other forms, including enormous faces of elec-trical energy and tentacles of soil, rock, and lightning. He starts to swallow the other Guardians and turn Quill into a battery for the energy he needs, but Quill draws on his happy memories with his teammates—his surro-gate family—to give him strength and clarity to break free from his biologi-cal family. When a bomb disintegrates the giant brain, Ego dissolves, taking with him Quill's opportunity to have similar powers and be with his biolog-ical father.[74]

Yet, through the pain of discovering that his real father was a monster and then enduring the horror of fighting and killing him, Quill realizes his true family (defined as those who care for him and willingly sacrifice on his behalf) is actually the rest of the Guardians. On several occasions the film makes this explicit, such as when Quill expresses excitement at finally find-ing his family (in the form of his father), and Gamora retorts, "I thought you already had.""[75] At another point, when Gamora's sister Nebula notes that the Guardians fight too much to be friends, Drax replies, "We're not friends. We're family."[76] Yondu, who cared for Quill during his formative years away from Earth, makes perhaps the most poignant observation. As he sacrifices himself to fly Quill away from Ego's imploding mass, Yondu remarks, "He may have been your father, boy, but he wasn't your daddy."[77]

Yondu's remark further establishes the film's definition of "family" as separate from biological paternity, and reinforces what Quill has both lost and gained. Altogether, the encounter has cost him a great deal: the illusion that his mysterious father was the being of light his mother thought he was, the adoptive father who actually cared for him, and the Walkman that was his last connection to his mother. However, as the Greek, Persian, Egyptian, and Yoruba myths anticipate, it is through his confrontation with the father figure that Quill achieves a renewed sense of self and reaffirms his true place in the universe as alongside the Guardians of the Galaxy, his real family.

The references to the superhero teams, whether the Guardians of the Galaxy or the Avengers, as "family" will continue throughout the final chapters in the MCU narrative, namely the films *Avengers: Infinity War* and *Avengers: Endgame*. For now, though, in *Spider-Man: Homecoming*, like Quill, Peter Parker also finds himself caught between two father figures. On the one hand, in the wake of aiding Iron Man's team during the events of *Captain America: Civil War*, Stark has taken an interest in mentoring Parker. Living with his aunt and having lost his uncle, Parker admires Stark, who reciprocates this adoration with a fatherly, protective attitude. He allows Parker to keep the automated suit provided for the battle with Captain America, but does not mention that it is guarded by protocols termed "Training Wheels" and "Baby Monitor," intended to lock out the more advanced features. Stark tracks Parker's every move, allowing him to intervene when Adrian Toomes (as the "Vulture") incapacitates the teenager and drops him in a lake to drown. When Parker resists Stark's resulting admonishments to limit his superhero activities, he earns the stereotypical parental reply, "Because I said so," prior to the equally formulaic "It's never too early to start thinking about college."[78]

Of course, Parker does not listen and his next attempt to apprehend the Vulture is even more disastrous, as a ferry boat nearly sinks, endangering numerous innocent bystanders. Once again, Stark rescues Parker and their subsequent exchange is worth quoting at length for how it reveals the obvious father-son overtones to their relationship:

> STARK: Do you know I was the only one who believed in you? Everyone else said I
>   was crazy to recruit a fourteen-year-old kid.
> PARKER: I'm fifteen.

STARK: No, this is where you zip it, all right? The adult is talking. What if somebody died tonight? Different story, right, because that's on you. And if you died, I feel like that's on me. I don't need that on my conscience.

PARKER: Yes, sir. I'm sorry. I understand.

STARK: Sorry doesn't cut it.

PARKER: I just wanted to be like you.

STARK: And I wanted you to be better. It's not working out. I'm going to need the suit back.

PARKER: For how long?

STARK: Forever.

PARKER: No, no, please, this is all I have, I'm nothing without the suit.

STARK: If you're nothing without the suit then you shouldn't have it. God, I sound like my dad.[79]

To the uninformed observer or audience member witnessing this dialogue, the assumption would be that the two are father and son. Thus punished, Parker then comes into closer contact with a rival father-figure in the person of Adrian Toomes, who is both the Vulture and his girlfriend Liz's father. Further stereotypical father (-in-law) moments occur as Parker arrives to escort Liz to the Homecoming dance. Toomes jokes, "You want something to drink, a bourbon or scotch or something like that?" When Parker declines, Toomes laughs and says, "That's the right answer."[80] During the car ride to the dance, though, Toomes deduces that Parker is Spider-Man and, under the guise of a "dad talk," threatens him (as recounted in Chapter Two) before concluding with more hackneyed fatherly phrases: "Now, you go in there and show my daughter a good time—just not too good."[81]

Mythically, Stark and Toomes represent two different poles of the father archetype, at different points vacillating between these roles at various points in the film. Although primarily a mentor, Stark also functions as (to use Joseph Campbell's phrase) the negative, boundary-enforcing "ogre father" by disciplining Parker and enforcing prohibitions upon him, i.e., confiscating his suit and forbidding him to use his powers.[82] Toomes occupies the diametrically-opposed role, primarily serving as the threatening "ogre father," but at odd times offering mentoring advice, however cynical, about how Parker ought to live his life. Within the pantheon of world myths and religions, both act in manners comparative to Rustam, Huang Di, Kronos, or Set, who perceived the younger individual, whether son or nephew, as a threat and sought to destroy them. In the case of Stark, the attempt at destruction is symbolic, while with Toomes, it is literal.

Correspondingly, Parker reacts in the manner of Suhrab, Zeus, or Horus by rebelling forcefully against the domineering restrictions of the older father-figures. Using his first suit (made up of swim goggles, sweat pants, and a hooded shirt), employing his cell phone as a crude tracking device, and drawing on his friend Ned as an assistant, Parker engages Toomes once again and triumphs over him through sheer physical power. By defying the orders to abandon his Spider-Man identity and utilizing his low-tech equipment and his raw abilities alone, Parker also symbolically prevails over Stark. Indeed, he starts the movie in slavish devotion to the superhero billionaire, but by the end he confidently rejects Stark's offer to join the Avengers, which would have included an even more advanced suit. Having successfully rejected and conquered both poles of the father figure archetype, Parker independently establishes his own self-worth, showing that, as demonstrated previously by the ancient mythic traditions, the superhero can only truly know him or herself by overcoming the older generation.

In *Captain Marvel*, Carol Danvers also overcomes oppressive circumstances, which could also be categorized as familial, though in a looser, more adoptive sense. As partly recounted in Chapter Two, after crashing in an experimental fighter jet, Danvers gains powers from the mysterious Tesseract, but is also left with amnesia. The alien Kree, who pursued her and killed her mentor, Wendy Lawson, take an interest in her as a result. In order to co-opt her powers, the Kree abduct her, implant a chip in her neck to dampen the energy coursing through her body, and refashion her memories so that she believes she is a Kree named "Vers." Her mentor, Yon-Rogg, and the Kree "Supreme Intelligence," a disembodied entity that oversees the alien society, convince her that the Skrulls, another alien race, are responsible for her state. This conditioning is gradually undone, however, as Danvers finds her way to her true birthplace on Earth and encounters her previous "family," in the form of her best friend Maria Rambeau and Rambeau's daughter, Monica. As Danvers cries in anger and frustration about her confused identity, Maria embraces her, tells her, "Your name is Carol Danvers," and proceeds to explain how close they once were and how much she had admired her.

In the model of Quill's journey in *Guardians of the Galaxy: Volume 2*, Danvers is delivered from the clutches of an abusive family (adoptive, in this case) and restored to those who truly care for her, and thus fit a broader definition of "family." When she confronts the Kree again, she and the Supreme Intelligence debate these very points. "We found you," the Kree apparition tells her, "We embraced you as our own," to which Danvers replies, "You stole me! From my home, my family, my friends."[83] Still extolling their domination over Danvers, the Supreme Intelligence continues, "Without us, you're only human ... on Hala [the Kree home-world], you were reborn: Vers." Her identity rediscovered, Danvers indignantly responds by asserting her renewed sense of self, simply stating, "My name is Carol."[84]

Clearly there are parallels between Danvers' proclamation of renewed identity in the face of a constricting family and the Greek, Yoruba, and other myths described previously. However, the contention over who truly controls Danvers' powers, the Kree authorities or Danvers herself, brings to mind issues present in Hindu mythology, particularly its robust tradition of goddess narratives. In those stories, the goddess is said to represent a cosmic energy called *śaktī*, without which the gods are powerless. *Śaktī*, as the feminine principle and energy of the universe, animates and gives the male gods the strength to create and sustain existence.[85] One version of the origin of the goddess is found in the *Purāṇa* narrative tradition, which tells of a time when the male gods Viṣṇu, Śiva, Brahmā, and others pooled their energy to create a feminine deity who would defeat a demon that had vanquished them all.[86] Throughout the *Purāṇas* and other Hindu narratives, the goddess takes multiple forms that tend to break down into two general categories: the nurturing and docile consorts of the gods as opposed to fierce and powerful figures who exist independently. With her customary wit and ability to turn a phrase, Wendy Doniger has termed the two classes, respectively (and memorably), "Goddesses of breast and goddesses of tooth."[87] The former category contains goddesses such as Lakṣmī and Sarasvatī, the goddesses of fortune and wisdom, as well as the consorts of Viṣṇu and Brahmā, respectively. In the latter group, we find figures such as Durgā and Kālī, whose narratives and imagery depict them bloodily and violently crushing opposing demons, and even overcoming the male deities, until timely intervention brings them back under control before they threaten the entire cosmos itself.

In response to this division in goddess representations, some scholars, such as Tracy Pintchman, read a patriarchal discourse at work. By defining independent, strong goddesses as a dangerous force in need of limitation and the maternal, married goddesses as beneficial, a clear rhetoric regarding female gender role standards is delivered.[88] In village areas, though, goddess festivals and rituals have developed around Durgā and, especially, Kālī where devotees revel in the very fierceness and independence that unsettles male priestly hegemony, delighting in stories of how those powerful figures exercise their divine *śaktī* energy to destroy demons, surpass the gods themselves, and challenge the bonds of male domination.[89] As C. Mackenzie Brown observes based on the same case studies, for those Hindus, "Kālī has come to reveal the divine perfection, and consequently, perfect freedom also. It is a freedom that transcends the mores of everyday society and the ethical norms of the philosophers."[90]

In many ways, Danvers does precisely this as part of her reclamation of self in *Captain Marvel*. She, too, brims with energy that an authoritarian group wishes to claim for its own ends. After the Kree's duplicity is revealed,

Yon-Rogg tells Danvers, "I made you into your best self," thereby making a claim to ownership of her abilities. Both he and the Supreme Intelligence contend that her powers come from them and thus warn her, "What is given can be taken away," referencing the control chip on her neck, which they employ to temporarily short circuit her powers.[91] Danvers flatly rejects these premises, however, and like Kālī, who is often depicted completely wreathed in flame and towering over a supine Śiva, she concentrates her energy until it bursts from her fists, eyes, feet, and eventually sears outward from every inch of her body. The implanted control chip melts and Danvers is free from manipulation and restriction, her power (her *śaktī*, to use the Hindu term), now hers to use as she will. "I've been fighting with one hand tied behind my back," she realizes, "but what happens when I'm finally set free?"[92] In answer, she quickly overwhelms her putative masters and even defeats an attack on Earth from a fleet of Kree warships. As the culmination of her self-realization, she tersely rebukes Yon-Rogg's challenge to prove herself in a final sparring match with him by delivering an energy blast to his chest, punctuated by the simple affirmation "I have nothing to prove to you."[93] Through a painful process of self-discovery, in which her mentor is killed and she determines that her supposed benefactors were actually enemies, Danvers thus reclaims her true identity and discovers the full extent of her powers.

Altogether, the Phase Three films we have considered in this chapter demonstrate how, at this point in the MCU myth, there is a widespread reckoning of inner tensions that have been brewing in some cases since the superheroes' origins in Phase One and certainly since the purity dilemmas of Phase Two. The narrative manifests these tensions with episodes

Like Hindu goddesses imbued with the cosmic energy of *śaktī*, Carol Danvers (Bree Larson) emanates the raw power of the Tesseract and uses it to overcome the domineering control of the alien Kree. From *Captain Marvel* (2019).

involving intra-familial strife that resonate strongly with ancient myths of familial and inter-generational conflict. The result has been a mix of grievous loss but also the opening up of new possibilities, with the balance between those outcomes varying depending on the superhero(es) involved. With the Avengers, the outlook is perhaps the most grim as their close-knit, family-like unit has been torn asunder and consumed in a cycle of violence, leaving Tony Stark and Steve Rogers estranged and reexamining their roles as superheroes. In the case of Rogers, he has even surrendered his shield and, as evidenced by the final frames of the film, painted his traditional red, white, and blue uniform entirely black.

In their respective battles with familial enemies, the other MCU superheroes are similarly scarred and forced to reevaluate their identities. Throughout, this is represented in the loss of personal objects: Thor loses Mjolnir, Quill's Walkman is smashed, the Wakandan heart-shaped herb is burned, and Spider-Man must (temporarily) relinquish his suit. More seriously, most also suffered the death of a mentor or loved one, whether it was Odin (and all of Asgard), Zuri and King T'Chaka, Yondu, or Wendy Lawson. Each object and person epitomized an aspect of that particular superheroes' personality and their loss signifies a transition. As we saw, the superheroes react in different ways, though a common thread is a reaffirmation of other pillars of their identity or the discovery of new paths forward, though the cost and pain has been great.

Within the larger MCU narrative, the overarching story that interweaves the various films into a cogent single myth, events are moving at this point that intervene before the superheroes have progressed very far at all on these new passages. In the after-credits scene of *Thor: Ragnarok*, as the Asgardian refugee transport moves through space, a massive battleship appears, dwarfing the cruiser by comparison. This is the ship of Thanos, the mad Titan, who represents nothing less than Death personified. Previously appearing only in glimpses and terrified hints and whispers, such as those of Gamora and Nebula, who (displaying their own tension-filled family situation) are his adopted daughters, the battleship's arrival signals Thanos' full-fledged advent in the MCU myth. With that, the MCU superheroes, like their shaman ancestors and other epic figures of world religions and mythologies from ages before, must do battle with the power of Death itself. We begin our discussion of that struggle and its mythic symbolism in the next chapter.

FIVE

Death Stalks the MCU

Thanos Among the Monsters
of the MCU and World Mythology

Boswell: *"But is not the fear of death natural to man?"*
Johnson: *"So much so, Sir, that the whole of life is but keeping away the thoughts of it."*
—*The Life of Samuel Johnson*, James Boswell, p. 123

[Myth] is nearly always rooted in the experience of death and the fear of extinction.
—Karen Armstrong, *A Short History of Myth*, p. 3

It's Thanos! He's a plague, Tony. He invades planets, he takes what he wants, and he wipes out half the population.
—Bruce Banner, played by Mark Ruffalo,
Avengers: Infinity War (2018)

Thanos has been inside my head for six years since he sent an army to New York. And now he's back.
—Tony Stark, played by Robert Downey Jr.,
Avengers: Infinity War (2018)

Avengers: Infinity War (2018) immediately establishes itself as of a different tone and gravity than previous entries in the MCU, setting the stage for grim and momentous developments as the mythology reaches the concluding chapters of its narrative. Rather than the triumphant fanfare of the opening *Marvel* trademark, there is instead a static-laden voice-over of a desperate plea for help from the Asgardian refugee ship last seen at the end of *Thor: Ragnarok*. As threatened in the after-credits scene of that film, the massive battleship looming over the cruiser has launched an attack and the dead and dying lay sprawled across the interior of the ship. Standing, silhouetted against the stars, is a massive, towering figure. He dwarfs Thor and Loki in size as he stalks into the midst of the crippled and dying to deliver some of the first lines of the film. This imposing figure, known as

Thanos, tells them the following: "I know what it's like to lose. To feel so desperately that you are right, yet to fail nonetheless. It's frightening. Turns the legs to jelly. But I ask you, to what end? Dread it, run from it, destiny arrives all the same. And now, it's here. Or should I say, I am."[1]

Created originally by comic writer Jim Starlin, Thanos (whose name stems from the Greek "Thanatos"—"Death") first appeared in an issue of *Iron Man* in the early 1970s. Hailing from the planet "Titan," he was son of the world's ruler "Mentor" and, in an obvious nod to Greek mythology where love and death are relatives, brother to "Eros." In that initial appearance, we are told, "the seed of evil sprouted and flowered in him, consuming his entire soul," until he murdered his own mother, raised an army of outcasts and monsters from across the galaxy, and conquered Titan.[2] One of the most famous storylines involving the character occurred in the 1990s as Thanos, out of a desire to become the lover of Death (personified as a woman in a dark, flowing cloak), swore to kill half of all beings in existence, thereby enlarging Death's realm at the expense of the living. To do so, he gathered the "Infinity Stones," special gems representing the elements of Space, Time, Reality, Power, Soul, and Mind, which stem from the beginnings of the universe and wield incredible power. Though he succeeds in wiping out half of all beings, Thanos is ultimately undone by, among other things, doubts about his own worthiness to possess such power.[3]

In the MCU, prior to *Avengers: Infinity War* Thanos appeared only in brief moments or was mentioned in occasional remarks by characters, but even this was enough to establish him as a looming threat. In the after-credits scene of *Marvel's The Avengers,* he is revealed as the force behind Loki's invasion of the Earth. He also serves as the authority behind Ronan in *Guardians of the Galaxy,* where he is referred to as the "most powerful being in the universe" and also a sadistic torturer.[4] In a post-credits scene after *Avengers: Age of Ultron,* he is shown donning the special gauntlet made to channel the power of the Infinity Stones. In prior films, the Infinity Stones were introduced as the Tesseract (Space), the Aether (Reality), the Orb (Power), Doctor Strange's amulet (Time), and the gem in Loki's Scepter, then Vision's head (Mind). As in the comics, by collecting and uniting all six Infinity Stones, Thanos will be rendered nearly omnipotent and have the ability—as befits his morbid name—to accomplish his overriding ambition of consigning half the population of all living beings in the universe to death.

Contrary to the comics, in the MCU, Thanos has no deficit in self-confidence, nor is he in pursuit of the affections of any other being, as a female personification of death is absent. In this narrative, he alone represents the power of death, both in name and action, as *Avengers: Infinity War* demonstrates vividly in its early moments. After the brief speech quoted earlier, the Hulk attacks Thanos, but the Titan quickly gains the advantage and beats the gamma giant unconscious. Thor leaps in next, but is subdued even more rapidly. After defeating two of the most powerful superheroes in the MCU, Thanos then murders Heimdall and, after an attempt at deception by Loki goes awry, slowly and excruciatingly strangles the trickster, all while Thor is forced to watch in anguish.

This display alone sets Thanos apart from previous villains and monsters in the MCU. Those distinguished primarily by strength (such as Abomination or Winter Soldier) are obviously outclassed, as shown by the Titan's thrashing of the Hulk, and villains who rely on technology (namely Toomes as "Vulture," Cross as "Yellowjacket," Ava Starr as "Ghost," Ivan Vanko as "Whiplash," and Obadiah Stane as "Iron Monger") would be unable to compete with the powers Thanos wields through only one Infinity Stone. As the film progresses, we also see that Thanos' ability to scheme, strategize, and plot is at least on par with the likes of the Red Skull, Aldrich Killian, Helmut Zemo, and N'Jadaka.

Some MCU villains, however, do attain a level of power at which they can threaten an entire planet, such as Loki, Ronan, and Ultron. In addition to his strength, shapeshifting, and magical powers, Loki is also a keenly intelligent being who puts the Bifrost and the Chitauri army to devastating use on Jotunheim and Earth, respectively. Ronan, on the other hand, is a fanatical Kree warrior driven by issues of cultural purity to try to exterminate the rival Xandarians, seeing them as a disease that can only be cured by destroying the entire planet with the Power Stone. In the same vein, Ultron speaks at times like a prophet and interprets the devastation he intends to wreak on the Earth as salvation. Though each, at least in their own minds, aspires to grandeur, they cannot measure up to Thanos, as the Titan and his followers readily observe. About Loki, whose motivation stems from feelings of inadequacy compared to Thor, Thanos' servant "the Other" comments, "Your ambition is little and born of childish need."[5] Similarly, Thanos himself calls the prideful Ronan a "boy" and tells him, "Your demeanor is that of a pouty child."[6] With ambitions on the universal as opposed to merely planetary scale, we can see why the Titan would see the plans of Loki, Ronan, and Ultron as child's play. Indeed, two of the three gain their stature from serving as Thanos' subordinates, all three hold power through only a single Infinity Stone (with Ultron initially achieving sentience through the Mind Stone), whereas the Titan eventually gains control of all six gems.

A few remaining villains possess higher potency and aspirations, such as Dormammu, who threatens to pull the Earth and the rest of the universe into the Dark Dimension. Ego, a planet unto himself, also strives to absorb the known cosmos. To this we can add the Thor villains Hela, who aims to conquer the Nine Realms and beyond, and Malekith, who sought the Aether to annihilate all life. As impressive in scope as each sounds, they are still bound in ways that Thanos is not and ultimately fall short of his rank. Hela and Ego, ultimately, were rooted in their own planets and unable to exert their influence beyond those realms, whereas Dormammu and Malekith were both overcome by Infinity Stones, which the Titan comes to control, thus surpassing each villain preceding him in the larger narrative.

At every turn, then, Thanos is shown to be the most frightful and terrible figure of the MCU's mythology to this point, which is unsurprising for a character whose name and ambition are synonymous with death. With that in mind, it is perhaps more appropriate to look for comparable figures and ideas to the MCU's Thanos among the gods of death and destruction found in the world's religions and mythologies. As the quote from Samuel Johnson at the opening of the chapter suggests, death is one of the great common denominators of human experience and, as such, is a universal concern of religious narratives around the globe. Archeological evidence shows that tens of thousands of years ago, almost certainly by the Pleistocene and definitely by the Paleolithic, the human species had developed notions of death as a special state and constructed rituals (and potentially myths) around the burial of bodies, as demonstrated by the ornamentation and special care taken in the arrangement of corpses.[7] Later, more animistic religious traditions, as found in North America and Africa, wove tales of death as a mistake caused by a miscommunication or wrongly-informed choice, a tragic blunder at the beginning of time that has thereafter doomed humanity and all other creatures.[8]

In other cases, however, traditions within these geographic regions crafted stories that portrayed death as regrettable, but necessary for the greater good of life on Earth. The Dinka of Sudan, for example, held that the creator saw that space on earth would run out if the population of the living continued to grow. He then created death to lighten nature's burden.[9] The Kiowa of the southwest region of North America and the Modoc of what is now northern California provided similar reasons for the origin of death: if creatures were allowed to live forever, there would simply not be enough room for everyone who was eventually born.[10] Some stories acknowledge this fact, but also characterize the ensuing existence as a struggle to outpace or at least match the predatory appetite of death. The Buganda of Uganda, for example, personified Death as the brother-in-law of the first man, Kintu. As the matrilineal uncle of Kintu's children with his wife, Death came occasionally to claim them for his land, and in order to maintain his family, Kintu and his wife must have children faster than Death can come to take them away.[11] Across the world, one gets a similar sense from a Japanese myth in the *Kojiki*, which tells how Izanagi followed his sister Izanami into the underworld after she died. Incensed at his intrusion, she furiously pursued him, threatening to kill one thousand people a day in retaliation. Izanagi responded that he would then insure that one-thousand-five-hundred people were born each day to keep ahead of death's march.[12] As one final point of correspondence, these interpretations of death as necessary for balance, but also rapacious in its appetite, jibe well with the notion in the Hindu *Bṛhadāraṇyaka Upaniṣad*, which refers to death as hunger, with the whole universe as its food.[13]

Interestingly, Thanos provides the same concern for balancing the cosmic scales of life and death, of ensuring that resources are not overused, as the motivation for his quest to destroy half of all living things. His adopted daughter, Gamora, tells the other Guardians of the Galaxy this same message, relating, "The entire time I knew Thanos, he only ever had one goal: to bring balance to the universe by wiping out half of all life."[14] In a flashback to when she was a child, Gamora recalls when Thanos kidnapped her, immediately after slaughtering half her planet's population, including her parents. At the time, he symbolized the necessity of balance by perching a double-bladed knife on her finger, implicitly juxtaposing the harmony of equilibrium with the violence he believed was needed to achieve it. All the while, as he instructs her in the balancing of the knife, he takes a calm, almost fatherly tone with the young Gamora, which he returns to years later as he demands to know the location of the Soul Stone. To reaffirm the worthiness of his intentions, he uses the story of her planet as an example of what he desires for the entire universe, saying that her people were starving amid a society verging on collapse, but after wiping out half of the population, her civilization now thrives. Speaking in terms recognizable from the Dinka, Kiowa, or Modoc myths, he says, continuing his fatherly tone:

> THANOS: Little one, it is a simple calculation. This universe is finite, its resources finite. If life is left unchecked, life will cease to exist. It needs correction.
> GAMORA: You don't know that!
> THANOS: I'm the only one who knows that. At least, I'm the only one with the will to act on it.[15]

In this exchange, Thanos positions himself as the sole corrective power in the universe, the only one (or so he claims) to realize, like the traditions we examined above, that while death is regrettable, it is necessary to forestall the greater disaster of overpopulation.

Later, on Thanos' now desolate home-world of Titan, he uses the Reality Stone to show Doctor Strange how prosperous and advanced his world once was at its peak, before strained resources and overpopulation led to its destruction. As with Gamora, Thanos and Strange differ on the solution the Titan proposed for his people, and now intends for the entire universe.

THANOS: Titan was like most planets: too many mouths, not enough to go around. And when we faced extinction I offered a solution.

STRANGE: Genocide?

THANOS: But random, dispassionate, fair to rich and poor alike…. With all six stones, I could simply snap my fingers and they would all cease to exist. I call that mercy.[16]

In ways eerily similar to the Native American, African, and Japanese mythic ways of understanding death, Thanos pictures himself as a harsh, but also necessary and impartial force in the cosmos. Without the mercy, as he calls it, of his death-dealing activities, there would only be more suffering as life chokes on itself. Thanos' stated mission in the MCU taps into these strains of world mythology that see death as serving a vital role, as much as humans might fear and resist it. This is why, according to the Dinka, out of a greater wisdom, the creator made death. For the Kiowa, the trickster Saynday let death into the world for the same reason, taking the advice of the ant-woman that there would be no room for the living if they did not die. Later, she feels differently when her own son is killed, but Saynday merely remarks that death is now here to stay.[17] The MCU portrays Thanos as seeing himself play the same role in the universe, performing the unattractive but crucial work of keeping life in check with death.

Monotheistic religious traditions overlap in some ways with this representation of death, but as we might expect, orient their understanding of human mortality towards their conception of the singular deity. In turn, there are interesting parallels with Thanos that emerge from those traditions. For Islam, which etymologically means "submission," death is simply another factor of God's plan to which an obedient Muslim should yield. On this point, according to the Qur'ān, Allah has said, "We have not granted everlasting life to any other human being before you either, even Muhammad…. Every soul is certain to taste death: we test you all through the bad and the good, and to us you will return."[18] The passage's invocation of Muhammad powerfully delivers the message of death's ubiquity, for if immortality could be expected of anyone, it would be the one considered the last of the prophets.

For this reason, one version of the death of Muhammad himself is interesting for illustrating this theme, and also for other purposes, such as the way that it personifies death. In that narrative, Muhammad falls gravely ill and his daughter, Fatima, sees a "tall stranger … his face stern and lean, his eyes large and dark," lurking at their doorstep.[19] She is understandably frightened, but Muhammad knows immediately that the figure is Azrael, the angel of death, sent by Allah to take his life. Rather than give in to fear, Muhammad models for Fatima, and all other Muslims, an obedient nature in the face of Allah's edict. He tells her, "My daughter, do not weep too much, for death is an experience that awaits us all; it is merely fate fulfilled ... none of us can escape His decree."[20] Azrael, like Thanos, is an imposing and fearful figure, but unlike the Titan, he operates under the auspices of a more benevolent entity who ultimately cares for all beings.

Judaism, based on the ancient Hebrew texts, also locates the ultimate source and authority over death with a single deity. Even as the Garden of Eden and Cain versus Abel myths suggest the entrance of death into the world was due to human error, in this way paralleling strands of thought in the Native American and African stories we examined, the Hebrew texts far more frequently attribute mortality to the will of God. For instance, one exemplary passage reads this way: "The Lord puts to death and gives life, casts down to Sheol and brings up again."[21] In Hebrew cosmology, Sheol exists as a shadowy underworld, comparable (and most likely drawn from) the traditions of other Mesopotamian peoples, which we will discuss below.[22] From this understanding, God exerts all power over life and death, and it is the believer's lot to accept blessings in this life and the prospect of the next existence in Sheol.

Early Christianity, as was its wont, built on the preexisting Hebrew traditions, making references to Sheol in its scriptures, as well as another destination called "Gehenna," that existed as a place of fiery retribution.[23] However, Christianity also reoriented views of death at the same time in two significant ways. First, rather than a force of nature to be endured, through the crucifixion of Jesus, death was seen as conquered and overcome, as Paul claimed in one of his letters to the early community: "the last enemy to be destroyed is death."[24] Second, even more than Islam with Azrael and certainly beyond what is found in Judaism, early Christianity linked death with a fearsome figure of evil, namely the fallen angel, Satan. This relationship appears explicitly in some New Testament texts, such as *Hebrews*, which says, "through death, he [Jesus] might destroy the one who has the power of death, that is, the devil."[25] This conflation of Satan with death continued through the early centuries of Christianity, as the devil was identified as the serpent in the *Genesis* story of Eden and otherwise blamed for human mortality, until the period of the late Middle Ages, when portrayals of death and Satan were slowly disentangled.[26] A strong connection persisted, however, as seen in Milton's *Paradise Lost*, where Death is the child produced by the union of Satan and Sin.[27]

In all, compared across these three monotheistic traditions, Islam and Christianity, by identifying mortality with a terrifying figure (Azrael and Satan, respectively), bear certain relations to the MCU's depiction of Thanos. Yet, in the case of these religious traditions, death's power is undercut by the action or oversight of an even greater force, whether it is Allah or Jesus. Within those traditions, both work to remove the horror of death in ways not present in the MCU, although the notion of sacrifice overcoming or at least mitigating mortality is a theme we will return to in Chapter Six.

Another thread across world mythologies that perhaps better approximates the MCU's framing of Thanos personifies death as a regal or noble figure who is nevertheless, as a communication of the innate dreadfulness of mortality, flanked by or associated with gruesome and ghastly servants. In Greece, the Lord of the Underworld, Hades, is considered a divinity, but his godhood is balanced by fearsomeness. For instance, like other Greek gods, he drives a golden chariot, but in his case it is pulled by coal-black horses. Further setting him apart, he is known as the "subterranean Zeus," but the Olympian gods and goddesses despise and shun his realm.[28] As Harris and Platzner describe traditions surrounding his representation, Hades was considered a god of high and potent stature, but one who also possessed a "grim and pitiless personality, his implacability reflecting the harsh quality of a natural law that condemns all living things to death."[29]

The MCU portrays Thanos in much the same way, showing that he and his followers believe he is like Hades as an extension of the universal constant of death, and thus allowed to construe his mercilessness as mercy. As an example, one of Thanos' servants, the so-called "Ebony Maw" (also simply called "the Maw," bringing to mind the Hindu *Upaniṣad*'s concept of death as hunger), attempts to convey this sense surrounding his master as they walk among the dead on the Asgardian ship. "Hear me and rejoice," Ebony Maw declares, "you have had the privilege of being saved by the Great Titan. You may think this is suffering. No. It is salvation. Universal scales tip toward balance because of your sacrifice. Smile. For even in death you have become children of Thanos."[30] As one would do with a figure of royalty, Ebony Maw heralds the arrival and presence of Thanos, adding a nearly messianic element to the perceived majesty of his master. Indeed, contributing to this royal mystique, the first full view of Thanos that the MCU provides its viewers, found in *Guardians of the Galaxy*, shows the Titan in his golden armor, perched atop a floating throne, acolytes bowed around him.

The god Yama occupies an analogous role in Hinduism, aligning with both Hades and Thanos. His Sanskrit epithet "*Dharmarāja*," or "Lord of the Eternal Law," once again speaks to the idea of death as regrettable but also inextricably woven into the nature of existence. In Hinduism, this deep connection to the eternal law of *dharma* has also tended to confer on Yama the sense of great wisdom and knowledge. Under certain circumstances he imparts these teachings to mortals, as he does with the young Brahmin Naciketas, who was sent mistakenly to the land of the dead and, as a recompense, is instructed by Yama in esoteric rituals and mystical understandings.[31] In another famous story, found in the *Mahābhārata*, a woman named

Thanos (Josh Brolin), the MCU's personification of Death, sits upon his floating throne. Images such as these in the MCU confer an air of royalty and regality upon the figure, even as he behaves in a thoroughly brutal fashion. From *Guardians of the Galaxy* (2014).

Sāvitrī sees her husband, Satyavat, collapse beside her while walking in the forest. Before long, "she saw a person in a yellow robe and turban, a handsome man resplendent like the sun, smoothly black and red-eyed. He had a noose in his hand and he looked terrifying as he stood gazing at Satyavat."[32] The approaching being is Yama, the god of death, come to claim Satyavat. Sāvitrī protests, hoping to save her husband's life, but in tones echoing Thanos and his minions' justifications, Yama tells her that the grand design of death is beyond a mortal's understanding and that his work is actually a kindness. Sāvitrī persists, however, hounding Yama with questions until she eventually extracts a boon from him—that she bear children by Satyavat—which can only be fulfilled if her husband is returned to life. Rather than display anger, Yama is actually pleased with her cleverness and bestows yet more knowledge upon her.

At the same time that he is seemingly wise and just, the other aspects of the story's description of Yama are telling. "Handsomeness" is juxtaposed with "terrifying," the "yellow robe" stands next to "red-eyed" (normally the attribute of demons in Hindu mythology), and besides wearing a turban, he also carries a noose. The regal stands next to the repulsive in the portrayal of Yama, as it does with Thanos in the MCU. One moment, the Great Titan stands in glittering, golden armor, wearing a crown-like helmet as Infinity Stones glow on his gauntlet, and the next instant he impales a helpless foe or grins as he strangles the life from a prisoner.

That royalty and nobility are but a veneer or a mask for something more horrible is shown by the creatures who often surround these gods of death. Hades is flanked by Cerberus, the enormous, three-headed dog who guards the gate of the underworld, as well as the ghastly boatman Charon and the hideous Furies. Besides appearing personally to claim souls, Yama also employs servants (called "*yamadūtas*") who are described as having crooked faces, yellow, red, or black bodies, fierce teeth and claws, and deformed arms and legs. These creatures accompany Yama, especially when he is to visit those who have led unjust lives. At those moments, in addition to the unsettling features he displayed in the forest with Sāvitrī, Yama takes on an even more intimidating form, with eyes as big as lakes and a voice like thunder.[33] For these reasons, despite being regarded as the *Dharmarāja*, for Hindus, "Yama is a deity who inspires dread. In India, talking about him or simply pronouncing his name is avoided."[34]

It is the same situation with Thanos, in both respects. For most of the three Phases of the MCU, he is spoken of only rarely and shown even less, though his influence ripples through the events of almost every episode of the narrative. Additionally, if we recall from Chapter Two, Monster Theory holds that the deformity of a figure communicates, through the myth, the disorder or chaos of which the character is a symbol. While Thanos is of massive size, like a Grendel or Humbaba or Polyphemus, he is not misshapen in quite the same way, as unlike those monsters, his morphology is still proportionate and his appendages are of humanoid form. Hades and Yama as well are both unsettling in their features, but not necessarily misshapen. All three figures, however, are served by beings who are misshapen, violent, and deformed, exhibiting classic monstrous features and tendencies. Just as Hades has Cerberus, Charon, and the Furies, and Yama has his *yamadūtas*, Thanos has the Chitauri and Leviathans (grotesque soldiers and beasts with spliced cybernetic and biological components, described in Chapter Two), the "Outriders" (multi-limbed, eye-less, black, dog-like monsters with bristling teeth), and main lieutenants called the "Children of Thanos." Of the latter, there is "Proxima Midnight" (a humanoid with curved horns), "Cull Obsidian" (a large bipedal, reptilian beast), "Corvus Glaive" (a creature with unnaturally long limbs and goblin-like ears), and the previously mentioned Ebony Maw (a thin being with shriveled hands and a face with no nose). As with Hades and Yama, Thanos' monstrosity is mediated through the figures around him.

As a commonality between the Greek, Hindu, and MCU mythologies, this move could be interpreted in several ways. For one, we could read it simply as a statement on the way death disrupts and throws chaos into life. On another note, this somewhat disjunctive relationship between the gods of death and their more (outwardly) horrifically monstrous followers could speak to the tension we have observed on more than one occasion during this discussion. Namely, though death can be seen as necessary

Thanos' loyal followers, the Children of Thanos, surround Loki after slaughtering the crew of the Asgardian refugee ship during the search for Infinity Stones. Their monstrosity expresses the Titan's hideous inner nature. From *Avengers: Infinity War* (2018). From left to right: Carrie Coon as Proxima Midnight, Tom Hiddleston as Loki, Tom Vaughan-Lawlor as Ebony Maw, Michael James Shaw as Corvus Glaive, and Terry Notary as Cull Obsidian.

in the course of existence, and hence noble in a sense, from a practical and experiential point of view, it is still terrible, painful, and discordant. The noble god thus stands for the necessity of death while the horror of mortality is still acknowledged, albeit mediated through other, more ghastly creatures associated with the divinity.

As much as Thanos might have in common with figures like Hades and Yama, he is arguably even more comparable to another class of mythologies which classify death as irremediably cruel and evil, with corresponding representations of the god of death. Within this category we can place Buddhism and its narratives of Māra, the "evil one." At times also referred to by epithets such as *"Antaka"* ("the Endmaker"), *"Maccurāja"* ("King of Death"), and *"Kaṇha"* ("the Dark One"), as discussed in Chapter Two, Māra is the lord of the realm of death and desire in which all beings are born, die, and are reborn through an endless cycle. The name "Māra" comes from the Sanskrit root *mṛ*, which means "death" and is distantly related to the English root that forms the word "mortal." As it is a causative construction, the most literally rendering of "Māra," then, might be "one who makes death," or more simply, "killer."[35] Despite having obvious demonic attributes, like Hades or Yama (a figure with whom he has notable connections), Māra is considered within Buddhism to hold godly stature as well, and he is portrayed as dwelling in a high heavenly realm, possessing a lustrous body, and holding sway over all the other gods and lower beings beneath him.[36]

But whereas Hades and Yama were seen in their respective traditions as fearful but noble, Māra within Buddhism, in keeping with that religion's skepticism toward divinities, is depicted as a fearful tyrant, in both senses, as one who inspires fear and is also full of fear, specifically of beings escaping his realm of birth, death, and rebirth. As we have seen, to avoid that circumstance, Māra uses an army of horrible creatures, akin to Thanos' Chitauri and Outriders, to try to kill Siddhartha Gautama before he might discover the path to Buddhahood, which leads outside the sphere of rebirth. In a similar attempt to keep others from escaping his control, Buddhist scriptures recount his tactic to shapeshift into a number of grotesque forms in the hopes of intimidating the Buddha and his followers as well as frighten them away from the path.[37] For these actions of despotically attempting to hold beings in the thrall of repeated suffering and death, in Buddhism Māra blends the status of god and demon, showing how Buddhists consider death itself to be an evil.

Elsewhere in the world, death is also personified as monstrous and evil. In Egypt, for example, the cosmic order of *ma'at* was eternally threatened by the serpent Apophis, whose darkness symbolized the horror of primordial chaos and death.[38] Ancient Aztec tradition talks of Mictlan, the god of the dead, who is known as the "all-devouring" and is said to possess multiple mouths to chew upon the deceased while he roams the underworld with the body of a bat. He is attended by other oversized bats, as the animals were thought to be ill-omened by Mesoamericans for their association with the night.[39] Mesopotamian narratives held a similarly dim view of the realm of the dead, its inhabitants, and death itself. In some traditions, this domain was ruled by the dread goddess Ereshkigal whose entire body, including face and lips, was black and dark "like tamarisk."[40] As described in certain myths, such as the *Epic of Gilgamesh*, death was also terrible for the punishments and deprivations one endured. Enkidu, who has been condemned to die by the gods, dreams of the gruesome world of the dead and relates his shocking vision to his friend, Gilgamesh: "a creature appeared with a lion's head, his face was ghastly, then a bird-man appeared and bound [my arms] behind me and forced me down to the underworld, the house of darkness … those who dwell there squat in the darkness, and dirt is their food, their drink is clay."[41] Looking around, Enkidu tells of seeing piles of crowns and discarded robes of priests, showing that the horror of death rules over, torments, and awaits all humanity, regardless of birth or station.

Though Thanos undoubtedly has certain commonalities with the sense of death as sad but necessary (found in Native American, African, and Japanese myths), potent and unavoidable (expressed in monotheistic religions), and grim but noble (articulated, for instance, in Greek and Hindu figures), the MCU positions him far more in the Buddhist, Egyptian, Mesoamerican, and Mesopotamian mode of a brutal and evil defiler. Bruce

Banner, one of the first of the Avengers to encounter Thanos, attempts to describe the nature and gravity of the Titan in this way: "He's a plague.... He invades planets, he takes what he wants, and he wipes out half the population."[42] Though the films show Thanos pretend toward nobility and espouse a higher purpose, the latter is maniacal and self-appointed, while the former is a mask for utter sadism.

One potential objection to the notion that Thanos stems from the harsher, more malevolent traditions of death gods lies in his seeming affection for his adopted daughter Gamora. Such attachments and displays, however, are not out of the question for deities or other figures representing death. Hades, out of desire and lust, kidnapped Persephone, keeping her as a virtual prisoner in his underworld realm, much as Thanos kidnaps Gamora and coerces her into remaining at his side. Mara in Buddhist mythology is thought to have his own daughters, named Rāga, Arati, and Taṇhā ("Lust," "Dissatisfaction," and "Thirst"), who he sends out on missions of seduction to entrap those mortals (such as Siddhartha Gautama, the one who would become the Buddha) who threaten his rule.[43] In the cases of both Hades and Mara, the familial connection these death gods possess evinces not love (though they believe it does), but rather rapacity and violence: the rape and abduction of Persephone is about Hades' craving to possess her, whereas the daughters of Mara are extensions of that deity's amalgamation of sex and destruction, as well as his longing to maintain control over all beings. In these relationships, which distort familial love with possession and control, we can see a metaphor for how death taints all life, seeking to grasp, control, and ultimately consume it. Thanos' relationship with Gamora is similar, as he exerts possession and control over her from the time she is a child, molding her into a tool to employ as an extension of his quest to acquire the Infinity Stones. Though he believes what he feels for her is love, she is under no such misapprehension, instead reacting to his sadism and domination by crying out, "This isn't love!"[44] Hence, if anything, Thanos' relationship with Gamora only tightens his link to other death gods, like Hades and Mara, whose twisted notions of "love" serve to communicate their malevolence.

As further examples of the Titan's vicious nature, the viewer sees him smile while Loki squirms at having to watch as Thor's face is burned by the Power Stone. Then, reversing the positions, he chokes Loki to death and grins as Thor shakes in helpless fury. To compel Gamora to reveal the location of the Soul Stone, Thanos dismembers and tortures his other adopted daughter, Nebula. Prior to that, he dares Quill to shoot Gamora, toying with the Guardians' affections for each other. We are also told that he coerced the dwarf Eitri into forging the gauntlet which will hold the stones by promising to let the dwarf's people live. When he received the gauntlet, he slaughtered the dwarves anyway and cut off Eitri's hands as further insurance against retribution. Looking ahead briefly to the final chapter of the MCU myth, *Avengers: Endgame*, Thanos tells Captain America, "In all my years of conquest, violence, slaughter, it was never personal. But I'll tell you now, what I'm about to do to your stubborn, annoying little planet. … I'm going to enjoy it. Very, very much."[45] Of course, his claims of dispassion during his atrocities are belied by the occasions given above, when he quite obviously took delight in the pain and destruction of others. His daughter Gamora likewise indicts him, saying, "You kill and torture and you call it mercy."[46] These acts and words, taken together with the hideous nature of his attendants and armies, serve to establish Thanos in the MCU myth as a figure of death who is relentless, ruthless, evil, and, beginning with *Avengers: Infinity War*, no longer in the background of the events of the MCU mythos, but at their center.

As described in the beginning of the chapter, Thanos makes his presence felt immediately, first by ravaging the Asgardian ship, killing scores of people, and taking the Tesseract, which houses the Space Stone. Prior to that film, he had already acquired the Power Stone from Xandar by devastating that planet. By an early point in *Avengers: Infinity War*, Thanos has thus already progressed one-third of the way to achieving the ultimate power of collecting all six Infinity Stones. These initial events also create an interesting distinction between the portrayal of Thanos in the comics and the MCU. In the original comics, Thanos is shown acquiring the Infinity Stones in the two-part special series *The Thanos Quest*. During

Despite his regal bearing and feints of rationality, Thanos' (Josh Brolin) brutality and underlying malevolence emerge. From *Avengers: Infinity War* (2018).

this chronicle of the Titan's search, he primarily employs trickery and guile to wrest the gems from their previous owners. For instance, he turns the strength of a being known as the "Champion" against himself and uses a robotic duplicate to fool the "Grandmaster," stealing the Power and Mind stones from them, respectively.[47] Thanos' tactics in the MCU are far less strategic, relying more on pure, brute force to gain the power he craves. That characterization works in the MCU mythology to enlarge and aggrandize Thanos as a threat and a symbol of remorseless mortality.

After taking possession of the first two Infinity Stones, Thanos heads to the strange settlement of "Knowhere" to find the Reality Stone. Encountering Thor adrift in the wreckage of the Asgardian ship, the Guardians of the Galaxy hear of Thanos' plan and deduce that the Titan's next destination will be Knowhere. Rocket and Groot depart with Thor to a place called Nidavellir to create a new, more powerful weapon for use against Thanos, while the other Guardians of the Galaxy head to Knowhere. Upon arrival, the latter group find the Titan threatening a being called the "Collector," who had taken possession of the Reality Stone (then perceived as the Aether) following the events of *Thor: The Dark World*. Gamora surprises Thanos and, using the same double-bladed knife he gave to her as a child, she seemingly kills him. The landscape then begins to shimmer and change, however, revealing that the entire scene has been an illusion. In fact, the planet of Knowhere is completely in flames and Thanos already possesses the Reality Stone, using it to fabricate the images he wished the Guardians of the Galaxy to see. In this way, he has lured Gamora, who alone knows the location of the Soul Stone, into his clutches.

The ability to twist, bend, or alter reality, at least in its appearances, occurs among many other figures of death and evil. Satan, just discussed within the Christian tradition as a personification of both death and evil, was considered apt to change shapes or create false images, as were his demonic minions, in order to fool the senses of those they wished to accost and torment.[48] In Buddhism, Māra also symbolizes death and evil and was similarly held as liable to assume any form he wished or manipulate appearances as desired. In order to distract, frighten, or otherwise discourage Buddhists from the path, Māra was known to manufacture loud cracking sounds in the earth, lustrous as well as revolting images, and apparitions of giant animals and phantom rock avalanches, among other images and shapes.[49] Throughout Mesopotamian, Indian, Chinese, African, and other mythologies, beings associated with evil and death are frequently shown as capable of warping reality or otherwise creating mirage-like images and phantasms.[50] Since both evil and death subvert, frustrate, and distort life in some fashion, we can speculate, following the Monster Theory introduced in Chapter Two, that these mythic characters are given the same capacity in their various narratives to garble and deform their bodies and the world around them. Thanos, now possessing the Reality Stone, draws level with these other figures of death and evil from around the world, showing his propensity to alter and pervert appearances.

Continuing on his quest to find the other three Infinity Stones, Thanos forces Gamora, through the torture of her sister, to reveal the location of the Soul Stone. They travel together to a planet called "Vormir," where at the edge of a deep precipice they encounter the Red Skull, who has become the guide to the stone. He explains that the Soul Stone can be possessed only with the sacrifice of another soul, specifically of someone the individual loves. At first, Gamora laughs, convinced that Thanos neither loves nor cares for anyone, but then realizes with horror that her death would indeed be a kind of sacrifice for him. She cries out and struggles as he drags her to the edge of the chasm and hurls her to her death, earning the Soul Stone.

In this way, Thanos, conforms to the type of the monstrous or—to use Campbell's phrase again—"ogre" father with which we became acquainted in the previous chapter. Like Kronos, who literally consumes his children to maintain power, Thanos expends his children to acquire power. In both *Guardians of the Galaxy* and *Guardians of the Galaxy: Volume 2*, we learn that the Titan regularly set Gamora and Nebula against one other, agonizingly punishing Nebula each time she lost by amputating part of her body and replacing it with cybernetics. This leads to deep enmity between the sisters, which is only overcome once they unite against their hated father. In the second of the two films, Nebula vows, "I will hunt my father like a dog, and I will tear him apart slowly, piece by piece until he knows some semblance of the profound and unceasing pain I know every single day."[51] With viciousness obviously learned from her father, Nebula attempts to carry out this threat, only to be captured and used as bait to ensnare Gamora, whom Thanos then murders. The generational "evil father" theme across films is even made explicit during the moments when the Guardians of the Galaxy meet Thor. Learning that Gamora is Thanos' daughter, Thor shares his own travails with Odin, Loki, and Hela, adding, "Families can be tough," which prompts Quill to relate his violent experience with his own father, Ego.[52] At that point in the narrative, the three characters, through their dialogue, bring into relief the mythic template of the "ogre father" in the MCU, of which Thanos is a clear participant.

For Thanos to take after Kronos, at least in part, is appropriate on several levels. First, they are both murderous fathers, but Kronos, in his role as "Father Time" (and part of the tradition that brings Western culture the paradigm of the "Grim Reaper," with his harvesting sickle) is also a death figure. It is then perhaps more than a coincidence that, after murdering his daughter, Thanos next pursues the Time Stone. This stone has been kept by

Doctor Strange, who was abducted (along with Iron Man and Spider-Man) to the planet Titan by the Ebony Maw. Joined eventually by Drax, Mantis, and Quill of the Guardians of the Galaxy, the superhero contingent form a plan to battle Thanos when he inevitably arrives. During the ensuing struggle, the group briefly subdue him, but he is ultimately too strong. Using the Power Stone to rip apart the orbiting moon and pelt the surface with meteors, drawing on the Reality Stone to hurl flames, or summoning his own titanic strength to shred Stark's armor, Thanos overcomes all of them. As the others lay beaten, Stark continues to fight until Thanos impales him with one of his own armor constructs. The Titan, holding the weapon in the Avenger's gut, hovers over him, and says, "You have my respect, Stark. When I'm done, half of humanity will still be alive. I hope they remember you."[53] Before he can kill Stark once and for all, however, Strange surrenders the Time Stone, leaving Thanos with only the Mind Stone left to attain.

That stone, belonging to the android Vision, has been defended during a massive battle between, on one side, the Avengers and the Wakandan army and, facing them, the Children of Thanos and their Outrider hordes. The conflict is especially violent and the alien army appears for a time to have an insurmountable advantage in numbers. When that edge appears telling, Thor arrives with his newly-forged axe "Stormbreaker" and drives Thanos' followers back. One by one, the superheroes are even able to kill the Children of Thanos, as Maximoff crushes Proxima Midnight under the grinding wheels of a giant machine, Banner explodes Cull Obsidian, and Vision impales Corvus Glaive. With Stark and Parker having earlier tossed Ebony Maw into the vacuum of space, all of Thanos' primary warriors and chief followers are dead. Meanwhile, outside Wakanda, the Avengers have seemingly won the battle.

The tide does not remain turned for long, however, as a portal opens and the Titan himself appears. Steve Rogers arrays the superheroes into a defensive line to protect the Vision, but Thanos wades through them easily, tossing Banner (wearing the "Hulkbuster" armor) into the side of a cliff, crumpling Rhodes' "War Machine" suit, and knocking Rogers unconscious. Only Wanda Maximoff remains and with her powers, themselves gained through Hydra's experiments with the Mind Stone in Loki's scepter, she holds Thanos at bay long enough to destroy the stone, and Vision along with it. With colossal audacity, Thanos approaches Maximoff, who has just destroyed the being she loved, and tells her, "Today I lost more than you could know, but now is no time to mourn." He then adds, ominously, "Now is no time at all."[54] Drawing on the Time Stone, the Titan reverses the actions of the previous moments, bringing Vision back to life, only to tear the Mind Stone from his head, killing him all over again. Thor enters the fray at this point, burying his axe in Thanos' chest and delivering what would normally be a mortal blow. For a figure of death, though, who has just reversed and re-instigated another creature's death mere moments prior, it is not enough. Exercising the full power of the combined Infinity Stones, Thanos snaps his fingers, and through that simple gesture, he exerts his wish of carnage across the entire universe. All of existence proceeds to rumble and shudder, with beings simply evaporating and vanishing. The superheroes lay defeated before an opponent, Death himself, who has proven vastly beyond their ability to stop.

With this outcome, the conclusion of *Avengers: Infinity War* corresponds to famous myths from Egypt, Greece, and India. In the former, the gods are left despondent when Set murders and dismembers Osiris, committing the kind of action the Egyptians most feared: the wanton chaos of a death that leaves the deceased without offspring or the possibility of an after-life, due to his body's mangled state. Such a nihilistic deed aligns Set, who has always had close parallels to notions of evil and chaos, to the primordial, death-dealing Apophis and leaves Isis, as well as the other gods, heartbroken and bereft.[55]

In ancient Greece, even Zeus and the other Olympians experience defeat at the hands of Typhon (also spelled "Typhoeus"), a monster born of Gaia's union with the underworld of Tartarus. A frightful beast, Typhon is described in this way: "up from his shoulders there grew a hundred snake heads, those of a bearded dragon, and the head licked with darting tongues and from the eyes on the inhuman heads fire glittered."[56] In Apollodorus' later, more elaborate version of the story, Typhon routes the Olympians and then overpowers Zeus, leaving him trapped in a cave with the sinews of his hands and feet cut.[57]

At times, the Hindu gods have fared equally poorly in battle, usually against a demon who, like Thanos, has gone on a quest to accumulate forbidden or difficult to achieve powers. Often these come in the form of a boon coerced from the creator god, Brahmā. One such demon, named Mahiṣa, knowing the gods to be male, chose the boon that he could only be killed by a woman. With the gods thus powerless against him, he wounds Viṣṇu, crushes Śiva's chest, and frightens off Yama, the god of death himself. After thus dethroning the gods, Mahiṣa takes control of the heavens and the deities must mournfully pass their time in remote caves.[58]

The demon Tāraka provokes a similar situation, having wrested the boon from Brahmā that only the son of the god Śiva (the famously celibate ascetic) could defeat him. Though they meet him in battle, the gods' collective might amounts to nothing against Tāraka: Viṣṇu's discus does not even scratch the demon's hide and Yama's staff taps against him uselessly. Tāraka drives the gods into hiding and exile, even forcing the seasons and celestial bodies like the sun and moon to do his bidding.[59]

In their failure against Thanos, the MCU superheroes are similarly dispossessed. When the Titan activates the stones in unison, he obtains his desire and half the universe is instantly consigned to death. In a wrenching sequence, character after character undergoes an experience one can liken to the words found in the Hebrew text *Genesis*: "By the sweat of your brow you will eat bread until you return to the ground, for from it you were taken. For you are dust, and to dust you shall return."[60] Comrade after comrade, friend after friend is forced to watch those whom they fought alongside reduced slowly, painfully to dust, disintegrating before their eyes. The Wakandan general Okoye sees T'Challa fragment into ashen pieces, Rogers watches Barnes disappear, Groot vanishes before Rocket's eyes, and so on. Perhaps most emotionally, Peter Parker, still on Titan, detects through his "spider sense" that something is not right and grabs hold of his mentor and father figure, Stark. Pitifully, he laments to him, "I don't want to go, please, I don't want to go, Mr. Stark. I'm sorry, Tony. I'm sorry."[61] Parker then dissipates into ash, leaving Stark horrified and almost alone, as all but Nebula have also disappeared. Though Stark has no speaking lines at that moment, the expression on his face evokes the words of Gilgamesh upon the death of Enkidu, his quest companion and dear friend: "When he heard the death rattle, Gilgamesh moaned like a doe. His face grew dark, and he said, 'Beloved, wait, don't leave me. Dearest of me, don't die, don't let them take you from me.'"[62]

The resonance of *Gilgamesh*, one of humanity's oldest myths, with the MCU, one of humanity's most recent myths, on the issue of death shows the importance of mortality to the collective imagination and concern of our species. As humans, we do not want to die and fear it so much that in our narratives we conjure monsters such as Māra, Mictlan, Set, and Thanos to express and hypostasize our unease at our powerlessness before this universal terror. Yet, in the realm of myth, we are anything but powerless, as is attested to in the eventual outcomes of the Egyptian, Greek, and Indian narratives outlined above. Though exiled each time, the gods rally against both Mahiṣa and Tāraka, creating beings (the goddess Durgā and the god Karttikeya, respectively) who exploit the loopholes in the demons' boons, leading to their destruction and overthrow. With the help of Hermes and Pan, Zeus recovers his lost sinews, regains his strength, and contends with Typhon again, battering the serpent dragon with thunderbolts before burying him beneath the volcano of Mount Aetna. In Egypt, in a move most likely connected to the mummification ritual, Isis reassembles her husband's body, becomes pregnant by him, and bears his child Horus, who restores justice by defeating Set. Osiris, then, ever after, is lord of the after-life and his example of victory over death was one that every ancient Egyptian hoped to replicate.

In this last instance, scholars have noted that, by using the case of Set's attack on Osiris as paradigmatic of death, the particularly Egyptian cultural view of mortality is revealed. Namely, death is a crime, an injustice, and "they could do something about it and restore the order that had been destroyed. Because death was not natural, because it did not lie in the nature of things, they could not accept it; they could and had to do something to counter it."[63] Likewise, the MCU superheroes find themselves confronted with death on a cosmic and intimately personal scale, and it is a situation they cannot accept. Yet, they are not pharaohs like the Egyptians nor are they gods like the Olympians or Hindu deities. As I have returned to again and again throughout this book, the more appropriate comparison for the MCU superheroes is the religious virtuoso, the one who encounters, mediates, and attempts to control the overwhelming powers of the sacred.

Specifically among that group, the MCU superheroes operate most like shamans who are, as Eliade observed across cultures from around the world, often the religious practitioners tasked with healing the desperately sick or curing those prematurely or wrongly claimed by death. As Eliade writes, in those cultures it is thought that "only the shaman can undertake a cure of this kind. For only he 'sees' the spirits and knows how to exorcise them; only he recognizes that the soul has fled, and is able to overtake it and return it to its body."[64] In Brazil, for instance, as evidenced by the ethnography of Michael Perrin on the Guajiro, shamans in that society have a standard recourse in situations where death has wrongfully claimed members of the community. Among the Guajiro, when a person has become a prisoner in the abode of death, the shaman will travel to that realm to retrieve the person's soul, restoring them to life.[65] The same could be said of the Gurung in Nepal, who are said to journey to the underworld to rescue souls stolen by demonic agents.[66] Indeed, this pattern recurs and has been repeated throughout the world, in South America, North America, Siberia, China, South Asia, and so on. As we will see in the next chapter, the MCU superheroes undertake a very similar kind of perilous journey to restore the lives of their lost comrades, once again challenging Thanos, as well as their own liminal instability, once and for all, triggering a climactic battle of apocalyptic imagery and proportions.

Six

The Superhero's Quest

*Journeys to the Underworld
and the Final Battle Against Death*

"*Every human society is, in the last resort, [people] banded
together in the face of death. The power of religion depends,
in the last resort, upon the credibility of the banners it puts
in the hands of [people] as they stand before death, or more
accurately, as they walk, inevitably, toward it.*"
—Peter Berger, *The Sacred Canopy*, p. 51

THANOS: *I am … inevitable.*
STARK: *And I … am … Iron Man.*
—*Avengers: Endgame* (2019)

In some world philosophies, as we saw in the last chapter, death is not necessarily the enemy of humanity. Rather, it is a force to put into perspective as part of a wider matrix of cosmic existence. To those thoughts already presented in the preceding pages, we can also add the Daoist *Dao De Ching*, which posits, "Life and Death stem from each other, and only seem to conflict," going on to argue that they flow into one another as complementary agents of change.[1] Another Asian classic of philosophy, the *Bushido* or "Code of the Samurai," suggests that the most important test of a person's life is how he or she faces death. Thus, all persons should cultivate a constant state of awareness and acceptance of their unavoidable and, in the language of both of the quotations offered above, inevitable demise.[2] Confronted with this inevitability of death, some world philosophies and religions therefore counsel that humans take a measured response of calm and acceptance.

As we saw in the last chapter, death has visited the MCU in the person of Thanos and left widespread destruction—the extinction of fifty percent of all living beings—in his wake. Unable to stop the Titan from accomplishing his goal, the MCU superheroes are thus left with the choice of whether to follow the path suggested by such works as the *Dao De Ching* and the *Bushido*, or to defy death against all odds and attempt to find some means to thwart the unstoppable force. As Tony Stark's sentiment in the second quote indicates, the superheroes choose the latter course of action, undertaking a perilous journey that recalls stories from numerous mythologies around the world. Ultimately, their actions also trigger a titanic final battle that resembles many cultures' visions of the end of the world. The final chapter of the MCU's twenty-two-film, three-Phase narrative thus ends, figuratively and literally, with a bang and in its conclusion the mythos not only delivers its own answer to the issue of human mortality, it also resolves the persistent matter of the liminality and instability of its superhero characters.

Upon Thanos' use of the six Infinity Stones to halve the population of all living beings (referred to in the film as the "Snap," after the Titan's snap of his fingers), the superheroes are left scattered and in disarray, with no knowledge of where the Titan has gone or even what they should do next. Carol Danvers, summoned by a distress call from Nick Fury, manages to locate Stark and Nebula, who are stranded in space, and return them to Earth to take stock of the scope of the disaster. At the Avengers' compound, Rogers and Stark see each other for the first time in years:

> STARK: I couldn't stop him.
> ROGERS: Neither could I.
> STARK: I lost the kid.
> ROGERS: Tony, *we* lost.[3]

Despite the momentary catharsis of the reunion, Stark quickly returns to his grievances against Rogers, including not signing the Sokovian Accords and hiding the truth about the murder of Stark's parents. Eventually, drained physically and mentally by his ordeal, Stark collapses. While he convalesces, Nebula informs the others of Thanos' probable location: a garden planet where he can reflect on his work after its completion. The remaining superheroes travel there without delay, intending to take possession of the Infinity Stones and reverse Thanos' "Snap." What they find, however, is that the Titan has destroyed the Stones through their own power. "The work is done," he gloats, "It always will be. I am inevitable."[4] Furious at their failure, both at the end of *Avengers: Infinity War* and then on this new planet, Thor beheads Thanos, but even killing Death at this point does not change what occurred. Thanos' words are a potent and succinct rendering of the ineluctable truth of mortality: it is inevitable, and always will be.

As displayed above, the Daoist and Japanese philosophies would advocate acceptance of that fact for one's own peace of mind, but this is something the superheroes still cannot do. Five years pass, the film tells us, and in that time certain of the Avengers show a complete inability to adapt to their new circumstances. Thor, for instance, has succumbed to depression and alcoholism, becoming nearly obese as he secludes himself from the remaining Asgardian citizens he is supposed to lead. Clint Barton, driven mad by the loss of his entire family in the "Snap", carries out vicious vigilante murders against crime organizations around the world. On the other hand, some have created new lives, such as Stark, who marries Pepper Potts, moves with her to the country, and has a child. Others carry on in their own fashion, such as Romanoff, who still coordinates small-scale activities from the Avengers' compound. For his part, Rogers runs support groups for those dealing with the loss of loved ones, friends, and family, counseling them on how to move on after the tragedy.

Yet, when Rogers meets Romanoff at the Avengers' compound, he voices the opposite, and decidedly non-Daoist, sentiment. "You know," he tells her, "I keep telling people they should move on and grow. Some do. But not us."[5] Even in the face of the irrefutable power of Thanos, of Death and its undeniable victory, the superheroes cannot bring themselves to surrender completely.

They receive another chance to renew the fight when Scott Lang suddenly appears, having been trapped in the Quantum Realm at the time of the "Snap." When he is released, the five years have only passed as five hours due to the time-warping qualities of the Quantum Realm. He travels to the Avengers' compound and informs Romanoff and Rogers of a startling potential plan: use the Quantum Realm to travel back in time, acquire the Infinity Stones for themselves, and then reverse Thanos' "Snap" in the present. Doing so will require undertaking a perilous journey through otherworldly lands (the Quantum Realm and the past), as well as provoking terrible powers and entities, but the possibility of restoring the dead to life is too tantalizing for Rogers, Romanoff, and eventually all the other remaining superheroes (including Banner, Thor, and Stark) to resist.

The quest they plan—called a "Time Heist" in the film—follows a well-trod path in world mythologies. With its ultimate goal of solving the mystery of death and returning the perished to life, this journey through time and space closely resembles the motif of the hero's descent into the underworld to gain the favor of, commune with, or even reclaim the dead. For example, in a Hopi story, a curious young man gains the aid of a shaman who administers a "strong medicine" that enables the youth to visit the spirit land. There he sees masses of skeletons living in a giant house, crowded in the dark, subsisting on smoke. An arrangement is agreed upon where the dead provide rain and good crops in exchange for offerings of smoke from the living.[6] An Australian story of a man named Yawalngaru is in a similar vein, though the benefit he gains for his people comes at greater cost. Wondering what the land beyond this life, called "Bralgu," is truly like, Yawalngaru paddles his canoe past all known landmarks and boundaries, eventually arriving at the spirit world. He participates in the dances of the dead, learns their laws, and brings back many gifts, such as special spears and the first yams. Touched by the land of the dead, though, Yawalngaru himself dies only a few days after returning.[7]

We find an even closer analogy in the story of Gilgamesh, who, after seeing his best friend Enkidu die, longs only for the chance to escape that same, sad destiny. "Must I die too?" he laments. "Must I become as lifeless as Enkidu? How can I bear this sorrow that gnaws at my belly, this fear of death that restlessly drives me onward?"[8] Out of the forlorn hope that he could escape death, Gilgamesh goes in search of Utnapishtim, the only human the gods have ever made immortal. The king travels over mountains, deserts, and through the deep tunnels where the sun passes into the earth at night, emerging on the other end in a garden. There he finds the tavern-keeper Shiduri, who engages him in a debate that echoes the inner turmoil the MCU superheroes face early in *Avengers: Endgame*. Upon hearing of Gilgamesh's intent, Shiduri recognizes his grief, but advises him to focus on the daily joys of life rather than be overwhelmed by sorrow. "Savor your food," she says, "make each of your days a delight ... let music and dancing fill your house, love the child who holds your hand." Gilgamesh refuses to be mollified, responding, "What can your words mean when my heart is sick for Enkidu who has died?"[9]

The contrast between these sentiments closely approximates the tension Rogers articulates in the film, publicly telling people to "move on" and live their lives, but privately confiding with Romanoff that he, nor any of the other superheroes, can bear to follow their own advice. When Lang presents the second chance of the "Time Heist," the Avengers react just as Gilgamesh does, choosing to undertake a difficult journey with an improbable chance for success rather than admit that they are helpless before the power of death.

Within the story of Gilgamesh, however, defiance is ultimately not enough to defeat mortality. The king muscles his way onto Utnapishtim's boat and finds the recluse's island, but the old man is just as skeptical as Shiduri was of the practicality of the quest. However, he believes the gods may consider immortality for the king if he can pass the test of remaining awake for seven days in a row. As sleep is considered a relative of death in many cultures, staying awake for a prolonged period could be seen as a test for defeating death. Almost comically, exhausted by his journey, Gilgamesh falls asleep nearly at once and instead of remaining awake for seven days, he sleeps for that entire time. Once awake, he realizes his failure and cries out, "Death has caught me, it lurks in my bedroom and everywhere I look, everywhere I turn, there is death."[10] As a coda of further tragedy, Utnap-ishtim gives Gilgamesh the consolation gift of a flower that can rejuvenate an older person into a youth, but the king loses this boon as well when it is eaten by a snake. In ancient Mesopotamia, then, as voiced by the myth of Gilgamesh, the message seems clear: no matter the stature of the hero, whether belonging to royalty or even having a partly divine nature, and no matter the effort put forth, death comes for everyone.[11]

Sadly, myths of those travelling to the underworld to save anoth-er's life, rather than their own, often meet with no more success than Gil-gamesh. The Greek myth of Orpheus is one famous example. When the musician's wife, Eurydice, is killed by a snakebite, he travels to the land of Hades, using his musical charms to elicit sympathy first from Charon the ferryman, then Cerberus, the ferocious three-headed guard-dog, and finally Hades himself. He is granted permission to lead Eurydice out of the underworld on the condition that he not look back at her until they have fully emerged from the land of the dead. Tragically, a mix of suspicion and curiosity to know if Eurydice is truly behind him leads Orpheus to look back just steps before the threshold of the upper-world, only to see her van-ish before him.[12] For some interpreters, this ending to the myth exempli-fies the Greeks' understanding that death is a line that cannot be crossed, as well as their "realistic assessment of whether such romantic notions as Love (Eros) have the power to overcome Death (Thanatos)."[13]

Across cultures, there are many other stories uncannily similar to the Orpheus narrative. The Modoc of the Pacific Northwest tell of a man named Kumokum who travels to the land of the dead to bring back his daughter. Surrounded by the skeletons of the dead, the chief of the under-world, impressed by the man's bravery, allows him to take his daughter back, but he must not look at her until they have reached their village. At first, like Orpheus, Kumokum is patient, but he eventually violates the pro-hibition and looks on to find only a pile of bones.[14] In a story from the Ser-rano of California, a hunter who follows his deceased wife to the land of the dead is also allowed to bring her back, but only if they do not have inter-course for three nights. They dutifully abstain until the fourth night, but since time works differently in the underworld, they have miscalculated, and he awakens to find her gone.[15] Within Japanese mythology, Izanagi, one of the primordial pair who helps create the world, descends into the under-world to attempt to bring back his wife Izanami, who has died giving birth to the god of fire. She agrees to come back with him on the condition that he not look at her, but, unable to contain his impetuous curiosity, he shines a light on her and sees her body, decaying and crawling with maggots. Seething with embarrassment and betrayal, Izanami herself chases Izan-agi from the underworld, threatening that he must never return.[16] In a story that resonates with both the Orpheus and Gilgamesh myths, a narrative from the Yukon of Northwestern Canada describes a grieving husband asking the lord of the underworld, Tipiknits, to return his wife to the realm of the living. Tipiknits agrees, but only if the man can stay awake all night. He falls asleep just before dawn and finds a rotten log lying beside him instead of his wife. As if this ending were not heartbreaking enough, when the man is sent away with instructions that he must not share any of his underworld experiences lest he die as well, he immediately informs his fellow villagers, wishing to die and rejoin his wife without delay.[17]

The consistency of the imagery and the message across these stories from Mesopotamia, Greece, Japan, and North America is striking. Despite the relative benevolence of the figures of death involved (whether it is Utnapishtim, Tipiknits, Izanami, or Hades) and the willingness of that being to give the human in question an opportunity to overcome mortality, for himself or for another, the hero cannot accomplish such seemingly simple tasks as staying awake or not turning around. While there are potential explanations for the prohibitions or tests involved—for instance, sleep being related to death as a loss of consciousness or not looking back as a metaphor for not acknowledging or facing death—at a simpler level, it is merely human nature to be curious or to grow weary. By that logic, it is also merely human nature to die. None of this bodes well for the Avengers' "Time Heist" and, arguably, they are in a worse position than their mythic predecessors, for Thanos is not as agreeable as Tipiknits or Hades. One thus gets the sense from these other-world narratives that the MCU superheroes will not have an easy or painless journey as they attempt to outmaneuver death.

Still, the quests of certain other heroes around the world create a possible template for how the Avengers' gambit might succeed. One instance comes from Eastern Tibet, where one recension of the *Epic of Gesar*, the warrior-king and culture hero, tells of his success in rescuing his mother's soul from a torturous after-life in a Hell realm.[18] Elsewhere in Asia, the legendary Chinese Buddhist monk Mu-lien (a figure adapted from the Indian Buddhist character Maudgalyāyana), known for his supernatural powers, was thought also to have visited his mother in Hell. Using powers on loan from the Buddha, as well as a personal intervention from the Buddha himself, Mu-lien releases his mother, along with other prisoners of Hell, into higher rebirths as "hungry ghosts." To further assist his mother and other beings in this state, which is still a miserable existence, Mu-lien institutes a "ghost festival" at which Buddhists make offerings dedicated to assisting these creatures.[19] In European traditions, early and medieval Christian lore contained a fascinatingly comparable narrative termed (by the Catholic Council of Trent) the "*Decensus ad Inferos*," or "Descent into Hell," or sometimes "Harrowing of Hell." By this tradition, Jesus was thought to have descended into Hell during the period of time between the crucifixion and his resurrection. Upon this descent, it was imagined that he either preached to or even deliberately released the Hebrew patriarchs, prophets, and other worthy souls who had been languishing in Hell without the benefit of the incarnation.[20]

Another tale of a descent into the underworld and a resultant triumph over deaths occurs in Mayan mythology. In the epic *Popul Vuh*, the heroic twins Hunahpu and Xbalanque journey to the horrible underground realm of Xibalba to face the Lords of Death, who have mutilated, sacrificed, and buried both their uncle and father. "Xibalba" itself is a term that comes from the Mayan root "to fear" and the trip the twins take to reach that land—over "Scorpion Road," "Blood River," and through whirlwinds and parched deserts—lives up to the name, and also resembles the road that Mayan mythology believes every deceased person must walk.[21] The Lords of Death expect the twins to fail the same tests as their forbears and thus fall victim to the malign powers of Xibalba. Hunahpu and Xbalanque, however, are not fooled by mannequins the Lords of Death put in place of themselves, nor do the twins sit on a heated bench, and finally they are able to keep a torch and cigar lit all night, without burning out, by using fireflies and a macaw's tail feather to make each only seem as if it were burning.[22] After passing those tests, the twins also survive the horrors of the Razor House, the Fire House, and the Bat House, among other places of terror, where eponymous threats attempt to kill them. Hunahpu and Xbalanque then find a way to trick the Xibalbans into thinking that they can make a "deathless sacrifice" by killing a victim and immediately resurrecting him. The Lords of Death allow the twins to practice on them, but once they have killed the Xibalbans, the heroes refuse to perform the revivification ceremony. The horrible underworld is thus conquered and the twins are able to exact terms such that, from then on, only the wicked among humanity must go to suffer torment in Xibalba.[23]

Consequently, all these stories from around the world exist on a spectrum of varying motivations and degrees of success and failure, but they all speak to the desire to thwart death and the challenges involved in such an audacious ploy. This establishes the mythic precedent, peril, and scope of what the MCU superheroes profess to attempt in their "Time Heist" bid to rescue all those who died in Thanos' "Snap." On a smaller scale, the MCU superheroes have already accumulated experience in this kind of otherworldly journey. Stark, for example, passed through the Tesseract portal to a distant sector of space during *Marvel's The Avengers*. Thor, Banner, and Valkyrie traversed an especially violent spatial disturbance travelling from Sakaar to Asgard in *Thor: Ragnarok*. Finally, Hank Pym and

Scott Lang have both descended deep into the Quantum Realm on several occasions, the former with the express purpose of rescuing Janet Pym from that dimension in *Ant-Man and the Wasp*. Aside from these particularly intense instances, as discussed in Chapter One, the MCU superheroes navigate different realms and dimensions on a regular basis, as Ant-Man moves through the microverse, Doctor Strange projects his astral body, Thor crosses the Bifrost, and the Guardians of the Galaxy voyage between solar systems.

These tendencies perfectly position the MCU superheroes for the challenge of accessing the Infinity Stones across the gulf of space and time. These talents and capacities also bring them into even closer alignment with the cross-cultural religious virtuoso known as the "shaman," whose similarities to the superheroes we have been noting since Chapter One. In many cultures, as explained in Chapter One and also at the end of the previous chapter, making expeditions to the underworld or otherworldly realm of the spirits is the special province of the shaman, who through these repeated trips comes to, as Coulianu puts it, "know the geography of the land of the dead" and is thus the one charged with bringing back lost souls.[24] As both Eliade and Stutley observe in their comparative surveys on shamanism, during cases of prolonged illness, or premature or suspicious death, the shaman will be called upon to travel to the otherworld to investigate the circumstances surrounding the afflicted, with the hope of bringing him or her back to life.[25] A series of cases Eliade details from Siberia illustrate this template, relating how the shaman travels over vast territories of mountains, deserts, and steppes, crossing bridges no wider than a hair, to finally confront the king of the dead, Erlik Khan. The shaman will then face several tests and, if Erlik Khan is pleased, he or she will be allowed to leave with the soul of the person concerned. If not, the shaman may him or herself be forced to join the realm of the dead permanently.[26]

A Kwaikutl story about a shaman named "Only One" illustrates this same tension and theme. Acquiring his powers after encountering a potent spirit in a cave, Only One receives his name after being the "only one" of a group able to endure the physical torment and sickness the spirit metes out by way of initiation. Only One is then even able to combat death, rescuing many souls on behalf of his and neighboring villages. As he continues to reclaim souls from the land of the ghosts, the Chief of the Ghosts creates more and more obstacles, hoping to entrap him, but each time Only One escapes.[27]

Examining this story, as well as thinking through the observations of Eliade and other scholars, it is plain that certain figures and aspects of the journeys described earlier in this chapter also possess some of the attributes of the shaman's journey, or contain figures who could loosely be termed "shamans." For instance, in his work on the figure of Mu-lien, Stephen Teiser argues that his popularity is largely due to the fact of his blending of Buddhist concepts with the abilities and activities connected to Asian shamanism.[28] However, as the general concept of the arduous journey to the underworld or otherworld in the hopes of defeating death, for themselves or others, is a characteristically shamanic trope, it would place the previously discussed stories of Gilgamesh, Orpheus, Jesus, Hunahpu and Xbalanque, and Gesar under that categorical umbrella. In that way, the shamanic notion of otherworldly contest with death can be seen as a worldwide mythic motif.

With the parameters of that motif established, we can assess more clearly the extent to which the Avengers' "Time Heist" fits that template. First, the nature of the quest, being a trip through another dimension (the Quantum Realm, depicted as a series of swirling, winding tunnels) to the lost land of the past, mimics the trip of the shaman and other heroes to the otherworld of the dead. As the Avengers begin their journey, it is even visually shown as a descent, for the platform the superheroes stand on opens into a gaping hole, pulling them downwards into the twisting cacophony of the Quantum Realm. It is also worth mentioning that in some traditions, shamans are thought to be able to travel not just across space, but also time, moving through the past or even the future, as needed.[29]

Second, certain magical equipment is often required to make the journey to the underworld possible. To visit the land of Tipiknits, the Yukon hunter in search of his wife uses an enchanted rope, the young Hopi man curious about the land of the dead employs a special garment with an eagle feather, Siberian shamans off to face Erlik Khan bring drums, and the hero twins of the *Popul Vuh* bring along their gaming equipment for the sacred Mayan ball game as protection against the Lords of Death in Xibalba.[30] The Avengers, for their part, rely on technologies that, even in the twenty-first century, appear nearly as magical and fantastic. Vials of "Pym particles" control their descent into the Quantum Realm, a large platform with shimmering mirrors opens the portal, a "Time GPS" on each superhero's wrist calibrates their journey to the correct span in time, and a size-reducing suit compatible with the "Pym particles" directs their transit through the underworld-like dimension. Just as every shaman has magical implements to make their otherworldly voyages possible, so do the Avengers.

Additionally, as we have seen, the journey to the otherworld is usually portrayed as a grueling trek across varied, demanding, and desolate terrain or landscapes. Gilgamesh, it is said, crossed mountains, seas, and deserts, before finally racing his way through a tunnel into the depths of the earth to find Utnapishtim. Siberian shamans, Eliade reports, similarly travel over lengths of steppes and climb forbidding mountains to reach the

Hank Pym (Michael Douglas) travels through the mysterious and dangerous Quantum Realm, which will be the superheroes' treacherous gateway to the past during their Time Heist to acquire the Infinity Stones. From *Ant-Man and the Wasp* (2018).

abode of Erlik Khan. Likewise, Yawlngaru canoed across the ocean to reach the realm of the spirits and Hunahpu and Xbalanque made their way over the Scorpion Road, the River of Blood, and other frightful geographies to find Xibalba. The Avengers also face a challenging journey as the Infinity Stones are scattered across the galaxy. They must visit the rocky, barren crags and caves of Morag for the Power Stone, climb snowy, windblown cliffs for the Soul Stone on Vormir, extract the Reality Stone (in the form of the Aether) from Jane Foster on Asgard, and circumvent guards and other obstacles on Earth during the Battle of New York to obtain the Space, Mind, and Time Stones, respectively. When the Tesseract (which holds the Space Stone) initially slips from their grasp, their journey becomes even more perilous as the only option is to take a further detour into the past by travelling to 1970s New Jersey.

As that diversion suggests, as another commonality, just like shamans and the other heroic figures we analyzed, the Avengers face tests, obstacles, and guardians throughout their quest. For his chance to return Eurydice to life, Orpheus must pass by Charon, Cerberus, and, most importantly, Hades. The figure "Only One" and the Siberian shaman must respectively overcome the Ghost Chief and Erlik Khan to rescue lost souls, and the Mayan hero twins must defeat the Lords of Death in Xibalba through various ordeals and trickery. In the same way, each of the Infinity Stones is guarded in some fashion and buffered by obstacles that must be overcome.

To obtain the Mind Stone, Rogers must outwit Hydra operatives posing as SHIELD agents, then fight a version of himself from the past. The Power Stone on Morag is held within an energy field and Nebula melts her robotic hand in order to remove it. Afterward, she is caught by none other than the past version of Thanos himself, which will ultimately have grave consequences for the superheroes. After pulling the Aether/Reality Stone from Jane Foster, Rocket must escape pursuing Asgardian sentries, as must Rogers and Stark when they arouse the suspicion of military police at the New Jersey base. The Hulk, meanwhile, must convince an initially obstinate Ancient One to surrender the Time Stone, which she does only after a lengthy conversation. Finally, Barton and Romanoff face the Red Skull on Vormir, as well as the even more costly trials associated with the Soul Stone, which will be discussed further below.

Another aspect of the underworld journey that the MCU myth replicates is encounters with the dead during the voyage itself. These encounters tend to be of great personal significance to the hero involved and often create powerful motivating factors for the quest as a whole. In the *Odyssey*, the sorceress Circe tells Odysseus to travel to the underworld to see the blind soothsayer Tiresias, who will give him guidance in finding a path back to his home of Ithaca. After making the difficult trek and giving the requisite offerings, the shadowy spirits of the dead appear, including Tiresias, comrades from the Trojan War, but also Odysseus' mother Anticleia. Odysseus tells her of the trauma of his voyage home and she relates her death from grief as she waited, seemingly without end, for him to return. She also goes on to relate the sorrow of his father and the troubles his wife Penelope and son Telemachus confront with their home overrun by suitors looking to usurp Odysseus' place. In a last heartbreaking moment, they move to embrace one last time, but cannot as she is only a shade of who she was.[31] Virgil's *Aeneid*, an epic of the founding of Rome, draws explicitly on the *Odyssey*, partly by containing its own scene in the underworld, in which Aeneas seeks out his late father, Anchises. When they meet, Anchises instructs Aeneas in the wonder that will be Rome, stoking his drive to establish the great city, as he "led his son through each new scene and fired his soul with a love of glory still to come."[32]

The MCU's Avengers have their own motivational and cathartic encounters with the dead during their journey. Accompanying Rocket to the Asgard of the past, Thor suffers an emotional breakdown when he sees Frigga, his mother, who coincidentally will die that very day. As a magical practitioner, Frigga recognizes that her son is from the future and, based on his disheveled, overweight appearance, deduces that "the future has not been kind" to him.[33] They talk and as Frigga counsels him, she suggests he admit that he has been a failure, both in the first war with Thanos and also as a leader for the remaining Asgardians. However, she then says, "Everyone fails at who they're supposed to be, Thor. The measure of a person, of a hero, is how well they succeed at being who they are."[34] These words have a deep impact on Thor and, before leaving with Rocket, he tries to summon Mjolnir, which still exists during this period of time. When the hammer arrives—which proves that, despite his failure against Thanos, his depression, his alcoholism, and the depths to which he has fallen, he is still worthy of its power—Thor laughs and cries in joy.

Meanwhile, the New Jersey detour to locate the Tesseract/Space Stone brings Stark and Rogers into contact with people important to them who have also since died. First, while hiding from the military police, Rogers accidentally wanders into the office of Peggy Carter, his love interest from the 1940s, who died of old age during *Captain America: Civil War*. As she holds a conversation on the other side of a window, unaware of his presence, Rogers watches her and sees that she still keeps a framed picture of him from before his super-soldier procedure. He lingers for several moments in that space, obviously longing for the time he lost in the nearly seventy years spent frozen in the ice. At the same time, in the basement of the installation, Stark encounters his father, Howard. As it turns out, during this time period, Stark's mother is pregnant with him at that very moment. Paradoxically, the son (who adopts an assumed name to allay suspicion) gives parenting advice to his own father, including a phrase that he will eventually hear from his father:

> TONY STARK: [My father] did drop the odd pearl.
> HOWARD STARK: How so?
> TONY STARK: "No amount of money ever bought a second of time."
> HOWARD STARK: Smart guy.
> TONY STARK: He did his best.
> HOWARD STARK: I'll tell you, that kid's not even here yet and there's nothing I wouldn't do for him.[35]

Stark then embraces his father, telling him, "Thank you," achieving closure after many years of not having had the chance to say goodbye. While during their underworld journeys, Odysseus sees his mother's ghost and is spurred to greater effort to get back to Ithaca, and Aeneas visits his father's spirit and finds even more motivation to found the settlement of Rome, Thor, Rogers, and Stark all experience personal revelations and catharsis during their encounters with the dead.

Finally, one other sequence during the Avengers' "Time Heist" resonates powerfully with the theme of sacrifice found frequently across cultures in the otherworldly journeys of the shaman. On Vormir, as was the case with Thanos and Gamora, the Red Skull leads Barton and Romanoff to the edge of a cliff and informs them that for the Soul Stone to be obtained, "you must lose that which you love. A soul for a soul."[36] In Siberian mythology, to gain a soul's freedom from the prisons of Erlik Khan can involve costly sacrifices, even the location of a surrogate to take the place of the lost individual.[37] Among the Warao of Venezuela, it is also thought that in order for the shaman to save a soul from death, he must provide a substitute in its stead to appease the spirits of the underworld.[38] Barton and Romanoff find themselves in the same position: in order to bring back those dead in Thanos' "Snap," they need to acquire the Soul Stone, and that can only be done through a sacrifice. One or the other of them must be that sacrifice.

At first, Barton and Romanoff laugh uncomfortably about their situation. Eventually, Barton thinks they have agreed to let him jump to his death, but Romanoff shows that she is determined for the sacrifice to be her. They embrace, even touching foreheads, having shared years of friendship and comradery. Then, they fight, each trying to get to the precipice before the other. Ultimately, Romanoff outmaneuvers Barton and falls to her death, winning the Soul Stone for the Avengers.

Interestingly, for such close friends, this is the third fight between Barton and Romanoff during the course of the MCU myth, though each is unusual in its own way. The pair first battle in *Marvel's The Avengers* when Barton is under Loki's mind control, then face one another again on opposite sides during *Captain America: Civil War*. These previous circumstances do not involve any true animosity, and neither does the third in *Avengers: Endgame*. Indeed, it is quite the opposite: on Vormir, they fight against one another to save one another.

In this way, the struggle between Barton and Romanoff on Vormir stands in utter contrast to the dynamic of Thanos and Gamora in *Avengers: Infinity War*. As we saw in the previous chapter, when he realizes the Soul Stone can only be acquired by sacrificing a life, Thanos sheds a tear, but then relentlessly drags his adopted daughter, screaming and fighting, to the edge of the mountain and hurls her to the rocks below. Thanos, in his egotism, construes the death of another as a sacrifice on his part, which is made even more inscrutable by the fact that his "sacrifice" is intended to secure the means for the deaths of further trillions of beings across the universe. Barton and Romanoff, on the other hand, fight to restore those trillions of lives. From that premise, they could easily fight to throw one another off the precipice and rationalize it as a small price to pay for the greater good. That they do not shows their primary commitment is not, like Thanos, to personal ambition, but to the loftier goal that animates their quest, namely restoring life. Semiotician James Liszka has argued in his "transvaluation theory" that in such parallel moments in narratives, where situations and motivations mirror one another, as we have with the sequences on Vormir in *Avengers: Infinity War* and then *Avengers: Endgame*, observing the subtle (or not very subtle) alterations in action are prime opportunities to reveal the differing values of characters in a myth.[39] This is precisely what we find between Thanos and the MCU superheroes: the former is revealed as self-centered and prone to view others as objects and means to ends, while the latter are other-centered and view their comrades, and other creatures, as ends in themselves. These differences are, of course, implicit in other interactions throughout the films, but the varying way in which the characters deal with the trope of the shamanic sacrifice brings into relief Thanos' will to destroy and the Avengers' determination to protect. Anthony Mills makes the argument that the theology of "interrelationality" (that is, the turn towards others) characterizes comics in the period of Stan Lee. Though Mills only tangentially deals with the MCU (and only the films from Phase One, at that), this argument of "other-centeredness" clearly applies to the situation between Barton and Romanoff, helping to shed light on the actions of both characters in this instance, as well as the contrast they create with the motivations of their archrival Thanos.[40]

Through their own version of the shaman's underworld journey, the MCU superheroes thus acquire all the Infinity Stones from the past, though the experience was perilous and the cost high. Back at the Avengers' Compound, the superheroes create their own gauntlet and, with the Hulk wielding all the power of the combined Infinity Stones, they brave a massive burst of energy as the gamma-irradiated giant performs his own "Snap."

Outside the compound, however, events are unfolding against them as the manipulation of time through their Quantum Realm activities produces the unintended consequence of alerting the Thanos of the past to their Infinity Stone quest. After capturing the Nebula from the future on Morag, Thanos replaces her with his own still-loyal Nebula from the past. She infiltrates the superheroes' facility and enables Thanos' battleship to come through time and space to loom over the Avengers' Compound. Raining rockets and bombs down on the complex, the warship obliterates the buildings and Thanos himself takes up position among the rubble, setting the stage for a cataclysmic final battle for possession of the Infinity Stones, and thus mastery over the entire universe.

Due to its scope and the symbolism it employs, this climactic struggle in *Avengers: Endgame* resembles visions of apocalyptic battles imagined within certain world religions, particularly those in the Western tradition. Some Christian traditions place great emphasis on *Revelation*, the last text of the New Testament, which contains imagery of a final battle between the forces of God and Satan, Jesus and the Anti-Christ. At that time, great turmoil and devastation will arise, described (in part) this way: "[there were] great earthquakes, and the sun turned as black as dark sackcloth and the moon became like blood. The stars in the sky fell like unripe figs shaken loose from the tree in a strong wind. Then the sky was divided like a torn scroll curling up, and every mountain and island was moved from its place."[41] Elsewhere in the New Testament, the earlier *Gospel of Mark* also imagines an end of the world with the sun darkened, the moon blacked out, and the stars falling from the sky, as buildings and whole cities are toppled.[42]

Based on these scriptural passages, movements have emerged over time within Christianity (especially its more Evangelical branches) that focus on an apocalyptic timeline termed "Pre-millennialism." In this conception of the end of the world, those faithful to this vision of Christianity would first vanish from the Earth in an event termed the "Rapture," which is followed by a seven-year-reign of global terror by a Satanically-powered Anti-Christ. At the end of this "Tribulation" period (as it is called within the religious subculture), a bloody war of unprecedented proportions will occur, followed by the reappearance of Jesus, who will usher in a thousand-year period of peace, hence the "Pre-millennial" term.[43]

On the face of it, certain superficial similarities obtain between the Pre-millennial timeline and the events of *Avengers: Infinity War* and *Avengers: Endgame*. Popular Evangelical imaginings of the Rapture, for instance, suggest that at the moment of disappearance, chaos will ensue around the world as cars are left driverless, planes lose passengers and pilots, families see mothers or fathers or babies vanish, and so on.[44] These very kinds of scenes play out in the after-credits scenes of *Avengers: Infinity War*, as cars without drivers run onto sidewalks, a pilotless helicopter crashes into a building, and people throughout the world turn to dust. From this point, an interregnal period roughly commensurate to the Tribulation (five versus seven years) takes place, followed by the final battle at the end of *Avengers: Endgame*.

On the other hand, there are also significant differences between the two visions. Those taken in Thanos' "Snap" are randomly selected and killed, not assumed into heaven as a divinely chosen few. Furthermore, the five-year interval after the "Snap," though challenging for the Earth and other populations around the universe, is not marked by the rise of an Anti-Christ figure, nor is the final battle the moment for the arrival of a single salvific entity who rescues the superheroes. Therefore, though the timeline of events for the concluding chapters of the MCU myth have very rough similarity to the Pre-millennial Christian vision of the end of the world, there are also even more compelling differences.

It is also important to note that Christian apocalypticism, whether Pre-Millennial or otherwise, has deep historical roots in preceding Western traditions. The imagery of *Revelation* and the *Gospel of Mark* stems in large part from language and terms in the Hebrew scriptures referring to the "Day of the Lord," when God would reward the faithful and punish the wicked. During this event, as the Christian New Testament also attests, there would be earthquakes, the blotting out of the sun and moon, and also the raising of the dead for a final judgment.[45] Even more proximate to the early Christian period, the Essene community of Qumran, who composed the texts known as the "Dead Sea Scrolls," further embellished this imagery and created detailed visions of a final battle between darkness and light, on both the earthly and cosmic scale.[46]

The Jewish and Essene concepts of the "Day of Lord" have their own historical roots, however, primarily in preceding Zoroastrian mythology from ancient Persia. Substantial historical evidence suggests ancient Persian influence on Judaism during the period of the "Babylonian captivity" and the much older Zoroastrian model of the end times, complete with a titanic final battle between the forces of good and evil, contains all of the building blocks of apocalyptic thought found in later Jewish and Christian traditions.[47] In the Zoroastrian version of the final confrontation at the end of days (called "Frashokereti" within the tradition), the sky will darken, the stars and sun will disappear, the earth will quake, and rivers of molten lava will spew forth from the ground. All the dead who have ever lived will be resurrected to take their place, based on the choices they made during their lifetimes, among the forces of either Angra Mainyu, the pernicious lord of evil, or Ahura Mazda, the god of light, purity, and good. In the ensuing battle, the forces of evil, including all its minions and human followers, will be consumed in the boiling lava, destroyed for all time, and the assembled devotees of good will inherit the cosmos.[48]

Outside the Western context, one also finds end of the world narratives in other cultures. Hinduism, for instance, has a tradition in the *Purāṇa* literature that the last manifestation of the god Viṣṇu in the world will be the form called "Kalkin." Riding astride a white horse, he will slaughter and destroy all the evildoers on the earth, cleansing the cosmos of immorality and licentiousness. In other Hindu versions of the end, destruction occurs on an even more cosmic scale, where Viṣṇu and/or Śiva will kindle a fire that dissolves the entire universe into boiling flames.[49] In Scandinavia, Norse mythology tells of the "Doom of the Gods," otherwise known as "Ragnarök," which in this context is even more extensive in its destruction than the MCU film of the same name. The original Norse version begins with the gradual deterioration of human existence into war, strife, famine, and cold, until a giant wolf swallows the sun and moon, while monsters, like the giants and the Midgard serpent, kept chained until this point, break loose to wreak havoc. As with other myths we have examined, the earth will then quake and the stars will fall from the sky. Odin, Thor, Heimdall, and the other gods will face the monsters, killing them, but also dying themselves in the process, before fire consumes the world. On a hopeful concluding note, after Ragnarök, the earth will be reborn, with life springing anew as another sun appears.[50]

The MCU's final battle with Thanos adopts many of the characteristics in the preceding mythic conceptions of a calamitous, end-of-times war. For example, when Thanos' battleship initially appears, it is a bright day, with the sun shining from a clear blue sky. After the missiles and bombs strike, the earth shakes, buildings are toppled, and the smoke and soot cover the sky, blotting out the sun. The forces of good and the forces of evil then assemble on opposing lines across the barren landscape, underneath this desolate sky. At first, it is only Stark, Rogers, and Thor against Thanos and the Titan's strength proves too much for even these three powerful Avengers to stop. Thanos then chooses to reveal the full measure of his might, calling down the entire army of Outriders, Chitauri, Leviathans, Children of Thanos, as well as other soldiers and beasts not seen yet in the MCU. As Rogers, the only superhero of the three left standing, braces for a hopeless fight against these legions, voices across his intercom and magical portals opening behind him show that the Avengers' own "Snap" has worked: all the people reduced to dust five years earlier have returned to life, and now the lost superheroes have gathered on the field to battle Thanos' forces. Over the following moments, the armies of Asgard, Kamar-taj, and Wakanda assemble alongside the other revived superheroes (including Spider-Man, Winter Soldier, Drax, Peter Quill, Wanda Maximoff, and many others). Just as found in Zoroastrian, Jewish, and Christian visions of the apocalypse, the dead on both sides (as the Children of Thanos were also all killed in the previous timeline) have returned to life and taken their place with either the forces of evil or the powers of good to enter into one last, massive battle.

That battle proceeds to sway back and forth as first one side, then the other gains advantage. Despite the staggering size of both armies and the punishment they inflict upon one another, the struggle devolves primarily into a contest between Thanos and a few select superheroes over possession of the Infinity Gauntlet. Though it appears the Titan has finally gained a hold on the glove, leading him to once again gloat that he is "inevitable," he is dismayed to find that Stark has tricked him. During their struggle, Stark removed the Infinity Stones and placed them on his armor. With another "Snap," even though the energy released kills him, Stark uses the Infinity Stones to wipe out Thanos and every last member of his army and minions. This act of self-sacrifice not only wins the battle for the superheroes, but by showing the utter elimination of the entire arrayed forces of evil, it also fulfills Zoroastrian, Jewish, Christian, Hindu, and Norse conceptualizations of the end battle as the moment when the powers of wickedness would be defeated and destroyed, once and for all.

In a fashion similar to ancient Western apocalyptic narratives, beneath a sun blocked out by smoke and ruin, the resurrected superheroes and their allies face the forces of evil in a final battle. From *Avengers: Endgame* (2019).

Stark's self-sacrifice also aligns closely with the shamanic journey the MCU superheroes have been travelling since gaining their powers in Phase One of the Marvel mythology. Prior to the beginning of the main battle, when Thanos confronts Rogers, Stark, and Thor, he taunts the three Avengers, telling them, "You could not live with your own failure. Where did that bring you? Back to me."[51] In a literal sense, this comment reflects the way the "Time Heist" has inadvertently brought their archenemy back into the fold. Taken in a more figurative manner, however, and with the further understanding of Thanos' function in the MCU as an allegorical figure for death, the Titan's taunt reveals the way in which the shaman, or any religious virtuoso, as the mediator between humanity and the force of the sacred, is on the frontline of the confrontation between humanity and its greatest enemy: Death. For the shaman and other religious specialists, all roads lead to death. As noted in Chapter One, this collision is preordained, as both the shaman and the MCU superhero partake in initiation rites symbolic of death and rebirth, meaning that they are forever marked by and drawn to death. During *Avengers: Infinity War*, Doctor Strange foresees this very outcome, using the Time Stone to look ahead to all possible futures. In order to save Stark's life and presumably allow him to later sacrifice it to ultimately defeat Thanos, Strange surrenders the stone to the

Tony Stark (Robert Downey, Jr.), having taken the Infinity Stones from Thanos, prepares to sacrifice his life to save the universe from death (Thanos). To Thanos' line "I am inevitable," he responds, "And I am Iron Man." From *Avengers: Endgame* **(2019).**

Titan. At the final battle in *Avengers: Endgame*, Strange gives Stark a signal referring back to this exchange and the Iron Man wrests the Infinity Stones away. Unaware of the theft, Thanos smugly declares, "I am inevitable," to which Stark, glowing and crackling with the uncontrollable energy, haltingly retorts, "And ... I am ... Iron Man."[52] His body unable to endure the surge of energy released, Stark, having killed the personification of Death, dies himself, confronting the mortality that has haunted him since his captivity in the cave where the "Iron Man" persona was born.

As much as this conclusion to the MCU myth creates a fascinating paradox about the nature of death, which we shall explore shortly, the final chapter of the twenty-two-film narrative is as personal as it is philosophical. As such, it also focuses intently on resolving the dilemmas and conflicted personalities—in short, the liminality—faced by most of the mythos' characters. For example, Nebula, who has dealt throughout the series with profound issues of self-loathing, is able to quite literally destroy her old self, using a blaster during the final battle to kill the version of herself from the past. Clint Barton's tension between family life and superhero duty, first introduced in *Avengers: Age of Ultron* and revisited at later points, achieves equilibrium once his family is resurrected in *Avengers: Endgame*. Natasha Romanoff, called the "Black Widow" due to her previously nefarious and murderous ways, first joins the Avengers due to having a kind of "red in her ledger," that is, a moral debt or imbalance that she wanted to wipe clean. Through her actions as an Avenger and a superhero, she is able to partly atone for these past deeds, but her conscience only rests, it appears, once she makes a final sacrifice on Vormir.

The changes are perhaps even more dramatic for the other superheroes. Originally averse to even saying the name "Hulk" in *The Incredible Hulk* and *Marvels' The Avengers*, Bruce Banner is shown as in perpetual conflict with his violent alter ego, to the point where the Hulk refuses to let Banner resurface during the two years from *Avengers: Age of Ultron* to *Thor: Ragnarok*. Then, vacillating to the opposite extreme, the Hulk rejects all pleas to manifest during the battles in *Avengers: Infinity War*. During the hiatus between Thanos' "Snap" and the events of *Avengers: Endgame*, Banner and the Hulk achieve a kind of détente where the intellect of the former coexists in the body of the latter. He explains the situation to his friends this way: "For years I've been treating the Hulk like he's some kind of disease, something to get rid of. But then I started looking at him as the cure. Eighteen months in the Gamma Lab, I put the brains and the brawn together and now look at me: Best of both worlds."[53] No longer a human and a monster struggling to coexist, Banner and the Hulk now occupy the same body harmoniously, their simmering category crisis finally resolved.

Though he still possesses certain problems of identity himself, Thor also makes peace with issues that had been festering in his life since the character's introduction in Phase One. Caught between the worlds of Asgard and Earth and buckling under the weight of his father's legacy, Thor takes his mother's advice, given during their encounter during the "Time Heist," and decides to aspire to be the person he is, rather than live the life into which he has been pressured. As a result, he relinquishes leadership of New Asgard to Valkyrie and goes off to chart his own path. Arguably, Thor's is the saddest character arc out of the Avengers, if not the entire complement of MCU superheroes as, during the course of the mythos' development, he has lost his mother, father, brother, close comrades, and the land he knew as home.

Steve Rogers has also been caught in unfortunate circumstances, though in his case it is as a result of being displaced in time. His self-sacrifice in 1945 led to a reawakening seventy years later in a world he did not recognize where almost everyone he knew was dead. This status frequently put Rogers out of step with those around him during the course of the MCU narrative. During the "Time Heist" detour to 1970, seeing his lost love, Peggy Carter, only intensified the feeling of loss that had continually haunted him. Rogers volunteers for the task of returning the Infinity Stones to their rightful temporal locations, but when the time to return arrives, he instead chooses to remain in the past. Having accomplished his task regarding the stones, he returns to the 1940s to dance with Peggy Carter, as he promised he would in *Captain America: The First Avenger*, and live out his natural life from that point forward. The rupture in time that cleaved Steve Rogers/Captain America into a temporally-confused and confusing figure thus resolved, he reappears to his waiting friends as an elderly, happy man.

Tony Stark also achieves a peaceful, happy family life, but it primarily occurs during the five-year interval, where he marries Pepper Potts and has a daughter, Morgan. Initially, protecting this new domestic world outweighs the prospect of returning to the Avengers to participate in the "Time Heist," but the thought of restoring the lives of those unfairly taken, like his mentee Peter Parker, draws him in regardless. Ultimately, this leads to his death in the final battle of *Avengers: Endgame*, but as noted above, death has been stalking him, as it has the entire MCU, since the Phase One of the mythic narrative. From the moment he emerged from the cave in Afghanistan, Stark, like all the other MCU superheroes in their own ways, was privileged with power but also cursed by instability. In his case, that came from being both human and machine at once. In *Avengers: Infinity War* and *Avengers: Endgame*, Death (in the person of Thanos) has finally caught up to them, and Stark in particular. Thanos' goading declaration—"I am inevitable"—stands as an obvious expression of the remorseless, unavoidable nature of death, but Stark's response—"And I am Iron Man"—hits multiple registers. It not only represents the film series coming full circle, as these were the character's last words in the very first MCU film (*Iron Man*), but at a higher level, it also defiantly asserts individuality and identity in the face of the impersonal depredation of death.

This is the previously referred to paradox of death: even while killing Death, Stark dies, showing that death both can and cannot be defeated. By invoking and navigating that tension, the MCU myth taps into and channels themes found in some of humanity's oldest stories. For instance, as we saw previously in the Mayan *Popul Vuh*, the hero twins Hunahpu and Xbalanque descend to the terrible realm of Xibalba to rescue their father and uncle. Despite destroying the Lords of Death, however, they cannot resurrect either person; reviving them, even with all of their other supernatural powers, is still out of their grasp. Instead, all they can do is ensure that "their names will not be lost."[54] Gilgamesh, too, faces this dilemma, for in the wake of his quest's failure, he knows death is not far off. At first despondent, upon returning to Uruk, Gilgamesh then notices the city's imposing walls, its great temple, its orchards and gardens, and all the other wonders he has built in his time as king. The reader is left to wonder if perhaps Gilgamesh has had an epiphany, realizing that even if he cannot live on, perhaps the works he leaves behind will.[55]

Stark's positioning in the MCU mirrors both of these mythic responses to mortality. In the first instance, like the Mayan myth suggests, one way to escape death is for our names, our reputations to live on and be remembered by those around us. Stark draws on this as he declares, "And I am Iron Man," invoking a name that has (within the MCU's world, at least) achieved global fame. Additionally, rather than the orchards, temples, or massive city walls of which Gilgamesh can boast, the legacy of Tony Stark is more visible in the final tribute shown in the later moments of *Avengers: Endgame*. As almost all of the superheroes of the MCU stand assembled, Pepper Potts presents Stark's first chest-piece, emblazoned with the words "Proof That Tony Stark Has a Heart." Originally forged in desperation in the darkness of a cave many years earlier, the chest-piece now floats down the water in front of just a few of the individuals his life has touched.

As part of this memorial ceremony, Stark's immediate family and closest friends view a holographic message the Avenger recorded prior to embarking on the "Time Heist." The message is significant for understanding the shift Stark has undergone from his introduction in *Iron Man* to the end of the MCU myth in *Avengers: Endgame* and is worthwhile to quote in its near entirety:

> Everybody wants a happy ending. Right? But it doesn't always roll that way. Maybe this time. I'm hoping if you play this back, it's in celebration. I hope families are reunited, I hope we get it back and something like a normal version of the planet has been restored, if there ever was such a thing…. So I thought I better record a little greeting, in the case of an untimely death, on my part. I mean, not that death at any time isn't untimely. This time travel thing we're going to try and pull off tomorrow, it's got me scratching my head about the survivability of it all. Then again that's the hero gig. Part of the journey is the end.[56]

As this statement attests, Stark is not the same self-centered, egotistical, narcissist that Rogers once commented, early in their friendship, would not be the one to "make the sacrifice play."[57] Quite clearly, based on the travails he has faced through his time as a superhero, he has contemplated and even accepted his potential and actual mortality, putting it into the context of what his life has achieved and the greater balance of what it means to be a hero or, in other words, what it means to be related to and in the service of others. Arguably, the Iron Man suit and its related technologies, from their first iteration in *Iron Man* and thereafter, were a literal and figurative shield or barrier between Stark and his own mortality. By the time of *Avengers: Endgame*, as evidenced by the message left behind for his loved ones, he has shed that barrier and confronted the inevitability (as Thanos would put it) of his death. Significantly, even as he faces the Titan in those final moments and uses the technology of his armor to hold the Infinity Stones, he does not employ his helmet, confronting Thanos—confronting Death—barefaced and clear-eyed.

In so doing, these events call to mind the metaphor of "microscopes" and "telescopes" used by Wendy Doniger to describe how myths, through the focus on the experience of one individual (the narrow lens of the microscope), can sharpen the image of a grander, more remote and even overwhelming universal truth (the wider lens of the telescope). She writes, "In great myths, the microscope and the telescope together provide a parallax that allows us to see ourselves in motion against the stream of time, like stars viewed from two different ends of the earth's orbit, one of the few ways to see the stars move."[58] Through the MCU's depiction of Stark's choice to accept death, we see the evolution of one person portrayed against the backdrop of the universal, unavoidable truth of human mortality.

Just as it has with all the other MCU superheroes, Death has hunted Stark throughout his years as a superhero. In response, Stark shows increasing courage and humanity during those years until, as a stand-in for the rest of his comrades, Death finally claims him. However, in doing so, the mythic paradox of death means that even as he died, like the father and uncle of the hero twins and Gilgamesh before him, Stark thwarts death by becoming immortal in the memories and lives of his loved ones and all those he has touched. In its concluding film, the MCU mythos, like so many world mythologies and narratives before, simultaneously shows and comforts us that while death may be inevitable, what one does in life and how one meets its end, matters most of all.

Conclusion

A Myth for This (and Every) Age

What is transmitted across the mental ether is therefore not dreams but myths, composed of individual human experience and art. Myths reflect our desire to believe that people really can dream the same dream, a desire that is a hope—a dream, if you will—that we all share.
—Wendy Doniger (O'Flaherty), *Other People's Myths: The Cave of Echoes*, p. 164

Part of the journey is the end.
—Tony Stark (played by Robert Downey, Jr.), *Avengers: Endgame* (2019)

In July 2019, Marvel Studios released *Spider-Man: Far from Home*, the twenty-third film in the MCU franchise and the first since the events of *Avengers: Endgame*. Lingering outside of the events of the prior three phases, but also not quite constituting the beginning of a new phase, the film occupies something of an ambiguous narrative territory. Its events briefly deal with the aftermath of Thanos' "Snap," as well as the Avengers' revival of those claimed in that catastrophe. The deaths of other super-heroes, especially Tony Stark as Peter Parker's mentor, also receive atten-tion. The main action of the film concerns Parker's increasing acclimation to the role of Spider-Man in the midst of the challenges posed by Quen-tin Beck, also known as "Mysterio," a technology expert who uses holo-graphic projections to generate simulated threats, which he then pretends to defeat. Beck deceives Parker into turning over a critical piece of the late Stark's technology, and the remainder of the film involves Spider-Man attempting to retrieve it and reveal Mysterio's illusions. Given Beck's appropriation of what was originally superhero technology, as well as the prevailing atmosphere of deceit and deception, the film aligns in import-ant ways with the impurity theme we discussed in Chapter Three as prevalent in multiple sequel films, particularly in the Phase Two, of the MCU.

At any rate, having garnered over one billion dollars worldwide, *Spider-Man: Far from Home* shows the staying power and lasting appeal of the MCU even outside the preceding Avengers and Infinity Saga storylines.[1] The same month as the release of *Spider-Man: Far from Home*, Marvel Studios head Kevin Feige announced a slate of upcoming films for the Phase Four of the MCU, as well as a plethora of other media projects. In Feige's words, these ventures are entirely "about the new," emphasizing new characters, new looks at a few old characters, and, through increasing diversity, new potential audiences.[2] The newly announced films include *Black Widow, The Eternals, Doctor Strange in the Multiverse of Madness, Shang-Chi and the Legend of the Ten Rings*, and *Thor: Love and Thunder*. Keeping with Feige's focus on breaking new territory with the Phase Four, and presumably projects thereafter, even the films containing previously released characters will contain new twists. Reportedly, *Black Widow* will provide fresh insight into Natasha Romanoff's character through events set prior to *Avengers: Infinity War, Doctor Strange in the Multiverse of Madness* may serve as Marvel's "first horror" movie, and in *Thor: Love and Thunder*, Jane Foster will take up the role of Thor.[3] On the other hand, *The Eternals,* dealing with a group of beings created in the distant past of the MCU, and *Shang-Chi and the Legend of the Ten Rings*, a film focused on a martial-arts character, represent entirely different directions for the franchise. Added to this are a variety of projects in the media of television mini-series concentrating on the new adventures of old characters (such as *Falcon and the Winter Soldier* and *Hawkeye*), but also figures entirely new to the MCU, including *Moon-Knight, She-Hulk,* and *Ms. Marvel*.[4]

Even with proposed plans for sequels to *Black Panther, Captain Marvel,* and a *Guardians of the Galaxy Vol. 3*, as the comments by Feige and the slew of announced projects suggest, the MCU is moving into territories and directions it has not previously explored. This includes the potential addition of popular, long-running characters from the Marvel Comics tradition who have to this point not been part of the MCU due to copyright issues, such as the "Fantastic Four" and the mutant "X-Men," both of which have served as part of their own independent film series, with varying degrees of success.[5] Additionally, due to ongoing and tangled negotiations between Marvel and Sony Pictures, the corporation which owns the rights to Spider-Man, the Summer and Fall of 2019 saw a veritable roller-coaster of uncertainty about what part the character would play (if any) in future MCU films, demonstrating just how much vagueness still remains as to the form and content of future Phases of the franchise.[6] As an aside, it is interesting to consider how issues of copyright and corporate ownership of characters, if projected into the past, would have influenced or even nullified ancient myths, such as the Homeric epics, the Hindu *Rāmāyaṇa* and *Mahābhārata*, Buddhist scriptures, and many, many others which extensively borrowed characters and even entire narratives from preexisting sources. The capitalistic notion that a corporation can own a mythic character is, for good or ill, a clear and present distinction between ancient and modern mythologies. At any rate, with the movement to a Phase Four, the MCU will transition to a new era, as confirmed by the screenwriters of *Avengers: Endgame*, who referred to that film as "definitely the end" of all that had preceded it and a concluding chapter to a complete, twenty-two film narrative.[7] *Avengers: Endgame* thus marks the end of the first era of the MCU and a send-off for its initial cohort of main characters.

Speaking from the point of view of the overarching narrative, then, with the Avengers' defeat of Thanos, as described in the previous chapter, the old generation of superheroes steps aside, and a new complement takes their place. As with so much else in the MCU, there are mythic precedents and overtones to this transition. Just as the Vedic gods (such as Agni, Indra, and Varuṇa) made way for the classical gods of Hinduism (such as Viṣṇu, Śiva, Kriṣṇa, and Devī), or after Ragnarök the perished deities of Odin, Thor, Heimdall, and others are succeeded by a new generation, the old superheroes of the MCU hand down their places to a class of descendants. At the end of *Avengers: Endgame*, Steve Rogers bequeaths his shield to Sam Wilson, conferring upon him the title of "Captain America," *Spider-Man: Far from Home* shows Peter Parker as the technological successor of Tony Stark, and in the forthcoming *Thor: Love and Thunder*, Jane Foster will take over as Thor. At the end of the twenty-two films, the passing of a mythic age is marked also by the passing of the torch.

Additionally, in a style similar to other mythic narratives such as the *Mahābhārata*, the Christian book of *Revelation*, the Aboriginal Australian stories of the Dreamtime, or even Tolkien's *Lord of the Rings*, the MCU narrative demarcates the end of this mythic age through a cataclysmic battle. Whereas the *Mahābhārata* marks the transition from one age (*yuga*) to another via the Kurukṣetra War of the Pāṇḍavas and Kauravas, *Revelation* describes the coming of the Millennium after Armageddon, the Aboriginal Dreamtime comes to an end with the Battle of Uluru, and the Third Age of Middle-Earth concludes with the War of the Ring, the MCU's Phase Three ends in the Infinity War with Thanos, concluded in the ruins of the Avengers' compound in *Avengers: Endgame*.[8]

Although the details and content of Phase Four movies are still subject to a great deal of speculation, the announced topics display a tendency also found in world religions toward filling in gaps in the biographical span of a character or the course of mythic history in general. Due to the character's death in *Avengers: Endgame*, the film *Black Widow* will almost certainly take place prior to those events, purportedly describing the unexplored period of time Romanoff spent fleeing from authorities after the superhero/ superhero struggle in *Captain American: Civil War.*[9] By covering a period in the distant past of the MCU, *The Eternals* stands to fill in gaps of cosmic significance and scope in the greater history of the superhero universe. One finds the same drive to fill in narrative gaps in various world religions, particularly those with stories of a founder, such as Christianity and Buddhism. In the former, several apocryphal texts cover incidents not found in the canonical scriptures, including childhood and youth.[10] In Buddhism, there is a tradition of stories known as the "*Jātaka* tales," which recount Siddhartha Gautama's past lives and attempt to shed light through those births on aspects of his Buddhahood.[11] Though the MCU has set films in the past for previous Phases (such as *Captain America: The First Avenger* and *Captain Marvel*), these were origin stories meant to establish a superhero for modern events. With these Phase Four films, not to mention its slate of television programs, which similarly aims to fill in gaps and lacuna in the tapestry of the myth so far, the MCU exhibits this same tendency found in world religions.

Owing partly to correspondences such as the foregoing and those chronicled throughout the preceding chapters of this book, I have argued that the MCU echoes mythic and religious narratives throughout world traditions. Due to the interconnection of its twenty-two films into one coherent story, as well as its treatment of timeless human themes—such as the shadow-self and the monster, the ambiguity of the sacred through superhero liminality, and, not least of all, the terror of human mortality—the MCU deserves the status of modern mythology. To prove these premises, over the course of the book we have followed how the themes, characters, and events of the franchise's films parallel and resonate with mythic and religious narratives from regions such as Greece, Mesopotamia, India, China, Egypt, and North, South, and Mesoamerica, as well as the traditions of Christianity, Judaism, Islam, Buddhism, Hinduism, and Daoism, among others. With connections and resemblances this broad and deep, the MCU's foundation in the world's traditions of mythic narrative is evident.

As discussed in the introduction to this work, to this point the prevailing interpretation of the MCU has been political, seeing the films as a statement on the events of 9/11 and the ongoing, so-called "War on Terror."[12] Elements of these political overtones are undoubtedly present and can be found in moments such as Stark's struggles against terrorists in Afghanistan (*Iron Man*), the degree to which the Chitauri attack on New York visually resembles 9/11 (*Marvel's The Avengers*), the Mandarin's rhetoric (*Iron*

Man 3), and the explicit reference to the villain Ronan as a fundamental-ist and terrorist (*Guardians of the Galaxy*). Yet, taken in context with the entire twenty-two films, these moments are relatively infrequent and are often even undermined within their respective narratives. For example, it is revealed that the true villain in *Iron Man* is Obadiah Stane, an Ameri-can arms-profiteer who serves as Tony Stark's shadow-self. In *Iron Man 3*, a similar trick is played, with the Mandarin and his incendiary speeches exposed as the cover for the actual enemy, Aldrich Killian. While the themes of 9/11 and terrorism are present in some aspects of the MCU, they are primarily the background and veneer for themes extending far deeper into the well-spring of world religions and mythologies.

Having thus completed a study that analyzes the films from that van-tage, we can also take stock of how it relates to the wider field of Religious Studies. First, by showing how the MCU can be broadly and extensively sit-uated among the world's mythic and religious traditions, it demonstrates the validity of the study of popular culture in Religious Studies. On this point, Bruce David Forbes, in the introduction to an edited volume on reli-gion and popular culture in America, has written the following:

> Approaching the study of religion through popular culture can help us learn more about widespread perceptions of religion, and the role religion plays in the everyday lives of people. The analysis of popular culture also can provide insights about how reli-gions change and are changed by the cultures that surround them.[13]

At times, however, some scholars in Religious Studies, such as David Chidester, have also critiqued or at least strongly cautioned against consid-ering popular culture phenomena within the context of the field.[14] Often this evaluation characterizes popular culture tropes, when they abut or resemble mythic or religious tropes, as purely imitative rather than origi-nal. On that point, Catherine Albanese, for instance, has written that "pop-ular culture always pieces and patches together its universe of meaning, appropriating terms, inflections, and structurations from numerous over-lapping contexts and using them as so many *ad hoc* tools to order and express."[15] Rather than myths unto themselves, this perspective interprets popular culture as, at most, echoes of what has come before.

To an extent, this admittedly applies to the MCU as certain charac-ters and names (including Thor and even Thanos) were pulled directly from preexisting traditions. On the other hand, it is important to consider the consequences of disqualifying or relegating to a lesser status those phe-nomena that borrow or echo preexisting traditions. Indeed, if this were implemented throughout the field, we ought to be prepared for the top-ics relevant to our studies to decrease dramatically. The Hebrew Bible, for example, draws extensively on Mesopotamian mythology, and the

Christian scriptures in turn echo the Hebrew Bible. In the Mediterranean, Homer pulled from older myths, and Virgil then built on Homer's work. In India, there was close interconnection and borrowing between Hindu and Buddhist traditions, in China the same relationship obtained between Buddhism, Daoism, and Confucianism, and so forth around the world. Mythic, religious, and literary traditions have always been enmeshed in webs of dialogue, borrowing, and interaction, laterally between one another and diachronically with older traditions, as observed by literary scholars such as Mikhail Bakhtin and Harold Bloom. The former championed the concept of the "dialogic" as a way of understanding multiple forms of communication, while the latter argued that almost all literary works should be considered products of "belatedness," or a reaction to preceding works and schools of thought.[16]

Mythic and religious traditions throughout history have always dwelt in overlapping contexts and appropriated terms, piecing together new significations and structures from what came before. The MCU is no different, adapting the symbolism and role of the shaman, the morphology of the monster, the terror of death, and the other themes we have discussed, and portraying them to audiences with, instead of characters like Gilgamesh, Arjuna, or Glooscap, the superheroes Iron Man, Captain America, the Hulk, and others. This fits the stipulation of some scholars, such as Henry Murray, who have argued that new mythologies are possible, "provided these are comparable in certain essential respects to mythologies of ancient origin."[17] As we have seen, this is certainly the case, but it only captures a portion of the mythic process at work. The MCU has both echoed previous mythic forms along the lines of what Murray and others suggest, but also re-envisioned these older forms into new situations, adapting ancient myths and questions for modern times and audiences. The characters and figures of the MCU face issues and struggles that are ancient, yet they are also certainly different and reflective of contemporary society (i.e., Tony Stark's mediation of humanity and technology, or Bruce Banner's monstrosity as an after-effect of radiation). Analyzing the popular culture form of the MCU within the field of Religious Studies helps us to reveal these dynamics and facts.

A second key contribution of this study is its use of wide-ranging comparison to put the MCU into the broader context of world narrative traditions. Broad comparison provides the opportunity to discern the larger patterns that connect those traditions, which William Paden has called the "templates for insight into human world-making."[18] As with the relevance of popular culture for Religious Studies, the method and even the viability of comparison has been a simmering controversy in the field. In a landmark essay, Jonathan Z. Smith famously called the comparative enterprise in Religious Studies an exercise in "homeopathy" or "contagion" that thrives on abstracted similarities that exist only in the eye of the beholder.[19] Comparison, however, as pointed out by Oliver Freiberger, is cognitively unavoidable, as our minds operate by classifying, constructing categories, and otherwise sorting like from unlike.[20] It is not a matter, therefore, of whether one does comparison in the study of Religious Studies, but what kind of comparison one undertakes. In this work, I have used comparison to reveal the "templates of insight," as Paden refers to them, which run through the MCU, uniting and putting it in conversation with other world mythic and religious traditions.

Finally, a consideration of the mythic import behind the MCU at least allows us to speculate that the source of its tremendous global popularity might be found in its deep roots in and resemblances to classic narratives, as well as its evocation of timeless questions of human experience. It is possible, as some have argued, that the reason for the preeminence of superheroes can be found in wish fulfillment, the comforting duality of right and wrong, or nostalgia for simpler times.[21] We must ask ourselves, though, if any of those reasons are enough to account for the tens of billions of dollars the films alone (not counting merchandise or video sales) have generated, the eruption of crowds into ecstatic cheers and applause during key scenes at screenings, or the emotional outpouring of letters and videos sent by fans to the screenwriters of *Avengers: Endgame* upon the conclusion of the series.[22] As Bruce David Forbes has argued, "Popular culture and traditional religions function in similar ways, providing meaning and helping people cope with life's problems."[23] Coming from the vantage of Theology and looking almost exclusively at the role of the superhero in the comic tradition rather than films, Greg Garrett makes an analogous point, arguing, "All those hero myths that have lasted—those whose stories touch something fundamental in all of us—have lasted largely because they have found new ways to tell us an old, old story."[24] This sentiment clearly applies to the MCU, which by drawing on mythic archetypes and essential questions of human life, has clearly touched a deep nerve among a vast number of people, creating a worldwide fandom.

Since the MCU portrays its characters, like Steve Rogers, Tony Stark, Bruce Banner, and others, not as gods, but also as something more than human, they could be said to occupy a delicate mythic balance as beings who are relatable to audiences, but simultaneously aspirational. As such, the MCU can weigh narratives of cosmic and grandiose drama against intimate questions of what it means to be human. Am I a hero or a monster? To whom do I owe my loyalties? Why do we have to die? By posing those questions in new forms and for a contemporary audience, the MCU serves the same purpose as mythologies throughout history, namely as a guide

The original Avengers assembled. From *Marvel's The Avengers* (2012). From left to right: Robert Downey, Jr., as Tony Stark/Iron Man, Mark Ruffalo as Bruce Banner/Hulk, Chris Evans as Steve Rogers/Captain America, Chris Hemsworth as Thor, Scarlett Johansson as Natasha Romanoff/Black Widow, and Jeremy Renner as Clint Barton/Hawkeye.

through the dilemmas and perils of the human experience. In her overview of the concept of myth through human history, Karen Armstrong has suggested much the same thing, arguing that any myth is "designed to help us to cope with the problematic human predicament" and, in the midst of that search, helps "people to find their place in the world and their true orientation."[25] Robert Ellwood paints the same picture of the role of myth across human history, saying that it is the role of such sacred narratives to

> reveal to us the creative imagination, the vision, the fears, and the sometimes bumbling responses of our ultimate human ancestors to the vast and baffling universe of which we find ourselves a tiny fragment. Those first humans still dwell deep within us, both alien and familiar, and their dreads and dreams can still shape our own consciousness.[26]

As we have seen, those dreads and dreams have found their way down through the ages of time into the new avatar of the MCU characters and stories, serving as new mythic guides to very old questions.

On that point of myth as a guide, when analyzing the Greek story of Theseus and the Minotaur, Joseph Campbell briefly remarks on the symbolic meaning of Ariadne's thread, used by the hero to find his way back out of the treacherous labyrinth. "It is indeed very little that we need!" Campbell comments, referring to the slenderness and seemingly insubstantial nature of the thread, "but lacking that, the adventure into the labyrinth is without hope."[27] If we take human existence as the labyrinth, the threads we use to guide our way are the stories we and our cultures produce and cherish, and the characters—Gilgamesh, Cúchulainn, Siddhartha Gautama, Tony Stark, Steve Rogers—created to stand for all of us. All of these characters and stories participate in the common human mythic heritage. It is no wonder, then, that the MCU carries on this tradition, the "Marvel"-ous mythology that it is.

Chapter Notes

Preface and Acknowledgments

1. Campbell, Joseph. *The Hero with a Thousand Faces*. Princeton: Princeton University Press, 1949, p. 4.

Introduction

1. Travis Clark, "The Eight Marvel Cinematic Universe Movies that Made Over $1 Billion at the Global Box Office," *Business Insider*, 4/29/19. Accessed 6/11/19. https://www.businessinsider.com/marvel-cinematic-universe-movies-to-make-1-billion-at-the-box-office-2019-4; Rebecca Rubin, "*Avengers: Endgame* Crushes $2 Billion Milestone in Record Time," *Variety*, 5/5/19. Accessed 6/7/19. www.variety.com/2019/film/news/avengers-endgame-2-billion-record-time-1203205293.

2. Those moments included the return of heroes thought dead from the events of the previous installment *Avengers: Infinity War* and the self-sacrifice of Tony Stark to save the world from Thanos, the MCU's main villain. Though such videos are notoriously ephemeral, links to these theater outbursts can be found at Toontastic, "Avenger Endgame Crazy MCU Fans Reaction," *Youtube*, 4/27/2019, 1:23, https://www.youtube.com/watch?v=UMnaNp9xngY, accessed 6/15/2019; Reza Sulfan, "Audience Reaction Ending Endgame Iron Man," *Youtube*, 4/27/2019, 1:17, https://www.youtube.com/watch?v=lDrkijN_vFM, accessed 6/15/2019.

3. *Avengers Assemble!: Critical Perspectives on the Marvel Cinematic Universe*, New York: Wallflower Press, 2018.

4. Jeffrey Brown, *The Modern Superhero in Film and Television: Popular Genre and American Culture*, New York: Routledge, 2017, p. 71. For other examples of this interpretation, see Derek Sweet, "America Assemble: The Avengers as Therapeutic Public Memory," in *Assembling the Marvel Cinematic Universe*, pp. 64–75; and Sasha-Mae Eccleston, "Enemies, Foreign and Domestic: Villainy and Terrorism in Marvel Studio's *Thor*," in *Assembling the Marvel Cinematic Universe*, pp. 168–184; *Portraying 9/11: Essays on Representation in Comics, Literature, Film, and Theater*, edited by Veronique Bragard, Christophe Dony, and Warren Rosenberg, Jefferson, NC: McFarland, 2011; Roz Kaveney, *Superheroes!: Capes and Crusaders in Comics and Films*, New York: I.B. Tauris, 2008; Tom Pollard, *Hollywood 9/11: Superheroes, Supervillains, and Superdisasters*. New York: Routledge, 2011.

5. See, respectively, Angela Watercutter, "*Captain Marvel* is about Female Power—not Empowerment," *Wired*, 3/11/2019. Accessed 3/24/2020. https://www.wired.com/story/captain-marvel-is-about-female-power-not-empowerment/; Tre Johnson, "*Black Panther* is a Gorgeous, Ground-breaking Celebration of Black Culture," *Vox*, 2/23/2018. Accessed 3/24/2020. https://www.vox.com/culture/2018/2/23/17028826/black-panther-wakanda-culture-marvel; Jamil Smith, "The Revolutionary Power of *Black Panther*," *Time*. Accessed 3/24/2020. https://time.com/black-panther/.

6. From "Beowulf: The Monsters and the Critics," Sir Israel Gollancz Memorial Lecture, Proceedings of the British Academy, 1936, pp. 245–95.

7. See *Four Theories of Myth in Twentieth Century History*. Iowa City: University of Iowa Press, 1987, p. 1.

8. See Bruce Lincoln, *Theorizing Myth: Narrative, Ideology, and Scholarship*. Chicago: University of Chicago Press, 1997; Russell McCutcheon, *Manufacturing Religion: The Discourse on Sui Generis Religion and the Politics of Nostalgia*. New York: Oxford University Press, 1997. See also Andrew von Hendy, *The Modern Construction of Myth*. Bloomington: Indiana University Press, 2002.

9. See William Doty, *Mythography: The Study of Myths and Rituals*. Second edition. Tuscaloosa: University of Alabama Press, 2000, pp. 5–16.

10. "Introduction," in *Sacred Narrative: Readings in the Theory of Myth*, Berkeley: University of California Press, 1984, p. 1.

11. "The Role of Myth in Life," in *Sacred Narrative: Readings in the Theory of Myth*, Berkeley: University of California Press, 1984, p. 204.

12. *Myth: Key Concepts in Religion*, New York: Continuum, 2008, pp. 1–2.

13. *The Politics of Myth: A Study of C.G. Jung, Mircea Eliade, and Joseph Campbell*, Albany: SUNY Press, 1999, p. 177.

14. *The Implied Spider: Politics and Theology in Myth*. New York: Columbia University Press, 1998, p. 54.

15. *Manufacturing Religion*, p. 18.

16. *Imagining Religion: From Babylon to Jonestown*. Chicago: University of Chicago Press, 1982, p. 21.

17. Robert Segal, "In Defense of the Comparative Method," *Numen*. 48.3, 2001, p. 352.

18. "Elements of a New Comparativism," in *A Magic Still Dwells: Comparative Religion in the Post-Modern Age*. Edited by Kimberley Patton and Benjamin Ray. Berkeley: University of California Press, 2000, p.182. See also Wesley Wildman, "Comparing Religious Ideas: There's Method in the Mob's Madness," in *Comparing Religions: Possibilities and Perils*, edited by Thomas Idinopoulos, Brian Wilson, and James Hanges. Leiden: Brill, 2006, pp. 77–113.

19. "Juggling Torches: We Still Need Comparative Religion," in *A Magic Still Dwells: Comparative Religion in the Post-Modern Age*. Edited by Kimberley Patton and Benjamin Ray. Berkeley: University of California Press, 2000, p. 163.

20. *The Implied Spider*, p. 61.

21. *The Myth of the Superhero*, Baltimore: Johns Hopkins Press, 2013, p. 11.

22. Peter Coogan, *Superhero: the Secret Origin of a Genre*, Monkeybrain Books, 2006, p. 124; Chris Knowles, *Our Gods Wear Spandex: The Secret History of Comic Book Heroes*. San Francisco: Weiser Books, 2007, pp. 23–31.

23. See Danny Fingeroth, *Superman on the Couch: What Superheroes Really Tell Us about Ourselves and Our Society*, New York: Continuum, 2004, p. 16, as well as Andrew Bahlmann, *The Mythology of the Superhero*, Jefferson, NC: McFarland, 2016, and Alex Romagnoli and Gian Pagnucci, *Enter the Superheroes: American Values, Culture, and the Canon of Superhero Literature*. Lanham, MD: Scarecrow Press, 2013.

24. *Superheroes and Gods: A Comparative Study from Babylonia to Batman*, McFarland, 2008.

25. Peter Suderman, "How Marvel Built Such an Impressive Movie Universe," *Vox*, 5/9/16. Accessed 6/7/19. www.vox.com/2016/5/9/11595344/marvel-cinematic-universe-captain-america-avengers.

On the narrative interconnectivity of the MCU, see also Maya Phillips, "The Narrative Experiment that is the Marvel Cinematic Universe," *The New Yorker*, 4/26/19. Accessed 6/11/19; Perry Dantzler, "Multiliteracies of the Marvel Cinematic Universe," in *Assembling the Marvel Cinematic Universe: Essays on the Social, Cultural, and Geopolitical Domains*, edited by Julian Chambliss, William Svitavsky, and Daniel Fandino, Jefferson, NC: McFarland, 2018, pp. 14–31; Rick Altman, *A Theory of Narrative*, New York: Columbia University Press, 2008.

26. On this point see, Patrick Shanley, "Can Anyone Besides Marvel Make a Cinematic Universe Work?" *Hollywood Reporter*, 3/29/18. Accessed 6/7/19. www.hollywoodreporter.com/heat-vision/marvel-cinematic-universe/why-is-it-one-works-1096504

27. See *Superheroes: A Modern Mythology*, Jackson: University of Mississippi Press, 1992, pp. 43–45.

28. For example, in the case of Gilgamesh, see Stephen Mitchell, "Introduction" in *Gilgamesh*, New York: Simon & Schuster, 2004. For this phenomenon in the narratives of the life of the Buddha,

see John Strong, *The Buddha: A Beginner's Guide*, New York: Oneworld Publications, 2009. Regarding Rama and the Rāmāyāṇa, see *Many Rāmāyāṇas: the Diversity of a Narrative Tradition in South Asia*, edited by Paula Richman, Berkeley: University of California Press, 1991.

29. "Power and Responsibility … and Other Reflections on Superheroes," in *What is a Superhero?* Edited by Robin Rosenberg and Peter Coogan. New York: Oxford University Press, 2013, p. 126.

30. "Introduction," *A Magic Still Dwells: Comparative Religion in the Post-Modern Age*, edited by Kimberley Patton and Benjamin Ray, Berkeley: University of California Press, 2000, p. 18.

31. *Do the Gods Wear Capes? Spirituality, Fantasy, and Superheroes*. New York: Continuum Press, 2011, 143.

32. *Marvel's The Avengers*. Directed by Joss Whedon (2012; Burbank, CA: Burbank, CA: Marvel Studios.) DVD.

33. *Avengers: Age of Ultron*. Directed by Joss Whedon (2012; Burbank, CA: Burbank, CA: Marvel Studios.) DVD.

34. *Marvel's The Avengers*. Directed by Joss Whedon (2012; Burbank, CA: Burbank, CA: Marvel Studios.) DVD.

35. See both *Authors of the Impossible: The Paranormal and the Sacred*, Chicago: University of Chicago Press, 2010 and *Mutants and Mystics: Science Fiction, Superhero Comics, and the Supernatural*, Chicago: University of Chicago Press, 2011.

36. Dave Itzkoff, "'Avengers,' the Most Lucrative Movie Franchise Ever, is Wrapping Up. Why?" *New York Times*. 4/23/18. Accessed 6/7/19. https://www.nytimes.com/2018/04/23/movies/avengers-infinity-war-disney-marvel.html.

37. Long Grove, IL: Waveland Press, 1992 [1948], p. 29.

38. *Religious Encounters with Death: Insights from the History and Anthropology of Religions*, edited by Frank Reynolds and Earle Waugh, Pennsylvania State University Press, 1977, p. 2.

39. *Supergods: What Masked Vigilantes, Miraculous Mutants, and a Sun God from Smallville Can Teach Us About Being Human*, New York: Spiegel and Rau, 2011, p. xvii.

Chapter One

1. *Ritual: Perspectives and Dimensions*. New York: Oxford University Press, 1997, p. 94.

2. *The Rites of Passage*. Translated by M.B. Visedom and G.L. Caffee. Chicago: University of Chicago Press, 1960 [1909], pp. 2–3.

3. See Catherine Bell, *Ritual: Perspectives and Dimensions*, pp. 94–102 for a complex and informative discussion and comparison of the range of such rituals.

4. Princeton: Princeton University Press, 1949.

5. On the importance of the origin story in the superhero genre, see Richard Reynolds, *Superheroes: A Modern Mythology*, Jackson: University of Mississippi Press, 1992, pp. 12–16; Andrew Bahlmann, *The Mythology of the Superhero*; Peter Coogan, *Superheroes: the Secret Origin of a Genre*; Robin Rosenberg, *Superhero Origins: What Makes Superheroes Tick and Why We Care*, Create Space Publishing, 2013.

6. *Iron Man*, directed by Jon Favreau (2008; Burbank, CA: Marvel Studios), DVD.

7. *Ibid.*

8. *Ibid.*

9. *The Ritual Process: Structure and Anti-Structure*. New York: DeGruyter, 1969, p. 95.

10. *Ibid.*, pp. 97–102.

11. *The Sacred and the Profane: Nature and Religion*. Translated by Willard Trask. New York: Harcourt Brace, 1959, p. 190.

12. See Donald K. Swearer, *The Buddhist World of Southeast Asia*. Albany: State University of New York Press, 1995, pp. 49–51. Also on this symbolism, see John S. Strong, *The Legend and Cult of Upagupta: Sanskrit Buddhism in North India and Southeast Asia*, Princeton: Princeton University Press, 1992, p. 88.

13. David Long, *The Hajj Today: A Survey of the Contemporary Pilgrimage to Makkah*, Albany: State University of New York Press, 1979, pp. 14–15.

14. For a discussion on how the symbolism of the grave can also serve as symbolism of the womb, see Eliade, *The Sacred and the Profane*, p. 191.

15. *Thor*, directed by Kenneth Branagh (2011; Burbank, CA: Marvel Studios), DVD.

16. *Ibid.*

17. *Captain America: the First Avenger,* directed by Joe Johnston (2011; Burbank, CA: Marvel Studios), DVD.

18. *Ibid.*

19. *Black Panther,* directed by Ryan Coogler (2018; Burbank, CA: Marvel Studios), DVD.

20. *The Sacred and the Profane,* p. 190.

21. *Ant-Man,* directed by Peyton Reed (2015; Burbank, CA: Marvel Studios), DVD.

22. *Marvel's The Avengers,* directed by Joss Whedon (2012; Burbank, CA: Marvel Studios), DVD.

23. *Captain Marvel,* directed by Anna Boden and Ryan Fleck (2019; Burbank, CA: Marvel Studios), DVD.

24. E. J. Michael Witzel, "Shamanism in Northern and Southern Eurasia: Their Distinctive Method of Change of Consciousness," *Social Science Information,* 50:1, 2.

25. Margaret Stutley, *Shamanism: an Introduction.* New York: Routledge, 2002, p. 3.

26. "Introduction," in *Shamanism in Asia,* edited by Peter Knecht and Clark Chilson, New York: Routledge, 2003, p. 5.

27. For a cognitive evolutionary approach to some of these potential commonalities, see Manvir Singh, "The Cultural Evolution of Shamanism," *Behavioral Brain Sciences,* 2018, pp. 1–62.

28. *The Origins of the World's Mythologies,* Oxford University Press, 2012, p. 382.

29. Mircea Eliade, *Shamanism: Archaic Techniques of Ecstasy,* Translated by Willard Trask, Princeton: Princeton University Press, 1964, p. 34. See also pp. 33–61.

30. *Ibid.,* p. 38.

31. F. George Heyne, "The Social Significance of the Shaman among the Chinese Reindeer Evenki," in *Shamanism in Asia,* edited by Peter Knecht and Clark Chilson, New York: Routledge, 2003, p. 39.

32. See *Civilized Shamans: Buddhism in Tibetan Societies.* Washington: Smithsonian Institution Press, 1993, pp. 7–8.

33. *The Tibetan Book of the Dead: the Great Liberation Through Hearing in the Bardo.* Translated with commentary by Francesca Fremantle and Chögyam Trungpa. Boston: Shambhala Press, 1987, p. 77.

34. *Shamanism: an Introduction,* p. 7.

35. For numerous examples and descriptions of these various actions, see Eliade, *Shamanism: Archaic Techniques of Ecstasy,* pp. 208–309.

36. Takiguchi Naoko, "Liminal Experiences of Miyako Shamans," in *Shamanism in Asia,* edited by Clark Chilson and Peter Knecht. New York: Routledge, 2003, pp. 153–154.

37. F. Georg Heyne, "The Social Significance of the Shaman among the Chinese Reindeer Evenki," in *Shamanism in Asia,* edited by Peter Knecht and Clark Chilson, New York: Routledge, 2003, pp. 31, 39.

38. *The Incredible Hulk,* directed by Louis LeTerrier (2008; Burbank, CA: Marvel Studios and Universal Pictures), DVD. The Incredible Hulk's origin story in the original comic version instead involves Bruce Banner's accidental exposure to the detonation of a "gamma bomb," reflecting the era's fear of advancements in atomic and related weaponry. See Stan Lee and Jack Kirby, *The Incredible Hulk,* Issue #1 (May 1962).

39. *Marvel's The Avengers,* directed by Joss Whedon (2012; Burbank, CA: Marvel Studios), DVD.

40. *The Avengers: Age of Ultron,* directed by Joss Whedon (2015; Burbank, CA: Marvel Studios), DVD.

41. Eliade, *Shamanism: Archaic Techniques of Ecstasy,* pp. 47–51.

42. Ioan Coulianu, *Out of this World: Otherworldly Journeys from Gilgamesh to Albert Einstein.* Boston: Shambhala Press, 1991, 38–44. See also, Eliade, *Shamanism: Archaic Techniques of Ecstasy.*

43. Takiguchi Naoko, "Liminal Experiences of Miyako Shamans," in *Shamanism in Asia,* edited by Clark Chilson and Peter Knecht. New York: Routledge, 2003, p. 157.

44. *Ant-Man,* directed by Peyton Reed (2015; Burbank, CA: Marvel Studios), DVD.

45. F. Georg Heyne, "The Social Significance of the Shaman among the Chinese Reindeer Evenki," in *Shamanism in Asia,* edited by Peter Knecht and Clark Chilson, New York: Routledge, 2003, p. 35.

46. *Doctor Strange,* directed by Scott Derrickson (2016; Burbank, CA: Marvel Studios), DVD.

47. *Ibid.*

48. F. Georg Heyne, "The Social Significance of the Shaman among the Chinese Reindeer Evenki," in *Shamanism in Asia,*

edited by Peter Knecht and Clark Chilson, New York: Routledge, 2003, p. 31.

49. *Thor: Ragnarok*, directed by Taika Waititi (2017; Burbank, CA: Marvel Studios), DVD.

50. *Marvel's The Avengers*, directed by Joss Whedon (2012; Burbank, CA: Marvel Studios), DVD.

51. *Ibid.*

52. This ability particularly evokes the "subtle body" projection thought to be a part of Chinese and Tibetan shamanism. See Stephen Teiser, *The Ghost Festival in Medieval China*, Princeton: Princeton University Press, 1988, pp. 144–145. See also Ioan M. Lewis, *Ecstatic Religion: An Anthropological Study of Spirit Possession and Shamanism*, revised edition. New York: Penguin Books, 1978, pp. 55–56.

53. *Guardians of the Galaxy*, directed by James Gunn (2014; Burbank, CA: Marvel Studios), DVD.

54. *Doctor Strange*, directed by Scott Derrickson (2016; Burbank, CA: Marvel Studios), DVD.

55. *Thor*, directed by Kenneth Branagh (2011; Burbank, CA: Marvel Studios), DVD.

56. Eliade, *Shamanism: Archaic Techniques of Ecstasy*, p. 31; Stutley, *Shamanism: An Introduction*.

57. "Liminal Experiences of Miyako Shamans," in *Shamanism in Asia*, edited by Clark Chilson and Peter Knecht. New York: Routledge, 2003, p. 153.

58. "Straddling a Boundary: The Superhero and the Incorporation of Difference," in *What is a Superhero?* Edited by Robin Rosenberg and Peter Coogan. New York: Oxford University Press, 2013. Emphasis in the original.

59. Iron Man, directed by Jon Favreau (2008; Burbank, CA: Marvel Studios), DVD.

60. *Ibid.*

61. *Ibid.*

62. *Marvel's The Avengers*, directed by Joss Whedon (2012; Burbank, CA: Marvel Studios), DVD.

63. *The Incredible Hulk*, directed by Louis Le Terrier (2008; Burbank, CA: Marvel Studios and Universal Pictures), DVD.

64. *Ibid.*

65. *Guardians of the Galaxy*, directed by James Gunn (2014; Burbank, CA: Marvel Studios), DVD.

66. For the original line, which actually reads, "With great power there must also come—great responsibility!," see *Amazing Fantasy* #15 (August 1962), writer: Stan Lee, Penciler: Steve Ditko.

67. *The Ritual Process*, p. 109.

68. *The Rites of Passage*, p. 114.

69. Émile Durkheim, *The Elementary Forms of Religious Life*, translated by Carol Cosman. New York: Oxford University Press, 2001, p. 221. While Durkheim's attempt to reconstruct what he considers "primal" and thus "original" religion is problematic, certain of his insights, such as the tendency across cultures to protectively separate that which is considered sacred, are still quite relevant.

70. *Patterns in Comparative Religion*, translated by Rosemary Sheed. Lincoln: University of Nebraska Press, 1996 [1958], p. 384.

71. Angela Sumegi, *Understanding Death: An Introduction to Ideas of Self and the Afterlife in World Religions*. Malden, MA: John Wiley and Sons (Wiley-Blackwell), 2014, p. 36; See also, Johnannes, Wilbert, *Mystic Endowment: Religious Ethnography of the Warao Indians*. Cambridge: Harvard University Press, 1993.

72. *Marvel's The Avengers*, directed by Joss Whedon (2012; Burbank, CA: Marvel Studios), DVD.

73. *Ibid.*

Chapter Two

1. *The Symbolism of Evil.* Translated by Emerson Buchanan. Boston: Beacon Press, 1967, p. 258.

2. Dustin Rowles, "George R. R. Martin Sounds Off on 'Ant-Man' and Marvel's Villain Problem," Uproxx: the Culture of What's Buzzing," 7/23/15. http://uproxx.com/tv/george-r-r-martin-on-antman-marvel's-villain-problem. Accessed 7/12/19.

3. Carl Jung, *The Archetypes and the Collective Unconscious.* Second edition. Translated by R.F.C. Hull. Princeton: Princeton University Press, 1990 [1959], pp. 284–285.

4. *Ibid.*, p. 20.

5. R.C. Zaehner, *Zurvan: a Zoroastrian Dilemma.* New York: Oxford University Press, 1955, pp. 54–79.

6. Mircea Eliade, *Mephistopheles and the*

Androgyne: Studies in Religious Myth and Symbol. Translated by J.M. Cohen. New York: Sheed and Word, 1965, pp. 83–85.

7. Stephen Batchelor, *Living with the Devil: A Meditation on Good and Evil.* New York: Riverhead Books, 2004, p. 28.

8. Jeffrey Cohen, Monster Culture: Seven Theses, in *Monster Theory: Reading Culture*, Minneapolis: University of Minnesota Press, 1996, p. 6. For the application of many of these same ideas to the genre of horror films, see Noel Carroll, *The Philosophy of Horror, or Paradoxes of the Heart.* New York: Routledge, 1990.

9. *Monsters: Evil Beings, Mythical Beasts, and All Manner of Imaginary Terrors.* Philadelphia: University of Pennsylvania, 2003, p. 12.

10. *Religion and Its Monsters*, New York: Routledge, 2002, p. 18.

11. *Iron Man*, directed by Jon Favreau (2008; Burbank, CA: Marvel Studios), DVD.

12. *Ibid.*

13. *Monsters: Evil Beings, Mythical Beasts, and All Manner of Imaginary Terrors*, pp. 174–175.

14. *Monsters of Our Own Making: The Peculiar Pleasures of Fear.* Lexington: University of Kentucky Press, 2007, p. 97.

15. Calvert Watkins, *How to Kill a Dragon: Aspects of Indo-European Poetics*, New York: Oxford University Press, 1995, p. 300.

16. For excellent translations of this myth see *Hindu Myths: A Sourcebook*, translated by Wendy Doniger O'Flaherty, New York: Penguin Press, 1976, pp. 74–76, or *The Rig Veda*, translated by Wendy Doniger O'Flaherty, New York: Penguin Press, 1981, pp. 148–151.

17. Geoffrey Parrinder, *African Mythology*. London: Hamlyn Publishing, 1967, p. 95.

18. *African Myths and Tales*, edited by Susan Feldmann. New York: Dell Publishing, 1963, pp. 97–99.

19. *American Indian Mythology*, Richard Erdoes and Alfonso Ortiz. New York: Pantheon Books, 1984, pp. 223–225.

20. *Beowulf: A New Verse Translation*, Seamus Heaney. New York: W.W. Norton and Company, 2000, pp. 157–183.

21. Warner, *Monsters of Our Own Making*, pp. 145–146.

22. *American Indian Mythology*, pp. 182–184.

23. *Ant-Man*, directed by Peyton Reed (2015; Burbank, CA: Marvel Studios), DVD.

24. *Ibid.*

25. *Ibid.*

26. *Monster Culture*, p. 6.

27. *Ant-Man*, directed by Peyton Reed (2015; Burbank, CA: Marvel Studios), DVD.

28. *Deadly Powers: Animal Predation and the Mythic Imagination.* New York: Prometheus Press, 2011. For a variant on this theme, often with interesting feminist insights, see also Marian Warner, *Monsters of Our Own Making: The Peculiar Pleasures of Fear.* Lexington: University of Kentucky Press, 2007.

29. *Spider-Man: Homecoming*, directed by Jon Watts (2017; Burbank, CA: Marvel Studios), DVD.

30. *Ibid.*

31. *Ibid.*

32. *Buddhacarita*, 13:9–10; see also, for English translation, *Life of the Buddha*, by Ashvaghosha, translated by Patrick Olivelle, New York: New York University Press, 2009, p. 377.

33. *The Connected Discourses of the Buddha*, translated by Bhikkhu Bodhi, Boston: Wisdom Publications, 2000, p. 200.

34. *Ibid.*, p. 210.

35. *Matthew* 4:1–10, *Luke* 4:1–13. These and all other quotations or references from the Bible are taken from the New Revised Standard Version.

36. For the comic version of this origin story, see *Amazing Fantasy #15* (August 1962), Writer: Stan Lee, Pencils: Jack Kirby, Inker: Steve Ditko. Marvel Comics. This version of events is also shown in the films *Spider-Man*, directed by Sam Raimi (2002; Burbank, CA: Sony Pictures), DVD and *The Amazing Spider-Man*, directed by Marc Webb (2012; Burbank, CA: Sony Pictures), DVD.

37. *Captain America: Civil War*, directed by Anthony and Joe Russo (2016; Burbank, CA: Marvel Studios), DVD.

38. *The Incredible Hulk*, directed by Louis LeTerrier (2008; Burbank, CA: Marvel Studios), DVD.

39. *Ibid.*

40. *Ibid.*

41. *Beowulf*, pp. 65, 113.

42. *The Odyssey*, translated by Robert Fagles, New York: Penguin Press, 1996, pp. 217–220.

43. *Gilgamesh: A New English Version,* Stephen Mitchell, New York: Free Press, 2004, pp. 119–123.

44. *Ibid.,* p. 124.

45. *The Incredible Hulk,* directed by Louis LeTerrier (2008; Burbank, CA: Marvel Studios), DVD.

46. *Avengers: Age of Ultron,* directed by Joss Whedon (2015; Burbank, CA: Marvel Studios), DVD.

47. *Captain America: The First Avenger,* directed by Joe Johnston (2011; Burbank, CA: Marvel Studios), DVD.

48. *Ibid.*

49. *Ibid.*

50. *Ibid.*

51. *Ibid.*

52. *Guardians of the Galaxy,* directed by James Gunn (2014; Burbank, CA: Marvel Studios), DVD.

53. Charles Kimball, *When Religion Becomes Evil: Five Warning Signs.* San Francisco: HarperCollins, 2002, p. 44 (Emphasis in the original.)

54. Mark Juergensmeyer, *Terror in the Mind of God: The Global Rise of Religious Violence.* Third Edition. Berkeley: University of California Press, 2005.

55. For a survey of movements and instances of religious violence across the world, see *Violence and the World's Religious Traditions: An Introduction,* edited by Mark Juergensmeyer, Margo Kitt, and Michael Jerryson. New York: Oxford University Press, 2016. For the particular region of South Asia, see *Religion and Violence in South Asia,* edited by John R. Hinnells and Richard King. New York: Routledge Press, 2007. Additional work on violence within the Buddhist tradition can be found in *Buddhist Warfare,* edited by Mark Juergensmeyer and Michael Jerryson, New York: Oxford University Press, 2010, and Michael Jerryson, *Buddhist Fury: Religion and Violence in Southern Thailand.* New York: Oxford University Press, 2011. A more theoretical approach can be found in Bruce Lincoln, *Holy Terrors: Thinking about Religion After September 11.* Chicago: University of Chicago Press, 2003.

56. *Guardians of the Galaxy,* directed by James Gunn (2014; Burbank, CA: Marvel Studios), DVD.

57. *Ibid.*

58. Ovid, *The Metamorphoses,* trans-lated by Horace Gregory, New York: Viking Press, 1958, p. 135.

59. *The Odyssey,* p. 274.

60. *Beowulf,* p. 89–93.

61. John Milton, *Paradise Lost,* edited by Gordon Testkey. New York: W. W. Norton Critical Editions, 2005, p. 5. It is worth noting that, while Milton himself had no use for the concept of a "heroic" Satan, an entire group of Romantic poets led by Percy Shelley and Lord Byron, inspired by Milton, saw the figure in just this way. On that point, see Kenneth Gross, "Satan and the Romantic Satan: a Notebook," in *Re-Membering Milton: Essays on the Texts and Traditions,* ed. Mary Nyquist and Margaret W. Ferguson (New York: Methuen, 1987).

62. *Paradise Lost,* p. 6.

63. *Ibid.* p. 25.

64. *Doctor Strange,* directed by Scott Derrickson (2016; Burbank, CA: Marvel Studios), DVD.

65. *Ibid.*

66. *Ibid.*

67. *Ibid.*

68. *Black Panther,* directed by Ryan Coogler (2018; Burbank, CA: Marvel Studios), DVD.

69. *Ibid.*

70. On the symbolic uses of inversion as a mythical trope, see Bruce Lincoln, *Discourse and the Construction of Society: Comparative Studies of Myth, Ritual, and Classification.* New York: Oxford University Press, 1992, p. 159.

71. *Black Panther,* directed by Ryan Coogler (2018; Burbank, CA: Marvel Studios), DVD.

72. *Ibid.*

73. *Ibid.*

74. *Ibid.*

75. *Paradise Lost,* p. 10.

76. *Monster Culture,* p. 5.

77. For instance, see Jeffrey Burton Russell, *The Prince of Darkness: Radical Evil and the Power of Good in History,* Ithaca: Cornell University Press, 1988, pp. 112–115.

78. This occurs throughout the Pali *Mārasamyutta of the Samyutta Nikāya* and the later Sanskrit *Perfection of Wisdom in Eight Thousand Lines.* For a detailed discussion of different forms assumed by Mara and their doctrinal and sectarian significance, see Michael Nichols, *Malleable Māra: Transformations of a Buddhist*

Symbol of Evil, Albany: State University of New York Press, 2019, pp. 21–24, 43, 63–64, 113–119, 146–148, 183, 198–99.

79. *Marvel's The Avengers*, directed by Joss Whedon (2012; Burbank, CA: Marvel Studios), DVD.

80. *Religion and Its Monsters*, pp. 4–5.

81. *Monster Culture*, p. 7.

82. *Deadly Powers: Animal Predation and the Mythic Imagination*, New York: Prometheus Books, 2011.

83. *Myths of Mesopotamia: Creation, Flood, Gilgamesh and Others*. Translated by Stephanie Dalley. New York: Oxford University Press, 1989, p. 237.

84. *Buddhacarita*, 13:19–20; *Life of the Buddha, by Aśvaghosha*, translated by Patrick Olivelle, New York: New York University Press, 2009, p. 381–383.

85. *Lucifer: the Devil in the Middle Ages.* Ithaca: Cornell University Press, 1984, p. 131.

86. *Marvel's the Avengers*, directed by Joss Whedon (2012; Burbank, CA: Marvel Studios), DVD.

87. *Ibid.*

88. *American Indian Mythology*, edited by Erdoes and Ortiz, pp. 192–193.

Chapter Three

1. *Avengers: Age of Ultron*, directed by Joss Whedon (2015, Burbank, CA: Marvel Studios), DVD.

2. *The Symbolism of Evil*, p. 25.

3. *Purity and Danger: An Analysis of Concepts of Pollution and Taboos.* New York: Routledge Press, 1966, p. 36.

4. *Ibid.*, p. 37.

5. *Ibid.*, pp. 54–58.

6. *Ibid.*, p. 97.

7. Julia Kristeva, *Powers of Horror: An Essay on Abjection*, translated by Leon Roudiez. New York: Columbia University Press, 1982, p. 4.

8. *The Elementary Forms of Religious Life*, p. 221.

9. See John Howard Lawson, *Theory and Technique of Playwriting and Screenwriting.* New York: G.P. Putnam's Sons, 1949.

10. See *Spider-Man*, directed by Sam Raimi (2002; Burbank, CA: Sony Pictures), DVD; *Spider-Man 2*, directed by Sam Raimi (2004; Burbank, CA: Sony Pictures), DVD; *Spider-Man 3*, directed by Sam Raimi (2007; Burbank, CA: Sony Pictures), DVD.

11. *Batman Begins*, directed by Christopher Nolan (2005; Burbank, CA: Warner Bros.), DVD; *The Dark Knight*, directed by Christopher Nolan (2008; Burbank, CA: Warner Bros.), DVD; *The Dark Knight Rises*, directed by Christopher Nolan (2012; Burbank, CA: Warner Bros.), DVD.

12. See *Man of Steel* directed by Zack Snyder (2013; Burbank, CA: Warner Bros.), DVD; *Batman Versus Superman*, directed by Zack Snyder (2016; Burbank, CA: Warner Bros.), DVD.

13. *Iron Man 2*, directed by Jon Favreau (2010; Burbank, CA: Marvel Studios), DVD.

14. *Ant-Man and the Wasp*, directed by Peyton Reed (2018; Burbank, CA: Marvel Studios), DVD.

15. *Guardians of the Galaxy: Volume 2*, directed by James Gunn (2017; Burbank, CA: Marvel Studios), DVD.

16. *Marvel's The Avengers*, directed by Joss Whedon (2012; Burbank, CA: Marvel Studios), DVD.

17. For a more detailed description of these purity laws in ancient India, see *Dharmasūtras, the Law Code of Ancient India*, translated by Patrick Olivelle. New York: Oxford University Press, 1999. For background on the class system, see Louis Dumont, *Homo Hierarchicus: the Caste System and Its Implications*, translated by Mark Sainsbury, Louis Dumont, and Basia Gulati, Berkeley: University of California Press, 1980. For an especially trenchant critique of the social and political elements of the caste system, see Brian K. Smith, *Classifying the Universe: the Ancient Indian Varṇa System and the Origins of Caste*, New York: Oxford University Press, 1994.

18. *Dharmasūtras*, p. 289.

19. *Ibid.*, p. 303.

20. *Ibid.*, p. 289.

21. Wendy Doniger O'Flaherty, *The Origins of Evil in Hindu Mythology*, Berkeley: University of California Press, 1976, pp. 104–111 and pp. 151–152.

22. For an in-depth discussion of these various themes and their associated myths, see Wendy Doniger O'Flaherty, *Śiva: the Erotic Ascetic*, New York: Oxford University Press, 1973.

23. *The Origins of Evil in Hindu Mythology*, pp. 160–164 and 278–279.

24. *Gaṇeśa: Lord of Obstacles, Lord of Beginnings*, New York: Oxford University Press, 1985, p. 65.

25. Sven Bretfeld, "Purifying the Pure: the *Visuddhimagga*, Forest-Dwellers, and the Dynamics of Individual and Collective Prestige in Theravāda Buddhism," in *Discourses of Purity in Transcultural Perspective*, edited by Matthias Bley, Nikolas Jaspert, and Stefan Köck. Boston: E.J. Brill, 2015, p. 333.

26. Hermann Josef Röllicke, "Some Brief Notes on Chinese Daoism," in *Discourses of Purity in Transcultural Perspective*, edited by Matthias Bley, Nikolas Jaspert, and Stefan Köck. Boston: E.J. Brill, 2015, p. 46.

27. Paolo Santangelo, "From 'Clean' to 'Pure' in Everyday Life in Imperial China," in *Discourses of Purity in Transcultural Perspective*, edited by Matthias Bley, Nikolas Jaspert, and Stefan Köck. Boston: E.J. Brill, 2015, pp. 83–96.

28. *A Treasury of Chinese Literature*, edited by Raymond Van Over. Greenwich, CT: Fawcett Premier Publishing, 1972.

29. Edward T.C. Werner, *Myths and Legends of China*, New York: Dover Publications, 1994 [1922], pp. 371–372. See also Tao Liu Sanders, *Dragons, Gods, and Spirits from Chinese Mythology*. New York: Schocken Books, 1980.

30. See Mary Boyce, *Zoroastrians: Their Religious Beliefs and Practices*. Boston: Routledge and Kegan Paul, 1979, pp. 13–14; Jon Davies, *Death, Burial, and Rebirth in the Religions of Antiquity*. New York: Routledge, 1999, pp. 43–44.

31. For instance, though the examples are more extensive and widespread in the texts, see *Leviticus* chapters 11–15 and *Deuteronomy* 14. It is worth noting that food purity rules in Islam have some similarities to those found in Judaism, as evidenced by this passage in the *Qur'ān*, 16:115: "[God] has forbidden you only these things: carrion, blood, pig's meat, and animals over which any name other than God's has been invoked." See *The Qur'ān: A New Translation*, translated by M.A.S. Abdel Haleem. New York: Oxford University Press, 2010, p. 173.

32. 5:-13.

33. 24:10–16.

34. See Susan Haber, edited by Adele Reinhartz, *"They Shall Purify Themselves": Essays on Purity in Early Judaism*. Atlanta: Society of Biblical Literature, 2008, pp. 18–19.

35. *1 Samuel* 17:1–51.

36. *2 Samuel* 11:1–27.

37. *Ibid.*, 12:15–18.

38. For a key work on the topic, see Robert Parker, *Miasma: Pollution and Purification in Early Greek Religion*, New York: Clarendon Press, 1983. Also see Walter Burkert, *Greek Religion*, translated by John Raffan. Cambridge: Harvard University Press, 1985, pp. 75–82. On the subject of internal, rather than external, purity concerns, see Andrej Petrovic and Ivana Petrovic, *Inner Purity and Pollution in Ancient Greek Religion*, New York: Oxford University Press, 2016.

39. "Concepts of Purity in Ancient Greece," in *Purity and the Forming of Religious Traditions in the Ancient Mediterranean World and Ancient Judaism*, edited by Christian Frevel and Christophe Nihan, Boston: E.J. Brill, 2013, p. 259.

40. Sophocles, *The Three Theban Plays*, translated by Robert Fagles, New York: Penguin Publishing, 1982, p. 164.

41. *Ibid.*, p. 185.

42. For the incident regarding Odysseus and the Cyclops Polyphemus, see *The Odyssey*, pp. 227–228.

43. *Iron Man 3*, directed by Shane Black (2013; Burbank, CA: Marvel Studios), DVD.

44. *Ibid.*

45. For a comparison of these Indo-European figures, see Norman Cohn, *Cosmos, Chaos, and the World to Come*, 2nd Edition, New Haven: Yale University Press, 2001, pp. 42–47. For a discussion of the chaos dragon in the comic book or graphic novel genre, specifically regarding the Batman and Joker characters, see Michael Nichols, "'I Think You and I Are Destined to Do This Forever': A Reading of the Batman/Joker Comic and Film Tradition through the Combat Myth." *The Journal of Religion and Popular Culture*. 23:2, July 2011, pp. 236–250.

46. *Thor: The Dark World*, directed by Alan Taylor (2013; Burbank, CA: Marvel Studios), DVD.

47. *Ibid.*

48. *Captain America: The Winter Soldier*, directed by Anthony and Joe Russo (2014; Burbank, CA: Marvel Studios), DVD.

49. For background on Buddhist orthodoxy, especially in India, see Gregory Schopen, *Bones, Stones, and Buddhist Monks: Collected Papers on the Archaeology, Epigraphy, and Texts of Monastic Buddhism in India*, Honolulu: University of Hawai'i Press, 1997. In the case of ancient Jewish institutional purity, see Jacob Neusner, "The Idea of Purity in Ancient Judaism," *Journal of the American Academy of Religion*, 43:1 (Mar., 1975), pp. 15–26.

50. *Purity and Danger*, p. 114.

51. See Judith Bovensiepen, "*Lulik*: Taboo, Animism, or Transgressive Sacred? An Exploration of Identity, Morality, and Power in Timor-Leste," *Oceania*, 84:2 (2014), p. 121–137.

52. *Captain America: The Winter Soldier*, directed by Anthony and Joe Russo (2014; Burbank, CA: Marvel Studios), DVD.

53. Graeme McMillan, "Joss Whedon on 'Avengers 2,'" *The Hollywood Reporter*. 12/17/2014. https://www.hollywoodreporter.com/heat-vision/joss-whedon-avengers-2-strong-758819. Accessed 7/27/2019.

54. *Avengers: Age of Ultron*, directed by Joss Whedon (2015; Burbank, CA: Marvel Studios), DVD.

55. *Marvel's The Avengers*, directed by Joss Whedon (2012; Burbank, CA: Marvel Studios), DVD.

56. *Avengers: Age of Ultron*, directed by Joss Whedon (2015; Burbank, CA: Marvel Studios), DVD.

57. *Ibid.*

58. *Ibid.*

59. *Ibid.*

60. *Ibid.*

61. *Ibid.*

62. *Purity and Danger*, p. 4.

63. *The Symbolism of Evil*, p. 30.

64. *Captain America: The Winter Soldier*, directed by Anthony and Joe Russo (2014; Burbank, CA: Marvel Studios), DVD.

Chapter Four

1. Certain elements of this chapter previously appeared as "Myths of Hero versus Hero: *the Iliad, the Mahābhārata*, and Marvel's *Civil War*," in *Cosmos and Logos: The Journal of Myth, Religion, and Folklore*. Vol. 3, August 2017, pp. 83–98. I thank the editors of *Cosmos and Logos* for their permission to reprint that material.

2. *The Iliad, or the Poem of Force: A Critical Edition*. Edited and translated by James Holoka. New York: Peter Lang Publications, 2005, p. 53.

3. *Iliad*, translated by Robert Fagles. New York: Penguin Press, 1998, p. 77.

4. *Violence and the Sacred*, translated by Patrick Gregory. Baltimore: Johns Hopkins University Press, 1997, p. 31.

5. *Civil War*, writer: Mark Millar, pencils: Steve McNiven. New York: Marvel Comics, 2007. For an analysis of the political parallels and symbolism of the graphic novel, see *Marvel Comics' "Civil War" and the Age of Terror: Critical Essays on the Comic Saga*, edited by Kevin Michael Scott. Jefferson, NC: McFarland, 2015; *Portraying 9/11: Essays on Representations in Comics, Literature, Film, and Theater*, edited by Veronique Braggard, Christopher Dony, and Warren Rosenberg. Jefferson, NC: McFarland, 2011.

6. Jennifer Vineyard, "Why the Movie *Captain America: Civil War* Didn't Have the Comic Book's Dark Ending," 5/12/2016. Vulture. www.vulture.com/2016/05/captain-america-civil-war-ending-different.html. Accessed 8/8/2019.

7. *Captain America: Civil War*, directed by Anthony and Joe Russo (2016; Burbank, CA: Marvel Studios), DVD.

8. *Ibid.*

9. *Ibid.*

10. *Ibid.*

11. On the possible historical and social context of the *Iliad* and the possibility that this portrayal reflects a time period of cultural strain, see Barry Strauss, *The Trojan War: A New History*, New York: Simon & Schuster, 2006; A.R. Burns, *The Penguin History of Ancient Greece*, New York: Penguin Books, 1985; J.E. Lendon, *Soldiers and Ghosts: A History of Battle in Classical Antiquity*, New Haven: Yale University Press, 2005, pp. 22–38.

12. *Iliad*, p. 82.

13. *Ibid.*, pp. 211–212.

14. *Ibid.*, p. 224.

15. Hilary Mackie, *Talking Trojan: Speech and Community in the Iliad*. New York: Rowman & Littlefield Publishers, 1996.

16. There is an abundant literature on

the historical and social context of the *Mahābhārata*. See Alf Hiltebeitel, *Rethinking the Mahābhārata: A Reader's Guide to the Education of the Dharma King*, Chicago: University of Chicago Press, 2001; John Brockington, *The Sanskrit Epics*, Leiden: E.J. Brill, 1998; James Fitzgerald, "The Great Epic of India as Religious Rhetoric," *Journal of the American Academy of Religion*, 51:4, 1983, p. 613; Tamar Reich, "Sacrificial Violence and Textual Battles: Inner Textual Interpretation in the Sanskrit *Mahābhārata*," *History of Religions*, 41:2, 2001, pp. 149–150; Adam Bowles, *Dharma, Disorder, and the Political in Ancient India*, Leiden: E.J. Brill, 2007.

17. On the respectable qualities of the Kauravas and traditions venerating them, see David Gitomer, "King Duryodhana: the *Mahābhārata* Discourse of Sinning and Virtue in Epic and Drama," *Journal of the American Oriental Society*, 112:2, 1992, pp. 222–232.

18. *The Mahābhārata, Book 1: The Book of the Beginning, Vol. 1*. Translated and Edited by J.A.B. van Buitenen. Chicago: University of Chicago Press, 1973, p. 126.

19. *The Mahābhārata, Book 4: The Book of the Virāta and the Book of the Effort, Vol. 3*. Translated and edited by J.A.B. van Buitenen. Chicago: University of Chicago Press, 1978, p. 451.

20. *Ibid.*, p. 467.

21. *The Bhagavad Gītā in the Mahābhārata*, translated and edited by J.A.B. van Buitenen. Chicago: University of Chicago Press, 1981, p. 71.

22. *The Táin: Translated from the Irish Epic Táin Bó Cúailnge*, translated by Thomas Kinsella. New York: Oxford University Press, 2002, p. 134.

23. *Ibid.*, p. 147.

24. *Captain America: Civil War*, directed by Anthony and Joe Russo (2016; Burbank, CA: Marvel Studios), DVD.

25. See *The Mahābhārata, Book 1: The Book of the Beginning*, p. 449, and The Iliad, p. 541 and 548.

26. *Captain America: Civil War*, directed by Anthony and Joe Russo (2016; Burbank, CA: Marvel Studios), DVD.

27. *Ibid.*

28. *Ibid.*

29. *Ibid.*

30. *Iliad*, p. 440.

31. *Ibid.*, p. 519.

32. *Ibid.*, p. 550.

33. *Ibid.*, p. 553. On the practice of mutilation of the dead as a part—and violation—of the Greek heroic code, see J.E. Lendon, "Homeric Vengeance and the Outbreak of Greek Wars," in *War and Violence in Ancient Greece*, edited by Hans van Wees. Oakville, CT: Classical Press of Wales, 2009, pp. 1–30.

34. *Iliad*, p. 589.

35. *The Ritual of Battle: Krishna in the Mahābhārata*. Ithaca: Cornell University Press, 1996, p. 244.

36. *The Mahābhārata*, Edited by Vishnu S. Sukhthankar Poona. Bhandarkar Oriental research Institute, 1975, 7.121.30. Unfortunately, good English translations of the war sections of the epic are lacking, so I have instead included citations to the book, chapter, and verses of the Sanskrit critical edition.

37. *Ibid.*, 8.61.66ff and 9.57ff, respectively.

38. *Ibid.*, 7.164.70–106.

39. *Ibid.*, 8.66.62ff.

40. *Arjuna in the Mahābhārata: Where Krishna is, There is Victory*. Columbia: University of South Carolina Press, 1989, p. 155.

41. *The Táin*, pp. 120–121.

42. *Ibid.*, p. 151.

43. *Captain America: Civil War*, directed by Anthony and Joe Russo (2016; Burbank, CA: Marvel Studios), DVD.

44. *Ibid.*

45. *Ibid.*

46. *Ibid.*

47. *Ibid.*

48. *The Iliad, or the Poem of Force*, p. 61.

49. *Iliad*, p. 261.

50. *The Táin*, p. 184.

51. *The Iliad, or the Poem of Force*, p. 57.

52. *Violence and the Sacred*, p. 31.

53. *Captain America: Civil War*, directed by Anthony and Joe Russo (2016; Burbank, CA: Marvel Studios), DVD.

54. "Krishna in the *Mahābhārata*: the Death of Karṇa," in *Krishna: A Sourcebook*, edited by Edwin Bryant. New York: Oxford University Press, 2007, p. 27.

55. *The Mahābhārata: 4 The Book of Virāṭa, 5 The Book of the Effort*, p. 445.

56. *Ibid.*, p. 453.

57. Hiltebeitel, "Krishna in the *Mahābhārata*: the Death of Karṇa," p. 47. This is Hiltebeitel's translation.

58. *Ibid.*, p. 55.

59. *Captain America: Civil War*, directed by Anthony and Joe Russo (2016; Burbank, CA: Marvel Studios), DVD.

60. *Thor: Ragnarok*, directed by Taika Waititi (2017; Burbank, CA: Marvel Studios), DVD.

61. *Ibid.*

62. See H.R. Davidson, *Gods and Myths of Northern Europe*. New York: Penguin Press, 1965, pp. 144–146. To an extent, as we will note in chapter six, Thor's character arc is somewhat blunted by the events of *Avengers: Infinity War*, where he gains a new, cybernetic eye and forges a new hammer/axe for summoning lightning. With these two acquisitions, he no longer needs to rely on his inner strength alone, as Odin encouraged him to do.

63. For some interpretations of the Egyptian meanings behind this myth, see Donald Mackenzie, *Egyptian Myths and Legends*, New York: Gramercy Books, 1978, pp. 16–23, and H. Frankfort, *Ancient Egyptian Religion: An Interpretation*, New York: Columbia University Press, 1948, pp. 128–131. Also see the Introduction to *The Egyptian Book of the Dead: The Papyrus of Ani*, translated by E. A. Wallis Budge. New York: Dover Publications, 1967 [1895], p. xlix–lii.

64. Yuan Ke, *Dragons and Dynasties: An Introduction to Chinese Mythology*, translated by Kim Echlin and Nie Zhxiong. New York: Penguin Books, 1993, pp. 14–17.

65. *Ibid.*, pp. 41–51.

66. *The Persian Book of Kings: An Epitome of the Shahnama of Firdawsi*, translated by B.W. Robinson. New York: Routledge, 2002, pp. 32–36.

67. John Wyndham, *Myths of Ife*, London, 1921.

68. *Hesiod*, translated by Richard Lattimore. Ann Arbor: University of Michigan Press, 1959, pp. 131–153.

69. For a discussion of its appearance in the ancient Mediterranean world, especially Greece and Mesopotamia, see G.S. Kirk, *Myth: Its Meaning and Functions in Ancient and Other Cultures*. Berkeley: University of California Press, 1970, pp. 213–215.

70. Stephen Harris and Gloria Platzner, *Classical Mythology: Images and Insights*. 2nd Edition. Mountain View, CA: Mayfield Publishing Company, 1998, p. 51.

71. "Oedipus and the Greek Oedipus Complex," in *Interpretations of Greek Mythology*, edited by Jan Bremmer. Totowa, NJ: Barnes and Noble Books, 1986, p. 48.

72. *Guardians of the Galaxy*, directed by James Gunn (2014; Burbank, CA: Marvel Studios), DVD.

73. *Ibid.*

74. *Guardians of the Galaxy: Vol. 2*, directed by James Gunn (2017; Burbank, CA: Marvel Studios), DVD.

75. *Ibid.*

76. *Ibid.*

77. *Ibid.*

78. *Spider-Man: Homecoming*, directed by Jon Watt (2017; Burbank, CA: Marvel Studios), DVD.

79. *Ibid.*

80. *Ibid.*

81. *Ibid.*

82. See *The Hero with a Thousand Faces*, pp. 126–130. For more on the father archetype, see C.G. Jung, *The Archetypes and the Collective Unconscious*, pp. 85, 214.

83. *Captain Marvel*, directed by Anna Boden and Ryan Fleck (2019; Burbank, CA: Marvel Studios), DVD.

84. *Ibid.*

85. On the concept of *śaktī*, see Tracy Pintchman, *The Rise of the Goddess in the Hindu Tradition*. Albany: State University of New York Press, 1994, p. 110; David Kinsley, *Hindu Goddesses: Visions of the Divine Feminine in the Hindu Religious Tradition*. Berkeley: University of California Press, 1986, p. 49; June McDaniel, *Offering Flowers, Feeding Skulls: Popular Goddess Worship in West Bengal*. New York: Oxford University Press, 2004, p. 3.

86. For an English translation of this passage, see *Classical Hindu Mythology: A Reader in the Sanskrit Purāṇas*, edited and translated by Cornelia Dimmitt and J.A.B. Van Buitenen. Philadelphia: Temple University Press, 1978, p. 234.

87. See *Women, Androgynes, and Other Mythical Beasts*. Chicago: University of Chicago Press, 1980, pp. 90–91. On these division of Hindu goddesses into two disparate groups, also see McDaniel, *Offering Flowering, Feeding Skulls*, p. 5.

88. *The Rise of the Goddess in the Hindu Tradition*, pp. 193–213.

89. For examples of such traditions, see Hillary Rodrigues, *Ritual Worship of the Great Goddess: The Liturgy of the Durgā Pūjā with Interpretation*. Albany: State

University of New York Press, 2003, p. 289; See also, Kinsley, *Hindu Goddesses*, p. 120.

90. "Kālī, the Mad Mother," in *The Book of the Goddess: Past and Present*, edited by Carl Olson. New York: Crossroad Books, 1986, p. 122.

91. *Captain Marvel*, directed by Anna Boden and Ryan Fleck (2019; Burbank, CA: Marvel Studios), DVD.

92. *Ibid.*

93. *Ibid.*

Chapter Five

1. *Avengers: Infinity War*, directed by Anthony and Joe Russo (2018; Burbank, CA: Marvel Studios), DVD.

2. *The Invincible Iron Man*, #55. Writer: Jim Starlin, Inker: Mike Esposito. New York: Marvel, 1973.

3. *The Infinity Gauntlet: 1–6*. Writer: Jim Starlin, Pencils: George Perez and Ron Lim, Inker: Joe Rubenstein, Tom Christopher, and Bruce Solotoff. New York: Marvel, 1991.

4. *Guardians of the Galaxy*, directed by James Gunn (2014; Burbank, CA: Marvel Studios), DVD.

5. *Marvel's The Avengers*, directed by Joss Whedon (2012; Burbank, CA: Marvel Studios), DVD.

6. *Guardians of the Galaxy*, directed by James Gunn (2014; Burbank, CA: Marvel Studios), DVD.

7. E.O. James, *Prehistoric Religion: A Study in Prehistoric Archaeology*. London: Thames and Hudson Books, 1957, p. 29.

8. For numerous examples of this representation of the origin of death in Africa, see Feldmann, *African Myths and Tales*, pp. 107–121. For examples in North America, see Erdoes, *American Indian Myths and Legends*.

9. Parrinder, *African Mythology*, p. 56.

10. Erdoes, *American Indian Mythology*, pp. 188–190.

11. Benjamin Ray, *African Religions: Symbol, Ritual, and Community*. Second Edition. Upper Saddle River, NJ: Prentice Hall, 2000, pp. 10–11.

12. *The Kojiki: an Account of Ancient Matters*, translated by Gustav Heldt. New York: Columbia University Press, 2014, p. 16.

13. *The Upaniṣads*, translated by Patrick Olivelle, p. 37.

14. *Avengers: Infinity War*, directed by Anthony and Joe Russo (2018; Burbank, CA: Marvel Studios), DVD.

15. *Ibid.*

16. *Ibid.*

17. Erdoes, *American Indian Mythology*, p. 189.

18. *The Qur'ān: A New Translation*, translated by M.A.S. Abdel Haleem. New York: Oxford University Press, 2010, pp. 204–205.

19. *Textual Sources for the Study of Islam*, edited and translated by Jan Knappert and Andrew Rippin. Chicago: University of Chicago Press, 1986, p. 82.

20. *Ibid.*, p. 83.

21. *1 Samuel* 2:6.

22. For other references in the Hebrew Bible to "Sheol" and its gloomy aspects, see *Psalm* 6:6, *2 Samuel* 22:5, *Job* 10:21–22, and *Numbers* 16:30–34.

23. For references to "Sheol" in Christian texts, see *Luke* 10:15 and 16:23, *Matthew* 11:23, and *Acts of the Apostles* 2:27 and 2:31. For references to "Gehenna," see *Matthew* 5:29 and 10:28, and *Mark* 9:44.

24. *1 Corinthians* 15:26.

25. *Hebrews* 2:14.

26. For a historical discussion of the gradual separation of death from Satan in the Christian tradition, see Jeffrey Burton Russell, *Satan and the Early Christian Tradition*, Ithaca: Cornell University Press, 1981, pp. 46 and 78; Russell, *Lucifer: the Devil in the Middle Ages*, p. 210.

27. P. 48.

28. See Burkert, *Greek Religion*, pp. 196 and 202, and Graves, *Greek Myths*, pp. 41–42.

29. *Classical Mythology: Images and Insights*, p. 128.

30. *Avengers: Infinity War*, directed by Anthony and Joe Russo (2018; Burbank, CA: Marvel Studios), DVD.

31. *Upanishads: A New Translation*, pp. 231–247.

32. *The Mahābhārata, Volume 2: 2 the Book of the Assembly Hall and 3 The Book of the Forest*, edited and translated by J.A.B. van Buitenen. Chicago: University of Chicago, 1975, p. 768.

33. Kusum P. Merh, *Yama: Glorious Lord of the Other World*. New Delhi: D.K. Printworld, 1996, pp. 175 and 188.

34. Gian Giuseppe Filippi, *Mrtyu: Concept of the Death in Indian Traditions*. New Delhi: D.K. Printworld, 1996, p. 1.

35. For a more extensive discussion of the epithets and linguistic valences of Māra, see Nichols, *Malleable Māra*, p. 3.

36. *Ibid.*, pp. 94–101. For descriptions of Māra's cosmic stature, see specifically *The Connected Discourses of the Buddha*, p. 227.

37. This occurs throughout the *Mārasaṃyutta* and *Bhikkhunīsaṃyutta* texts. See *The Connected Discourses of the Buddha*, pp. 195–220 and p. 221–230, respectively.

38. Cohn, *Cosmos, Chaos, and the World to Come*, p. 21.

39. Lewis Spence, *The Myths of Mexico and Peru*. New York: Dover Publications, 1994, pp. 95–96.

40. Dalley, *Myths from Mesopotamia*, p. 154.

41. *Gilgamesh*, pp. 142–144.

42. *Avengers: Infinity War*, directed by Anthony and Joe Russo (2018; Burbank, CA: Marvel Studios), DVD.

43. For two of the key instances of Māra's daughters in Buddhist texts available in English translation, see Bhikkhu Bodhi, *The Connected Discourses of the Buddha: A Translation of the Saṃyutta Nikāya*, Boston: Wisdom Publications, 2000; and Bijoya Goswami, *Lalitavistara*. Kolkata: The Asiatic Society, 2001.

44. *Avengers: Infinity War*, directed by Anthony and Joe Russo (2018; Burbank, CA: Marvel Studios), DVD.

45. *Avengers: Endgame*, directed by Anthony and Joe Russo (2019; Burbank, CA: Marvel Studios), DVD.

46. *Avengers: Infinity War*, directed by Anthony and Joe Russo (2018; Burbank, CA: Marvel Studios), DVD.

47. See *The Thanos Quest: Book 1—Schemes and Dreams*, Writer: Jim Starlin, Pencils: Ron Lim, Ink: John Beatty. New York: Marvel Comics, 1990, and *The Thanos Quest: Book 2—Games and Prizes*, Writer: Jim Starlin, Pencils: Ron Lim, Ink: John Beatty. New York: Marvel Comics, 1990.

48. Jeffrey Burton Russell, *Satan and the Early Christian Tradition*, pp. 173–174.

49. See *The Connected Discourses of the Buddha*, pp. 196, 199, 202, and 206.

50. For the more global comparative analysis of these occurrences, see Robert Ellwood, *Tales of Darkness: The Mythology of Evil*. New York: Continuum Books, 2009. On the particular case of India, two good references are N. N. Bhattacharyya, *Indian Demonology: the Inverted Pantheon*. New Delhi: Manohar Publishers, 2000, and Gail Hinich Sutherland, *Disguises of the Demon: The Development of the Yakṣa in Hinduism and Buddhism*, Albany: State University of New York Press, 1991.

51. *Guardians of the Galaxy: Volume 2*, directed by James Gunn (2017; Burbank, CA: Marvel Studios), DVD.

52. *Avengers: Infinity War*, directed by Anthony and Joe Russo (2018; Burbank, CA: Marvel Studios), DVD.

53. *Ibid.*

54. *Ibid.*

55. Jan Assmann, *Death and Salvation in Ancient Egypt*, translated by David Lorton. Ithaca: Cornell University Press, 2005, pp. 25–26. See also Jon Davies, *Death, Burial, and Rebirth in the Religions of Antiquity*. New York: Routledge, 1999, pp. 29–31; Erik Hornung, *The One and the Many: Conceptions of God in Ancient Egypt*, translated by John Bains. Ithaca: Cornell University Press, 1982, pp. 80–81; "Introduction," *The Egyptian Book of the Dead*, p. cxvi.

56. Lattimore, *Hesiod*, pp. 172–173.

57. Graves, *Greek Myths*, pp. 46–47; Harris and Platzner, *Classical Mythology*, p. 65.

58. For a prose English translation of this story, which is recounted in the Sanskrit *Devī-Mahātmya*, see R. K. Narayan, *Gods, Demons, and Others*. New York: Bantam Books, 1993, pp. 31–45.

59. See *The Birth of Kumāra by Kālidāsa*, translated by David Smith. New York: New York University Press, 2005, pp. 69–79.

60. *Genesis* 3:19.

61. *Avengers: Infinity War*, directed by Anthony and Joe Russo (2018; Burbank, CA: Marvel Studios), DVD.

62. Mitchell, *Gilgamesh*, p. 150.

63. Assmann, *Death and Salvation in Ancient Egypt*, p. 67. See also, "Introduction," *The Egyptian Book of the Dead*, pp. lii and cxiii, and Siegfried Morenz, *Egyptian Religion*, translated by Ann Keep. New York: Routledge Press, 2004 [1973], pp. 191–212.

64. Eliade, *Shamanism*, p. 216.

65. Michael Perrin, *The Way of the Dead*

Indian: Guajiro Myths and Symbols, Austin: University of Texas Press, 1987, pp. 7–8.

66. Stan Mumford, *Himalayan Dialogue: Tibetan Lamas and Gurung Shamans in Nepal*. Madison: University of Wisconsin Press, 1989, pp. 182–183.

Chapter Six

1. *The Way of Life According to Lao Tzu*, translated by Witter Bynner. New York: Perigee Books, 1994, p. 32.

2. *The Code of the Samurai: A Modern Translation of the Bushido Shoshinshu of Taira Shigesuke*, translated by Thomas Cleary. Rutland, VT: Tuttle Publishing, 1999, pp. 66–67.

3. *Avengers: Endgame*, directed by Anthony and Joe Russo (2019; Burbank, CA: Marvel Studios), DVD.

4. *Ibid.*

5. *Ibid.*

6. Erdoes, *American Indian Mythology*, pp. 442–445.

7. Ronald Berndt and Catherine Berndt, *The Speaking Land: Myth and Story in Aboriginal Australia*. Rochester, VT: Inner Traditions International, 1994, pp. 378–381.

8. Mitchell, *Gilgamesh*, p. 159.

9. *Ibid.*, pp. 168–169.

10. *Ibid.*, p. 193.

11. For further elaboration of this point, see G.S. Kirk, *Myth: Its Meaning and Functions in Ancient and Other Cultures*, Berkeley: University of California Press, 1970, p. 142.

12. Graves, *Greek Myths*, p. 44. Also see W. K. Guthrie, *Orpheus and Greek Religion: A Study of the Orphic Movement*, New York: W.W. Norton and Company, 1966.

13. Harris and Platzner, *Classical Mythology: Images and Insights*, p. 216. Also see Fritz Graf, "Orpheus: A Poet Among Men," in *Interpretations of Greek Mythology*, edited by Jan Bremmer. Totowa, NY: Barnes and Noble Books, 1986, p. 84.

14. Erdoes, *American Indian Mythology*, pp. 190–193. For a discussion of possible theories of diffusion between the ancient Greek stories and the North American versions, see Graf, "Orpheus: A Poet Among Us," pp. 80–106.

15. Erdoes, *American Indian Mythology*, pp. 438–439.

16. *Nihongi: Chronicles of Japan from the Earliest Times*, translated by W. G. Astin. London: George Allen and Unwin Ltd., 1956, pp. 30–31; *The Kojiki*, translated by Gustav Heldt, pp. 14–16.

17. Eliade, *Shamanism*, pp. 311–312.

18. For discussion of the figure of Gesar, see Geoffrey Samuel, *Tantric Revisionings: Understandings of Tibetan Buddhism and Indian Religion*. Burlington, VT: Ashgate Publishing, 2005, pp. 170–171.

19. Teiser, *The Ghost Festival in Medieval China*, pp. 6–7; Robert Campany, "To Hell and Back: Death, Near Death, and Otherworldly Journeys in Early Medieval China," in *Death, Ecstasy, and Otherworldly Journeys*, edited by John Collins and Michael Fishbane. Albany: State University of New York Press, 1995, pp. 354–356.

20. See Guy G. Stroumsa, "Mystical Descents," in *Death, Ecstasy, and Otherworldly Journeys*, p. 144. See also Jeffrey Burton Russell, *Satan: The Early Christian Tradition*, pp. 118–121, and *Lucifer: The Devil in the Middle Ages*, pp. 135–138.

21. Spence, *The Myths of Mexico and Peru*, pp. 37–38, 129.

22. *Popul Vuh: The Mayan Book of the Dawn of Life*, revised edition, translated by Dennis Tedlock. New York: Simon & Schuster, 1996, pp. 116–119.

23. *Ibid.*, pp. 120–138.

24. *Out of This World*, p. 233.

25. Eliade, *Shamanism*, pp. 217–218; Stutley, *Shamanism: An Introduction*, p. 87.

26. Eliade, *Shamanism*, pp. 201–203, 213.

27. Marion Wood, *Spirits, Heroes, and Hunters: Native American Indian Mythology*. New York: Peter Bedrick Books, 1981, pp. 58–62.

28. *The Ghost Festival in Medieval China*, pp. 140–149.

29. For instance, see *Tantric Revisionings*, pp. 78–79, 119.

30. See Eliade, *Shamanism*, p. 211 and 311; Erdoes, *American Indian Mythology*, p. 442; and Popol Vuh, p. 116.

31. *The Odyssey*, translated by Robert Fagles, pp. 251–256.

32. *The Aeneid*, translated by Robert Fagles, p. 212.

33. *Avengers: Endgame*, directed by Anthony and Joe Russo (2019; Burbank, CA: Marvel Studios), DVD.

34. *Ibid.*

35. *Ibid.*

36. *Ibid.*

37. Eliade, *Shamanism*, p. 216; Stutley, *Shamanism: An Introduction*, p. 85.

38. Johannes Wilbert, *Mystic Endowment: Religious Ethnography of the Warao Indians*. Cambridge: Harvard University Press, 1993, p. 99.

39. James Liszka, *The Semiotic of Myth: A Critical Study of the Symbol*. Bloomington: Indiana University Press, 1989.

40. See Anthony Mills, *American Theology, Superhero Comics, and Cinema: The Marvel of Stan Lee and the Revolution of a Genre*. New York: Routledge Press, 2014, pp. 169–184.

41. *Revelation*, 6:12–14.

42. *Gospel of Mark*, 13:24–27.

43. For historical background and context on Christian apocalyptic movements in general and Pre-millennialism in particular, see Paul Boyer, *When Time Shall Be No More: Prophecy Belief in Modern American Culture*. Cambridge: Harvard University Press, 1992; Norman Cohn, *The Pursuit of the Millennium: Revolutionary Millenarians and Mystical Anti-Christs of the Middle Ages*, revised edition, London: Temple Smith Publishing, 1970; John Collins, *The Apocalyptic Imagination: An Introduction to the Jewish Matrix of Christianity*, New York: Crossroads Publishing Company, 1984.

44. For a lengthy description of the forms the Rapture has assumed in Evangelical imaginations, see Boyer, *When Time Shall Be No More*, pp. 254–290.

45. See *Isaiah* 24–27, *Joel* 3, *Ezekiel* 37, and *Zechariah* 14.

46. Norman Cohn, *Cosmos, Chaos, and the World to Come*, pp. 187–193.

47. For this genetic link between the mythologies, see Norman Cohn, *Cosmos, Chaos, and the World to Come*, pp. 220–231.

48. *Ibid.*, pg. 97. See also Boyce, *Zoroastrianism*, pp. 28 and 129.

49. See Doniger-O'Flaherty, *The Origins of Evil in Hindu Mythology*, pp. 200–205, and *Classical Hindu Mythology*, translated by Dimmit and van Buitenen, p. 42.

50. H.R. Ellis Davidson, *Gods and Myths of Northern Europe*, pp. 37–38.

51. *Avengers: Endgame*, directed by Anthony and Joe Russo (2019; Burbank, CA: Marvel Studios), DVD.

52. *Ibid.*

53. *Ibid.*

54. *Popul Vuh*, translated by Dennis Tedlock, p. 141.

55. Mitchell, *Gilgamesh*, pp. 198–199.

56. *Avengers: Endgame*, directed by Anthony and Joe Russo (2019; Burbank, CA: Marvel Studios), DVD.

57. *Marvel's The Avengers*, directed by Joss Whedon (2012; Burbank, CA: Marvel Studios), DVD.

58. Wendy Doniger, *The Implied Spider*, p. 25.

Conclusion

1. Pamela McClintock, "Box Office: 'Spider-Man: Far From Home" Re-release Pays Off, Pic Nears $400 Million in U.S.," *Hollywood Reporter*, 9/1/2019. https://hollywoodreporter.com/heat-vision/spider-man-far-home-rerelease-pays-nears-400m-us-1235936. Accessed 9/15/2019.

2. Scott Huver, "Kevin Feige Reveals the Thinking Behind Marvel's Phase Four." *CNN*. 7/21/2019. https://cnn.com/2019/07/21/entertainment/kevin-feige-comic-con/index.html. Accessed 9/15/2019.

3. Devan Coggan, "Here Are All Marvel's Upcoming Phase 4 Movies," *Entertainment Weekly*. 9/5/2019. https://ew.com/movies/2019/07/22/marvel-phase-4-every-movie-and-tv-show/. Accessed 9/20/2019.

4. *Ibid.*

5. See Eliana Dockterman, "The Path to the X-Men Joining the Marvel Cinematic Universe Just Got a Lot Clearer." *Time*. 3/20/2019. https://time.com/5517975/marvel-cinematic-universe-x-men/. Accessed 9/25/2019.

6. Will Thorne, "Sony Picture's Chief on Spider-Man Split: 'For the Moment, the Door is Closed." *Variety*. 9/5/2019. https://variety.com/2019/film/news/spiderman-mcu-sony-pictures-chief-1203324907/. Accessed 9/19/2019. For a seeming resolution to the drama, see Mark Hughes, "Spider-Man Back in Marvel Cinematic Universe After Sony, Marvel Reach a Deal." *Forbes*. 9/27/2019. https://www.forbes.com/sites/markhughes/2019/09/27/spider-man-back-in-marvel-cinematic-universe-after-sony-

marvel-reach-new-deal/#53778a621a8f. Accessed 9/30/2019.

7. Scott Huver, "Avengers: Endgame Screenwriters Really Wanted to Deliver a Satisfying Conclusion," *CNN.* 8/13/2019. https://cnn.com/2019/08/13/entertainment/avengers-endgame-screenwriters/index.html. Accessed 9/18/2019.

8. For a comparative analysis of narratives of age-ending battles, see Michael Nichols, "How the World Ended: Myths of Retrospective Eschatology," *Cosmos and Logos: the Journal of Myth, Religion, and Folklore,* Vol. 2, 2016, pp. 1–12.

9. Eric Eisenberg, "Black Widow: What We Know So Far." *Cinemablend.* 7/31/2019. https://www.cinemablend.com/news/2477354/black-widow-what-we-know-so-far. Accessed 9/30/2019.

10. For an erudite discussion of these texts and their place within the wider early Christian tradition, see Bart Ehrman, *Lost Christianities: the Battles for Scripture and the Faiths We Never Knew.* New York: Oxford University Press, 2005.

11. For a discussion of these *jātaka* stories and translations of several of the most famous examples, see *Once the Buddha Was a Monkey: Ārya Śūra's Jātakamālā,* translated by Peter Khoroche. Chicago: University of Chicago Press, 2006.

12. To recap just a few examples discussed in more detail in the introduction, see Jeffrey Brown, *The Modern Superhero in Film and Television: Popular Genre and American Culture,* p. 71, and Terence McSweeney, *Avengers Assemble!: Critical Perspectives on the MCU,* pp. 23–24.

13. Bruce David Forbes, "Introduction," in *Religion and Popular Culture in America,* Revised Edition, edited by Bruce David Forbes and Jeffrey Mahan. Berkeley: University of California Press, 2005, p. 2.

14. David Chidester, "The Church of Baseball, the Fetish of Coca-Cola, and the Potlatch of Rock 'n' Roll: Theoretical Models for the Study of Religion in American Popular Culture," *Journal of American Academy of Religion.* 64:4, 1996, pp. 743–765.

15. Catherine Albanese, "Religion and Popular Culture: An Introductory Essay," *Journal of American Academy of Religion.* 59:4, 1991, p. 740.

16. See M.M. Bakhtin, *The Dialogic Imagination,* translated by Caryl Emerson and Michael Holquist. Austin: University of Texas Press, 1981, and Harold Bloom, *A Map of Misreading.* New York: Oxford University Press, 1975.

17. Henry A. Murray, "The Possible Nature of a 'Mythology' to Come," in *Myth and Mythmaking,* edited by Henry A. Murray. New York: George Braziller Press, 1960, p. 300.

18. William E. Paden, "Elements of a New Comparison," in *A Magic Still Dwells,* p. 190.

19. *Imagining Religion: From Babylon to Jonestown.* Chicago: University of Chicago Press, 1982, pp. 21–35.

20. *Considering Comparison: A Method for Religious Studies.* New York: Oxford University Press, 2019, pp. 52–53, 92–93.

21. See, respectively, Archie Bland, "Comic Book Superheroes: the Gods of Modern Mythology," *The Guardian.* 5/27/2016. https://theguardian.com/books/2016/may/27/comic-book-superheroes-the-gods-of-modern-mythology. Accessed 9/14/2019; Robin Rosenberg, "Our Fascination with Superheroes," in *What is a Superhero?,* pp. 3–18; Ben Saunders, *Do the Gods Wear Capes?: Spirituality, Fantasy, and Superheroes.* New York: Continuum Press, 2011, p. 32.

22. Scott Huver, "Avengers: Endgame Screenwriters Really Wanted to Deliver a Satisfying Conclusion," *CNN.* 8/13/2019. https://cnn.com/2019/08/13/entertainment/avengers-endgame-screenwriters/index.html. Accessed 9/18/2019.

23. Bruce David Forbes, "Introduction," in *Religion and Popular Culture in America,* p. 15.

24. Greg Garrett, *Holy Superheroes: Exploring Faith and Spirituality in Comic Books.* Colorado Springs: Piñon Press, 2005, p. 37.

25. *A Short History of Myth.* New York: Canongate Press, 2005, p. 6.

26. *Myth: Key Concepts in Religion,* p. 6

27. *The Hero with a Thousand Faces,* p. 23.

Filmography

The Amazing Spider-Man, directed by Marc Webb (2012; Burbank, CA: Sony Pictures), DVD.

Ant-Man, directed by Peyton Reed (2015; Burbank, CA: Marvel Studios), DVD.

Ant-Man and the Wasp, directed by Peyton Reed (2018; Burbank, CA: Marvel Studios), DVD.

The Avengers: Age of Ultron, directed by Joss Whedon (2015; Burbank, CA: Marvel Studios), DVD.

The Avengers: Endgame, directed by Anthony and Joe Russo (2019; Burbank, CA: Marvel Studios), DVD.

The Avengers: Infinity War, directed by Anthony and Joe Russo (2018; Burbank, CA: Marvel Studios), DVD.,

Batman Begins, directed by Christopher Nolan (2008; Burbank, CA: Warner Bros. Pictures), DVD.

Batman v. Superman: Dawn of Justice, directed by Zack Snyder (2016; Burbank, CA: Warner Bros. Pictures), DVD.

Black Panther, directed by Ryan Coogler (2018; Burbank, CA: Marvel Studios), DVD.

Captain America: Civil War, directed by Joe and Anthony Russo (2016; Burbank, CA: Marvel Studios), DVD.

Captain America: The First Avenger, directed by Joe Johnston (2011; Burbank, CA: Marvel Studios), DVD.

Captain America: The Winter Soldier, directed by Joe and Anthony Russo (2014; Burbank, CA: Marvel Studios), DVD.

Captain Marvel, directed by Anna Boden and Ryan Fleck (2019; Burbank, CA: Marvel Studios), DVD.

The Dark Knight, directed by Christopher Nolan (2008; Burbank, CA: Warner Bros. Pictures), DVD.

The Dark Knight Rises, directed by Christopher Nolan (2012; Burbank, CA: Warner Bros. Pictures), DVD.

Doctor Strange, directed by Scott Derrickson (2016; Burbank, CA: Marvel Studios), DVD.

Guardians of the Galaxy, directed by James Gunn (2014; Burbank, CA: Marvel Studios), DVD.

Guardians of the Galaxy: Volume 2, directed by James Gunn (2017; Burbank, CA: Marvel Studios), DVD.

The Incredible Hulk, directed by Louis LeTerrier (2008; Burbank, CA: Marvel Studios and Universal Pictures), DVD.

Iron Man, directed by Jon Favreau (2008; Burbank, CA: Marvel Studios), DVD.

Iron Man 2, directed by Jon Favreau (2010; Burbank, CA: Marvel Studios), DVD.

Iron Man 3, directed by Shane Black (2013; Burbank, CA: Marvel Studios), DVD.

Man of Steel, directed by Zack Snyder (2013; Burbank, CA: Warner Bros. Pictures), DVD.

Marvel's The Avengers, directed by Joss Whedon (2012; Burbank, CA: Marvel Studios), DVD.

Spider-Man, directed by Sam Raimi (2002; Burbank, CA: Sony Pictures), DVD.

Spider-Man: Far from Home, directed by Jon Watts (2019; Burbank, CA: Marvel Studios), DVD.

Spider-Man: Homecoming, directed by Jon Watts (2017; Burbank, CA: Marvel Studios), DVD.

Spider-Man 2, directed by Sam Raimi (2004; Burbank, CA: Sony Pictures), DVD.

Spider-Man 3, directed by Sam Raimi (2007; Burbank, CA: Sony Pictures), DVD.

Thor, directed by Kenneth Branagh (2011; Burbank, CA: Marvel Studios), DVD.

Thor: Ragnarok, directed by Taika Waititi (2017; Burbank, CA: Marvel Studios), DVD.

Thor: The Dark World, directed by Alan Taylor (2013; Burbank, CA: Marvel Studios), DVD.

Bibliography

African Myths and Tales, edited by Susan Feldmann. New York: Dell Publishing, 1963.

Albanese, Catherine. "Religion and Popular Culture: An Introductory Essay." *Journal of American Academy of Religion.* 59:4, 1991, p. 733–742.

Altman, Rick. *A Theory of Narrative.* New York: Columbia University Press, 2008.

Amazing Fantasy #15 (August 1962), writer: Stan Lee, Penciler: Steve Ditko.

American Indian Mythology, Richard Erdoes and Alfonso Ortiz. New York: Pantheon Books, 1984.

Armstrong, Karen. *A Short History of Myth.* New York: Canongate Press, 2005.

Arnaudo, Marco. *The Myth of the Superhero.* Baltimore: Johns Hopkins Press, 2013.

Assmann, Jan. *Death and Salvation in Ancient Egypt,* translated by David Lorton. Ithaca: Cornell University Press, 2005.

Bahlmann, Andrew. *The Mythology of the Superhero.* Jefferson, NC: McFarland, 2016.

Bakhtin, M.M. *The Dialogic Imagination,* translated by Caryl Emerson and Michael Holquist. Austin: University of Texas Press, 1981.

Batchelor, Stephen. *Living with the Devil: A Meditation on Good and Evil.* New York: Riverhead Books, 2004.

Beal, Timothy K. *Religion and Its Monsters.* New York: Routledge, 2002.

Bell, Catherine. *Ritual: Perspectives and Dimensions.* New York: Oxford University Press, 1997.

Beowulf: A New Verse Translation, Seamus Heaney. New York: W.W. Norton and Company, 2000.

Berndt, Ronald, and Catherine Berndt. *The Speaking Land: Myth and Story in Aboriginal Australia.* Rochester, VT: Inner Traditions International, 1994.

The Bhagavad Gītā in the Mahābhārata, translated and edited by J.A.B. van Buitenen. Chicago: University of Chicago Press, 1981.

Bhattacharyya, N. N. *Indian Demonology: the Inverted Pantheon.* New Delhi: Manohar Publishers, 2000.

The Birth of Kumāra by Kālidāsa, translated by David Smith. New York: New York University Press, 2005.

Bland, Archie. "Comic Book Superheroes: the Gods of Modern Mythology." *The Guardian.* 5/27/2016. https://theguardian.com/books/2016/may/27/comic-book-superheroes-the-gods-of-modern-mythology.

Bloom, Harold. *A Map of Misreading.* New York: Oxford University Press, 1975.

Boswell, James. *The Life of Samuel Johnson.* Garden City, NY: Garden City Books, 1945.

Bovensiepen, Judith. "*Lulik*: Taboo, Animism, or Transgressive Sacred? An Exploration of Identity, Morality, and Power in Timor-Leste." *Oceania* 84:2 (2014), pp. 121–137.

Bowles, Adam. *Dharma, Disorder, and the Political in Ancient India.* Leiden: E.J. Brill, 2007.

Boyce, Mary. *Zoroastrians: Their Religious Beliefs and Practices.* Boston: Routledge and Kegan Paul, 1979.

Boyer, Paul. *When Time Shall Be No More: Prophecy Belief in Modern American Culture.* Cambridge: Harvard University Press, 1992.

Bragard, Veronique, Christophe Dony, and Warren Rosenberg (eds.). *Portraying 9/11: Essays on Representation in Comics, Literature, Film, and Theater.* Jefferson, NC: McFarland, 2011.

Bremmer, Jan. "Oedipus and the Greek Oedipus Complex," in *Interpretations of Greek Mythology,* edited by Jan Bremmer. Totowa, N.J: Barnes and Noble Books, 1986.

Bretfeld, Sven. "Purifying the Pure: the *Visuddhimagga,* Forest-Dwellers, and the Dynamics of Individual and Collective Prestige in Theravāda Buddhism," in *Discourses of Purity in Transcultural Perspective,* edited by Matthias Bley, Nikolas Jaspert, and Stefan Köck. Boston: E.J. Brill, 2015.

Brockington, John. *The Sanskrit Epics.* Leiden: E.J. Brill, 1998.

Brown, C. Mackenzie. "Kālī, the Mad Mother," in *The Book of the Goddess: Past and Present,* edited by Carl Olson. New York: Crossroad Books, 1986, pp. 110–123.

Brown, Jeffrey. *The Modern Superhero in Film and Television: Popular Genre and American Culture.* New York: Routledge, 2017.

Buddha-Karita, or Live of Buddha by Ashvaghosha. Edited by E.B. Cowell. Amsterdam: Philo Press, 1970.

Burkert, Walter. *Greek Religion,* translated by John Raffan. Cambridge: Harvard University Press, 1985.

Campany, Robert. "To Hell and Back: Death, Near Death, and Otherworldly Journeys in Early Medieval China," in *Death, Ecstasy, and Otherworldly Journeys,* edited by John Collins and Michael Fishbane. Albany: State University of New York Press, 1995, pp. 343–360.

Campbell, Joseph. *The Hero with A Thousand Faces.* Princeton: Princeton University Press, 1949.

Carroll, Noel. *The Philosophy of Horror, or Paradoxes of the Heart.* New York: Routledge, 1990.

Chidester, David. "The Church of Baseball, the Fetish of Coca-Cola, and the Potlatch of Rock 'n' Roll: Theoretical Models for the Study of Religion in American Popular Culture." *Journal of American Academy of Religion* 64:4, 1996, pp. 743–765.

Civil War, writer: Mark Millar, pencils: Steve McNiven. New York: Marvel Comics, 2007.

Clark, Travis. "The Eight Marvel Cinematic Universe Movies that Made Over $1 Billion at the Global Box Office." *Business Insider,* 4/29/19. https://www.businessinsider.com/marvel-cinematic-universe-movies-to-make-1-billion-at-the-box-office-2019-4

Classical Hindu Mythology: A Reader in the Sanskrit Purāṇas, edited and translated by Cornelia Dimmitt and J.A.B. Van Buitenen. Philadelphia: Temple University Press, 1978.

The Code of the Samurai: A Modern Translation of the Bushido Shoshinshu of Taira Shigesuke, translated by Thomas Cleary. Rutland, VT: Tuttle Publishing, 1999.

Cohen, Jeffrey. "Monster Culture: Seven Theses," in *Monster Theory: Reading Culture.* Minneapolis: University of Minnesota Press, 1996.

Cohn, Norman. *Cosmos, Chaos, and the World to Come,* 2nd Edition. New Haven: Yale University Press, 2001.

Cohn, Norman. *The Pursuit of the Millennium: Revolutionary Millenarians and Mystical Anti-Christs of the Middle Ages,* revised edition. London: Temple Smith Publishing, 1970.

Collins, John. *The Apocalyptic Imagination: An Introduction to the Jewish Matrix of Christianity.* New York: Crossroads Publishing Company, 1984.

The Connected Discourses of the Buddha, translated by Bhikkhu Bodhi. Boston: Wisdom Publications, 2000.

Coogan, Peter. *Superhero: The Secret Origin of a Genre.* Monkeybrain Books, 2006.

Courtright, Paul. *Gaṇeśa: Lord of Obstacles, Lord of Beginnings*: New York: Oxford University Press, 1985.

Culianu, Ioan. *Out of this World: Otherworldly Journeys from Gilgamesh to Albert Einstein.* Boston: Shambhala Press, 1991.

Dantzler, Perry. "Multiliteracies of the Marvel Cinematic Universe," in *Assembling the Marvel Cinematic Universe: Essays on the Social, Cultural, and Geopolitical Domains,* edited by William Svitavsky Chambliss and Daniel Fandino. Jefferson, NC: McFarland, 2018, 168–184.

Davidson, H. R. *Gods and Myths of Northern Europe.* New York: Penguin Press, 1965.

Davies, Jon. *Death, Burial, and Rebirth in the Religions of Antiquity.* New York: Routledge, 1999.

Dharmasūtras, the Law Code of Ancient India, translated by Patrick Olivelle. New York: Oxford University Press, 1999.

Dockterman, Eliana. "The Path to the X-Men Joining the Marvel Cinematic Universe Just Got a Lot Clearer." *Time.* 3/20/2019. https://time.com/5517975/marvel-cinematic-universe-x-men/.

Doniger, Wendy. *The Implied Spider: Politics and Theology in Myth,* New York: Columbia University Press, 1998 (See also, "O'Flaherty, Wendy Doniger.")

Doty, William. *Mythography: The Study of Myths and Rituals.* Second edition. Tuscaloosa: University of Alabama Press, 2000.

Douglas, Mary. *Purity and Danger: An Analysis of Concepts of Pollution and Taboos.* New York: Routledge Press, 1966.

Dumont, Louis. *Homo Hierarchicus: the Caste System and Its Implications,* translated by Mark Sainsbury, Louis Dumont, and Basia Gulati. Berkeley: University of California Press, 1980.

Dundes, Alan. "Introduction," in *Sacred Narrative: Readings in the Theory of Myth.* Edited by Alan Dundes. Berkeley: University of California Press, 1984, pp. 1–3.

Durkheim, Émile. *The Elementary Forms of Religious Life,* translated by Carol Cosman. New York: Oxford University Press, 2001.

Eccleston, Sasha Mae. "Enemies, Foreign and Domestic: Villainy and Terrorism in Marvel Studio's *Thor,*" in *Assembling the Marvel Cinematic Universe,* edited by Julian Chambliss, William Svitavsky, and Daniel Fandino. Jefferson, NC: McFarland, 2018, 168–184.

The Egyptian Book of the Dead: The Papyrus of Ani, translated by E. A. Wallis Budge. New York: Dover Publications, 1967 [1895].

Ehrman, Bart. *Lost Christianities: the Battles for Scripture and the Faiths We Never Knew.* New York: Oxford University Press, 2005.

Eisenberg, Eric. "Black Widow: What We Know So Far." *Cinemablend.* 7/31/2019. https://www.cinemablend.com/news/2477354/black-widow-what-we-know-so-far.

Eliade, Mircea. *Mephistopheles and the Androgyne: Studies in Religious Myth and Symbol.* Translated by J.M. Cohen. New York: Sheed and Word, 1965.

Eliade, Mircea. *Patterns in Comparative Religion,* translated by Rosemary Sheed. Lincoln: University of Nebraska Press, 1996 [1958].

Eliade, Mircea. *The Sacred and the Profane: Nature and Religion.* Translated by Willard Trask. New York: Harcourt Brace, 1959.

Eliade, Mircea. *Shamanism: Archaic Techniques of Ecstasy,* Translated by Willard Trask. Princeton: Princeton University Press, 1964.

Ellwood, Robert. *Myth: Key Concepts in Religion.* New York: Continuum, 2008.

Ellwood, Robert. *The Politics of Myth: A Study of C.G. Jung, Mircea Eliade, and Joseph Campbell*. Albany: SUNY Press, 1999.

Ellwood, Robert. *Tales of Darkness: The Mythology of Evil*. New York: Continuum Books, 2009.

Filippi, Gian Giuseppe. *Mrtyu: Concept of the Death in Indian Traditions*. New Delhi: D.K. Printworld, 196.

Fingeroth, Danny. "Power and Responsibility ... and Other Reflections on Superheroes," in *What is a Superhero?* Edited by Robin Rosenberg and Peter Coogan. New York: Oxford University Press, 2013.

Fingeroth, Danny. *Superman on the Couch: What Superheroes Really Tell Us about Ourselves and Our Society*. New York: Continuum, 2004.

Fitzgerald, James. "The Great Epic of India as Religious Rhetoric." *Journal of the American Academy of Religion*, 51:4, 1983: pp. 611–630.

Forbes, Bruce David. "Introduction," in *Religion and Popular Culture in America*. Revised edition, edited by Bruce David Forbes and Jeffrey Mahan. Berkeley: University of California Press, 2005, pp. 1–20.

Frankfort, Henri. *Ancient Egyptian Religion: An Interpretation*, New York: Columbia University Press, 1948.

Freiberger, Oliver. *Considering Comparison: A Method for Religious Studies*. New York: Oxford University Press, 2019.

Garrett, Greg. *Holy Superheroes: Exploring Faith and Spirituality in Comic Books*. Colorado Springs, Co: Piñon Press, 2005.

Gilmore, David. *Monsters: Evil Beings, Mythical Beasts, and All Manner of Imaginary Terrors*. Philadelphia: University of Pennsylvania, 2003.

Girard, René. *Violence and the Sacred*, translated by Patrick Gregory. Baltimore: Johns Hopkins University Press, 1997.

Gitomer, David. "King Duryodhana: the *Mahābhārata* Discourse of Sinning and Virtue in Epic and Drama." *Journal of the American Oriental Society*, 112:2, 1992, pp. 222–232.

Goswami, Bijoya. *Lalitavistara*. Kolkata: The Asiatic Society, 2001.

Graf, Fritz. "Orpheus: A Poet Among Men," in *Interpretations of Greek Mythology*, edited by Jan Bremmer. Totowa, NJ: Barnes and Noble Books, 1986.

Gross, Kenneth. "Satan and the Romantic Satan: a Notebook," in *Re-Membering Milton: Essays on the Texts and Traditions*, ed. Mary Nyquist and Margaret W. Ferguson. New York: Methuen Press, 1987.

Günther, Linda-Marie. "Concepts of Purity in Ancient Greece," in *Purity and the Forming of Religious Traditions in the Ancient Mediterranean World and Ancient Judaism*, edited by Christian Frevel and Christophe Nihan. Boston: E.J. Brill, 2013.

Guthrie, W. K. *Orpheus and Greek Religion: A Study of the Orphic Movement*. New York: W.W. Norton and Company, 1966.

Haber, Susan, edited by Adele Reinhartz. *"They Shall Purify Themselves": Essays on Purity in Early Judaism*. Atlanta: Society of Biblical Literature, 2008.

Harris, Stephen, and Gloria Platzner. *Classical Mythology: Images and Insights*. 2nd Edition. Mountain View, CA: Mayfield Publishing Company, 1998.

Hesiod, translated by Richard Lattimore. Ann Arbor: University of Michigan Press, 1959.

Heyne, F. George. "The Social Significance of the Shaman among the Chinese Reindeer Evenki," in *Shamanism in Asia*, edited by Peter Knecht and Clark Chilson. New York: Routledge, 2003.

Hiltebeitel, Alf. "Krishna in the *Mahābhārata*: the Death of Karṇa," in *Krishna: A Sourcebook*, edited by Edwin Bryant. New York: Oxford University Press, 2007.

Hiltebeitel, Alf. *Rethinking the Mahābhārata: A Reader's Guide to the Education of the Dharma King*, Chicago: University of Chicago Press, 2001.

Hilterbeitel, Alf. *The Ritual of Battle: Krishna in the Mahābhārata.* Ithaca: Cornell University Press, 1996.

Hindu Myths: A Sourcebook. Translated by Wendy Doniger O'Flaherty. New York: Penguin Press, 1975.

Hinnells, John R., and Richard King (eds). *Religion and Violence in South Asia.* New York: Routledge Press, 2007.

Hornung, Erik. *The One and the Many: Conceptions of God in Ancient Egypt,* translated by John Bains. Ithaca: Cornell University Press, 1982.

Hughes, Mark. "Spider-Man Back in Marvel Cinematic Universe After Sony, Marvel Reach a Deal." *Forbes.* 9/27/2019. https://www.forbes.com/sites/markhughes/2019/09/27/spider-man-back-in-marvel-cinematic-universe-after-sony-marvel-reach-new-deal/#53778a621a8f.

Huver, Scott. "Avengers: Endgame Screenwriters Really Wanted to Deliver a Satisfying Conclusion." *CNN.* 8/13/2019. https://cnn.com/2019/08/13/entertainment/avengers-endgame-screenwriters/index.html.

Huver, Scott. "Kevin Feige Reveals the Thinking Behind Marvel's Phase Four." *CNN.* 7/21/2019. https://cnn.com/2019/07/21/entertainment/kevin-feige-comic-con/index.html.

The Iliad, translated by Robert Fagles. New York: Penguin Press, 1998.

The Infinity Gauntlet: 1–6. Writer: Jim Starlin, Pencils: George Perez and Ron Lim, Inker: Joe Rubenstein, Tom Christopher, and Bruce Solotoff. New York: Marvel, 1991.

The Invincible Iron Man, #55. Writer: Jim Starlin, Inker: Mike Esposito. New York: Marvel, 1973.

Itzkoff, David. "'Avengers,' the Most Lucrative Movie Franchise Ever, is Wrapping Up. Why?" *New York Times.* 4/23/18. https://www.nytimes.com/2018/04/23/movies/avengers-infinity-war-disney-marvel.html.

James, E. O. *Prehistoric Religion: A Study in Prehistoric Archaeology.* London: Thames and Hudson Books, 1957.

Jerryson, Michael. *Buddhist Fury: Religion and Violence in Southern Thailand.* New York: Oxford University Press, 2011.

Johnson, Tre. "*Black Panther* is a Gorgeous, Ground-breaking Celebration of Black Culture." *Vox,* 2/23/2018. Accessed 3/24/2020. https://www.vox.com/culture/2018/2/23/17028826/black-panther-wakanda-culture-marvel.

Juergensmeyer, Mark. *Terror in the Mind of God: The Global Rise of Religious Violence.* Third Edition. Berkeley: University of California Press, 2005.

Juergensmeyer, Mark, and Michael Jerryson (eds.). *Buddhist Warfare.* New York: Oxford University Press, 2010.

Juergensmeyer, Mark, Margo Kitt, and Michael Jerryson (eds.) *Violence and the World's Religious Traditions: An Introduction.* New York: Oxford University Press, 2016.

Julian Chambliss, William Svitavsky, and Daniel Fandino, Jefferson, NC: McFarland, 2018.

Jung, Carl. *The Archetypes and the Collective Unconscious.* Second edition. Translated by R.F.C. Hull. Princeton: Princeton University Press, 1990 [1959].

Katz, Ruth. *Arjuna in the Mahābhārata: Where Krishna is, There is Victory.* Columbia: University of South Carolina Press, 1989.

Kaveney, Roz. *Superheroes!: Capes and Crusaders in Comics and Films,* New York: I.B. Tauris, 2008.

Kimball, Charles. *When Religion Becomes Evil: Five Warning Signs.* San Francisco: HarperCollins, 2002.

Kinsley, David. *Hindu Goddesses: Visions of the Divine Feminine in the Hindu Religious Tradition.* Berkeley: University of California Press, 1986.

Kirk, G.S. *Myth: Its Meaning and Functions in Ancient and Other Cultures.* Berkeley: University of California Press, 1970.

Knecht, Peter, and Clark Chilson (eds.) *Shamanism in Asia*, New York: Routledge, 2003.

Knowles, Christopher. *Our Gods Wear Spandex: The Secret History of Comic Book Heroes*. San Francisco: Weiser Books, 2007.

The Kojiki: An Account of Ancient Matters, translated by Gustav Heldt. New York: Columbia University Press, 2014.

Kripal, Jeffrey. *Authors of the Impossible: The Paranormal and the Sacred*. Chicago: University of Chicago Press, 2010.

Kripal, Jeffrey. *Mutants and Mystics: Science Fiction, Superhero Comics, and the Supernatural*. Chicago: University of Chicago Press, 2011.

Kristeva, Julia. *Powers of Horror: An Essay on Abjection*, translated by Leon Roudiez. New York: Columbia University Press, 1982.

Lawson, John Howard, *Theory and Technique of Playwriting and Screenwriting*. New York: G.P. Putnam's Sons, 1949.

Lee, Stan (writer), and Jack Kirby (artist), *The Incredible Hulk*, Issue #1, New York: Marvel Comics (May 1962).

Lendon, J.E. "Homeric Vengeance and the Outbreak of Greek Wars," in *War and Violence in Ancient Greece*, edited by Hans van Wees. Oakville, CT: Classical Press of Wales, 2009.

Lewis, Ioan M. *Ecstatic Religion: An Anthropological Study of Spirit Possession and Shamanism*, revised edition. New York: Penguin Books, 1978.

Life of the Buddha, by Ashvaghosha, translated by Patrick Olivelle. New York: New York University Press, 2009.

Lincoln, Bruce. *Discourse and the Construction of Society: Comparative Studies of Myth, Ritual, and Classification*. New York: Oxford University Press, 1992.

Lincoln, Bruce. *Holy Terrors: Thinking about Religion After September 11*. Chicago: University of Chicago Press, 2003.

Lincoln, Bruce. *Theorizing Myth: Narrative, Ideology, and Scholarship*. Chicago: University of Chicago Press, 1997.

Liszka, James. *The Semiotic of Myth: A Critical Study of the Symbol*. Bloomington: Indiana University Press, 1989.

Lo Cicero, Don. *Superheroes and Gods: A Comparative Study from Babylonia to Batman*. Jefferson, NC: McFarland, 2008.

Long, David. *The Hajj Today: A Survey of the Contemporary Pilgrimage to Makkah*. Albany: State University of New York Press, 1979.

Mackenzie, Donald. *Egyptian Myths and Legends*. New York: Gramercy Books, 1978.

Mackie, Hilary. *Talking Trojan: Speech and Community in the Iliad*. New York: Rowman & Littlefield Publishers, 1996.

The Mahābhārata, edited by Vishnu S. Sukhthankar Poona. Bhandarkar Oriental research Institute, 1975.

The Mahābhārata, Book 1: The Book of the Beginning, Vol. 1. Translated and edited by J.A.B. van Buitenen. Chicago: University of Chicago Press, 1973.

The Mahābhārata, Book 2: The Book of the Assembly Hall and 3 The Book of the Forest, Vol. 2, edited and translated by J.A.B. van Buitenen. Chicago: University of Chicago, 1975.

The Mahābhārata, Book 4: The Book of the Virāta and the Book of the Effort, Vol. 3, edited and translated by J.A.B. van Buitenen. Chicago: University of Chicago Press, 1978.

Malinowski, Bronislaw. *Magic, Science, and Religion*. Long Grove, IL: Waveland Press, 1992 [1948].

Malinowski, Bronislaw. "The Role of Myth in Life," in *Sacred Narrative: Readings in the Theory of Myth*. Edited by Alan Dundes. Berkeley: University of California Press, 1984, pp. 193–206.

Marvel Comics' "Civil War" and the Age of Terror: Critical Essays on the Comic Saga, edited by Kevin Michael Scott. Jefferson, NC: McFarland, 2015.

McClintock, Pamela. "Box Office: 'Spider-Man: Far From Home" Re-release Pays Off, Pic Nears $400 Million in U.S." *Hollywood Reporter,* 9/1/2019. https://hollywoodreporter. com/heat-vision/spider-man-far-home-rerelease-pays-nears-400m-us-1235936.

McCutcheon, Russell. *Manufacturing Religion: The Discourse on Sui Generis Religion and the Politics of Nostalgia.* New York: Oxford University Press, 1997.

McDaniel, June. *Offering Flowers, Feeding Skulls: Popular Goddess Worship in West Bengal.* New York: Oxford University Press, 2004.

McMillan, Graeme. "Joss Whedon on 'Avengers 2.'" *The Hollywood Reporter.* 12/17/2014. https://www.hollywoodreporter.com/heat-vision/joss-whedon-avengers-2-strong-758819.

McSweeney, Terrence. *Avengers Assemble!: Critical Perspectives on the Marvel Cinematic Universe.* New York: Wallflower Press, 2018.

Merh, Kusum P. *Yama: Glorious Lord of the Other World.* New Delhi: D.K. Printworld, 1996.

Mills, Anthony. *American Theology, Superhero Comics, and Cinema: The Marvel of Stan Lee and the Revolution of a Genre.* New York: Routledge Press, 2014.

Milton, John. *Paradise Lost,* edited by Gordon Testkey. New York: W. W. Norton Critical Editions, 2005.

Mitchell, Stephen. *Gilgamesh.* New York: Simon & Schuster, 2004.

Morenz, Siegfried. *Egyptian Religion,* translated by Ann Keep. New York: Routledge Press, 2004 [1973].

Morrison, Grant. *Supergods: What Masked Vigilantes, Miraculous Mutants, and a Sun God from Smallville Can Teach Us About Being Human.* New York: Spiegel and Rau, 2011.

Murray, Henry A. "The Possible Nature of a 'Mythology' to Come," in *Myth and Mythmaking,* edited by Henry A. Murray. New York: George Braziller Press, 1960, pp. 300–353.

Myths of Mesopotamia: Creation, Flood, Gilgamesh and Others. Translated by Stephanie Dalley. New York: Oxford University Press, 1989.

Naoko, Takiguchi. "Liminal Experiences of Miyako Shamans," in *Shamanism in Asia,* edited by Clark Chilson and Peter Knecht. New York: Routledge, 2003.

Narayan, R.K. *Gods, Demons, and Others.* New York: Bantam Books, 1993.

Neusner, Jacob. "The Idea of Purity in Ancient Judaism." *Journal of the American Academy of Religion,* 43:1 (Mar., 1975), pp. 15–26.

Nichols, Michael. "How the World Ended: Myths of Retrospective Eschatology." *Cosmos and Logos: the Journal of Myth, Religion, and Folklore,* Vol. 2, 2016, pp. 1–12.

Nichols, Michael. "'I Think You and I Are Destined to Do This Forever': A Reading of the Batman/Joker Comic and Film Tradition through the Combat Myth." *The Journal of Religion and Popular Culture.* 23:2, July 2011, pp. 236–250.

Nichols, Michael. *Malleable Māra: Transformations of a Buddhist Symbol of Evil.* Albany: State University of New York Press, 2019.

Nichols, Michael. "Myths of Hero versus Hero: *the Iliad, the Mahābhārata,* and Marvel's *Civil War.*" *Cosmos and Logos: The Journal of Myth, Religion, and Folklore.* Vol. 3, August 2017, pp. 83–98.

Nietzsche, Friedrich. *Beyond Good and Evil: Prelude to a Philosophy of the Future.* Edited by Rolf-Peter Horstmann and Judith Norman. Translated by Judith Norman. New York: Cambridge University Press, 2002.

Nihongi: Chronicles of Japan from the Earliest Times, translated by W. G. Astin. London: George Allen and Unwin Ltd., 1956.

O' Flaherty, Wendy Doniger. *Women, Androgynes, and Other Mythical Beasts.* Chicago: University of Chicago Press, 1980.

The Odyssey, translated by Robert Fagles. New York: Penguin Press, 1996.

O'Flaherty, Wendy Doniger. *The Origins of Evil in Hindu Mythology.* Berkeley: University of California Press, 1976.

O'Flaherty, Wendy Doniger. *Other People's Myths: The Cave of Echoes.* Chicago: University of Chicago Press, 1988.

O'Flaherty, Wendy Doniger. *Śiva: the Erotic Ascetic.* New York: Oxford University Press, 1973.

Once the Buddha Was a Monkey: Ārya Śūra's Jātakamāla, translated by Peter Khoroche. Chicago: University of Chicago Press, 2006.

Ovid's The Metamorphoses, translated by Horace Gregory. New York: Viking Press, 1958.

Paden, William E. "Elements of a New Comparison," in *A Magic Still Dwells: Comparative Religion in the Post-Modern Age,* edited by Kimberley Patton and Benjamin Ray. Berkeley: University of California Press, 2000, pp. 182–192.

Parker, Robert. *Miasma: Pollution and Purification in Early Greek Religion.* New York: Clarendon Press, 1983.

Parrinder, Geoffrey. *African Mythology.* London: Hamlyn Publishing, 1967.

Patton, Kimberley, "Juggling Torches: Why We Still Need Comparative Religion," in *A Magic Still Dwells: Comparative Religion in the Post-Modern Age,* edited by Kimberley Patton and Benjamin Ray. Berkeley: University of California Press, 2000, pp. 153–171.

Patton, Kimberley, and Benjamin Ray. "Introduction," in *A Magic Still Dwells: Comparative Religion in the Post-Modern Age,* edited by Kimberley Patton and Benjamin Ray. Berkeley: University of California Press, 2000, pp. 1–22.

The Perfection of Wisdom Literature in Eight Thousand Lines, translated by Edward Conze.

Perrin, Michael. *The Way of the Dead Indian: Guajiro Myths and Symbols.* Austin: University of Texas Press, 1987.

The Persian Book of Kings: An Epitome of the Shahnama of Firdawsi, translated by B.W. Robinson. New York: Routledge, 2002.

Petrovic, Andrej, and Ivana Petrovic. *Inner Purity and Pollution in Ancient Greek Religion.* New York: Oxford University Press, 2016.

Phillips, Maya. "The Narrative Experiment that is the Marvel Cinematic Universe." *The New Yorker,* 4/26/19.

Pintchman, Tracy. *The Rise of the Goddess in the Hindu Tradition.* Albany: State University of New York Press, 1994.

Pitkethly, Clare. "Straddling a Boundary: The Superhero and the Incorporation of Difference," in *What is a Superhero?* Edited by Robin Rosenberg and Peter Coogan. New York: Oxford University Press, 2013, pp. 25–30.

Pollard, Tom. *Hollywood 9/11: Superheroes, Supervillains, and Superdisasters.* New York: Routledge, 2011.

Popul Vuh: The Mayan Book of the Dawn of Life, revised edition, translated by Dennis Tedlock. New York: Simon & Schuster, 1996.

Portraying 9/11: Essays on Representations in Comics, Literature, Film, and Theater, edited by Veronique Braggard, Christopher Dony, and Warren Rosenberg. Jefferson, NC: McFarland, 2011.

The Qur'ān: A New Translation, translated by M.A.S. Abdel Haleem. New York: Oxford University Press, 2010.

Ray, Benjamin. *African Religions: Symbol, Ritual, and Community.* Second Edition. Upper Saddle River, NJ: Prentice Hall, 2000.

Reich, Tamar. "Sacrificial Violence and Textual Battles: Inner Textual Interpretation in the Sanskrit *Mahābhārata,*" *History of Religions,* 41:2, 2001, pp. 142–169.

Reynolds, Frank, and Earl Waugh (eds.). *Religious Encounters with Death: Insights from the History and Anthropology of Religions.* Pennsylvania State University Press, 1977.

Reynolds, Richard. *Superheroes: A Modern Mythology.* Jackson: University of Mississippi Press, 1992.

Richman, Paula (ed.). *Many Ramayanas: The Diversity of a Narrative Tradition in South Asia.* Berkeley: University of California Press, 1991.

Ricoeur, Paul. *The Symbolism of Evil.* Translated by Emerson Buchanan. Boston: Beacon Press, 1967.

The Rig Veda. Translated by Wendy Doniger O'Flaherty. New York: Penguin Books, 1981.

Rodrigues, Hillary. *Ritual Worship of the Great Goddess: The Liturgy of the Durgā Pūjā with Interpretation.* Albany: State University of New York Press, 2003.

Romagnoli, Alex, and Gian Pagnucci. *Enter the Superheroes: American Values, Culture, and the Canon of Superhero Literature.* Lanham, MD: Scarecrow Press, 2013.

Rosenberg, Robin. "Our Fascination with Superheroes," in *What is a Superhero?,* edited by Robin Rosenberg and Peter Coogan. New York: Oxford University Press, 2013 pp. 3–18.

Rosenberg, Robin. *Superhero Origins: What Makes Superheroes Tick and Why We Care.* Create Space Publishing, 2013.

Rowles, Dustin. "George R. R. Martin Sounds Off on 'Ant-Man' and Marvel's Villain Problem," Uproxx: The Culture of What's Buzzing," 7/23/15. http://uproxx.com/tv/george-r-rmartin-on-antman-marvel's-villain-problem. Accessed 7/12/19.

Rubin, Rebecca. "*Avengers: Endgame* Crushes $2 Billion Milestone in Record Time," *Variety,* 5/5/19. www.variety.com/2019/film/news/avengers-endgame-2-billion-record-time-1203205293.

Russell, Jeffrey Burton. *Lucifer: the Devil in the Middle Ages.* Ithaca: Cornell University Press, 1984.

Russell, Jeffrey Burton. *The Prince of Darkness: Radical Evil and the Power of Good in History.* Ithaca: Cornell University Press, 1988.

Russell, Jeffrey Burton. *Satan and the Early Christian Tradition,* Ithaca: Cornell University Press, 1981.

Röllicke, Hermann Josef. "Some Brief Notes on Chinese Daoism," in *Discourses of Purity in Transcultural Perspective,* edited by Matthias Bley, Nikolas Jaspert, and Stefan Köck. Boston: E.J. Brill, 2015.

Samuel, Geoffrey. *Civilized Shamans: Buddhism in Tibetan Societies.* Washington: Smithsonian Institution Press, 1993.

Samuel, Geoffrey. *Tantric Revisionings: Understandings of Tibetan Buddhism and Indian Religion.* Burlington, VT: Ashgate Publishing, 2005.

Sanders, Tao Liu. *Dragons, Gods, and Spirits from Chinese Mythology.* New York: Schocken Books, 1980.

Santangelo, Paolo. "From 'Clean' to 'Pure' in Everyday Life in Imperial China," in *Discourses of Purity in Transcultural Perspective,* edited by Matthias Bley, Nikolas Jaspert, and Stefan Köck. Boston: E.J. Brill, 2015.

Saunders, Ben. *Do the Gods Wear Capes? Spirituality, Fantasy, and Superheroes.* New York: Continuum Press, 2011.

Schopen, Gregory. *Bones, Stones, and Buddhist Monks: Collected Papers on the Archaeology, Epigraphy, and Texts of Monastic Buddhism in India.* Honolulu: University of Hawai'i Press, 1997.

Segal, Robert. "In Defense of the Comparative Method." *Numen* 48.3, 2001, pp. 339–373.

Shanley, Peter. "Can Anyone Besides Marvel Make a Cinematic Universe Work?" *Hollywood Reporter,* 3/29/18. www.hollywoodreporter.com/heat-vision/marvel-cinematic-universe/why-is-it-one-works-1096504

Singh, Manvir. "The Cultural Evolution of Shamanism," *Behavioral Brain Sciences,* 2018, 1–62.

Smith, Brian K. *Classifying the Universe: the Ancient Indian Varṇa System and the Origins of Caste.* New York: Oxford University Press, 1994.

Smith, Jamil. "The Revolutionary Power of *Black Panther.*" *Time.* Accessed 3/24/2020. https://time.com/black-panther/

Smith, Jonathan Z. *Imagining Religion: From Babylon to Jonestown.* Chicago: University of Chicago Press, 1982.

Sophocles, *The Three Theban Plays,* translated by Robert Fagles. New York: Penguin Publishing, 1982.

Spence, Lewis. *The Myths of Mexico and Peru.* New York: Dover Publications, 1994.

Strenski, Ivan. *Four Theories of Myth in Twentieth Century History.* Iowa City: University of Iowa, 1987.

Strong, John. *The Buddha: A Beginner's Guide.* New York: Oneworld Publications, 2009.

Strong, John S. *The Legend and Cult of Upagupta: Sanskrit Buddhism in North India and Southeast Asia.* Princeton: Princeton University Press, 1992

Stroumsa, Guy. "Mystical Descents," in *Death, Ecstasy, and Otherworldly Journeys,* edited by John Collins and Michael Fishbane. Albany: State University of New York Press, 1995, pp. 139–154.

Stutley, Margaret. *Shamanism: an Introduction.* New York: Routledge, 2002.

Suderman, Peter. "How Marvel Built Such an Impressive Movie Universe." *Vox,* 5/9/16. www.vox.com/2016/5/9/11595344/marvel-cinematic-universe-captain-america-avengers

Sulfan, Reza. "Audience Reaction Ending Endgame Iron Man." *Youtube,* 4/27/2019, 1:17, https://www.youtube.com/watch?v=lDrkijN_vFM.

Sumegi, Angela. *Understanding Death: An Introduction to Ideas of Self and the Afterlife in World Religions.* Malden, MA: John Wiley and Sons (Wiley-Blackwell), 2014.

Sutherland, Gail Hinich. *Disguises of the Demon: The Development of the Yakṣa in Hinduism and Buddhism.* Albany: State University of New York Press, 1991.

Swearer, Donald K. *The Buddhist World of Southeast Asia.* Albany: State University of New York Press, 1995.

Sweet, Derek. "America Assemble: the Avengers as Therapeutic Public Memory," in *Assembling the Marvel Cinematic Universe: Essays on the Social, Cultural, and Geopolitical Domains,* edited by Julian Chambliss, William Svitavsky, and Daniel Fandino. Jefferson, NC: McFarland, 2018, 64–75.

The Táin: Translated from the Irish Epic Táin Bó Cúailgne, translated by Thomas Kinsella. New York: Oxford University Press, 2002.

Textual Sources for the Study of Islam, edited and translated by Jan Knappert and Andrew Rippin. Chicago: University of Chicago Press, 1986.

The Thanos Quest: Book 1—Schemes and Dreams, Writer: Jim Starlin, Pencils: Ron Lim, Ink: John Beatty. New York: Marvel Comics, 1990.

The Thanos Quest: Book 2—Games and Prizes, Writer: Jim Starlin, Pencils: Ron Lim, Ink: John Beatty. New York: Marvel Comics, 1990.

The Tibetan Book of the Dead: the Great Liberation Through Hearing in the Bardo. Translated with commentary by Francesca Fremantle and Chögyam Trungpa. Boston: Shambhala Press, 1987.

Tolkien, J.R.R. "Beowulf: The Monsters and the Critics," Sir Israel Gollancz Memorial Lecture, Proceedings of the British Academy, 1936, 245–95.

Toontastic, "Avenger Endgame Crazy MCU Fans Reaction." *Youtube,* 4/27/2019, 1:23, https://www.youtube.com/watch?v=UMnaNp9xngY.

A Treasury of Chinese Literature, edited by Raymond Van Over. Greenwich, CT: Fawcett Premier Publishing, 1972.

Trout, Paul. *Deadly Powers: Animal Predation and the Mythic Imagination.* New York: Prometheus Books, 2011.

Turner, Victor. *The Ritual Process: Structure and Anti-Structure.* New York: DeGruyter, 1969.

van Gennep, Arnold. *The Rites of Passage.* Translated by M.B. Visedom and G.L. Caffee. Chicago: University of Chicago Press, 1960 [1909].

Vineyard, Jennifer. "Why the Movie *Captain America: Civil War* Didn't Have the Comic Book's Dark Ending," 5/12/2016. *Vulture.* www.vulture.com/2016/05/captain-america-civil-war-ending-different.html. Accessed 8/8/2019.

von Hendy, Andrew. *The Modern Construction of Myth.* Bloomington: Indiana University Press, 2002.

Warner, Marina. *Monsters of Our Own Making: The Peculiar Pleasures of Fear.* Lexington: University of Kentucky Press, 2007.

Watercutter, Angela. "*Captain Marvel* is about Female Power—not Empowerment," *Wired,* 3/11/2019. Accessed 3/24/2020. https://www.wired.com/story/captain-marvel-is-about-female-power-not-empowerment/

Watkins, Calvert. *How to Kill a Dragon: Aspects of Indo-European Poetics.* New York: Oxford University Press, 1995.

The Way of Life According to Lao Tzu, translated by Witter Bynner. New York: Perigee Books, 1994.

Weil, Simone. *The Iliad, or the Poem of Force: A Critical Edition.* Edited and translated by James Holoka. New York: Peter Lang Publications, 2005.

Werner, Edward T.C. *Myths and Legends of China.* New York: Dover Publications, 1994 [1922].

Wilbert, Johnannes. *Mystic Endowment: Religious Ethnography of the Warao Indians.* Cambridge: Harvard University Press, 1993.

Wildman, Wesley. "Comparing Religious Ideas: There's Method in the Madness," in *Comparing Religions: Possibilities and Perils.* Edited by Thomas Idinopoulos, Brian Wilson, James Hanges. Leiden: Brill, 2006, pp. 77–113.

Witzel, E.J. Michael. *The Origins of the World's Mythologies.* New York: Oxford University Press, 2012.

Witzel, E.J. Michael, "Shamanism in Northern and Southern Eurasia: Their Distinctive Method Of Change of Consciousness." *Social Science Information,* 50:1, 2011.

Wood, Marion. *Spirits, Heroes, and Hunters: Native American Indian Mythology.* New York: Peter Bedrick Books, 1981.

Wyndham, John. *Myths of Ife,* London, 1921.

Yuan Ke, *Dragons and Dynasties: An Introduction to Chinese Mythology,* translated by Kim Echlin and Nie Zhxiong. New York: Penguin Books, 1993.

Zaehner, R.C. *Zurvan: A Zoroastrian Dilemma.* New York: Oxford University Press, 1955.

Index

Numbers in **bold italics** indicate pages with illustrations

197

CPSIA information can be obtained
at www.ICGtesting.com
Printed in the USA
LVHW041939090323
741281LV00003B/487